MANAGEMENT IN FRANCE

MANAGEMENT IN FRANCE

Jean-Louis Barsoux
and
Peter Lawrence

Department of Management Studies,
University of Loughborough

CASSELL

Cassell Educational Limited
Villiers House
41/47 Strand
London WC2N 5JE

First published in hardback 1990
Reprinted 1992

British Library Cataloguing in Publication Data

Barsoux, Jean-Louis
  Management in France.
  1. France. Management
  I. Title   II. Lawrence, Peter
  658'.00944

  ISBN 0-304-32525-2

Printed and bound in Great Britain by
Biddles Ltd, Guildford and King's Lynn

Contents

Coherent whole
Brilliance and its limitations
Aspects of management
Universal versus culture-bound
Restatement
A French malaise?
1992 and all that

Acknowledgements

An undertaking such as this would not have been possible without the assistance and co-operation of many people. First, a number of people helped us in a preliminary way, with insights into company organization and the nature of management work. In this connection we would particularly like to thank Ted Marsh of the Hawker Siddeley Group. Second, we are very grateful to M. Carron de la Carrière of the French Embassy together with John Ardagh and David Marsh for providing introductions to companies and senior managers in France. Third, we would like to thank all the companies that participated in the study – and more especially the managers within those firms who gave up their valuable time. We are also indebted to Marion Aitkenhead in the Department of Management Studies at Loughborough University for her secretarial help throughout the research.

All of this research was carried out under the auspices of the Economic and Social Research Council. It is customary in these circumstances to thank the research sponsors for their generous financial support, but, over and beyond this, we must praise the Council for its flexibility and responsiveness to the demands of international research.

Finally, we should thank Professor Geoffrey Gregory of the Department of Management Studies at Loughborough University, who has had sufficient faith in the researchers to allow them to proceed as they saw fit – and where necessary has provided additional funds for the research.

J-LB
PL

List of figures

List of abbreviations and acronyms

The following list gives some of the most common abbreviations and acronyms relating to French management.

APEC	Association Pour l'Emploi des Cadres
Bac	Baccalauréat (equivalent of 'A' levels)
BTS	Brevet de Technicien Supérieur
CCI	Chambre(s) de Commerce et d'Industrie
CCIP	Chambre de Commerce et d'Industrie de Paris
CEDEP	Centre Européen d'Education Permanente
CEGOS	Commission Générale d'Organisation Scientifique
Centrale	L'Ecole Centrale (private engineering grande école)
CGC	Confédération Générale des Cadres
CGD	Centre des Jeunes Dirigeants
CGT	Confédération Générale du Travail
CNOF	Comité Nationale de l'Organisation Française
CNPF	Conseil National du Patronat Français
CPA	Centre de Perfectionnement aux Affaires
CRC	Centre de Recherches et d'Etudes des Chefs d'Entreprises
Dauphine	Management University, Paris-IX
DESS	Diplôme d'Etudes Supérieures Spécialisées
DEUG	Diplôme d'Etudes Universitaires Générales
DUT	Diplôme Universitaire de Technologie (awarded by IUT)
ENA	Ecole Nationale d'Administration
ENE	Ecole Nationale d'Exportation
ESCAE	Ecole(s) Supérieure(s) de Commerce et d'Administration des Entreprises
ESCP	Ecole Supérieure de Commerce de Paris
ESSEC	Ecole Supérieure des Sciences Economiques et Commerciales
FNEGE	Fondation Nationale pour l'Enseignement de la Gestion des Entreprises
FO	Force Ouvrière
Gadz'arts	Alumni of l'Ecole des Arts et Métiers
GARF	Groupement des Agents Responsables de la Formation

HEC	Ecole des Hautes Etudes Commerciales
INSEAD	Institut Européen d'Administration des Affaires
INSEE	Institut National des Statistiques et des Etudes Economiques
ISA	Institut Supérieur des Affaires
ISSEC	Institut Supérieur de Sciences Economiques et Commerciales
IUT	Institut(s) Universitaire(s) de Technologie
LEST	Laboratoire d'Economie et de Sociologie du Travail
PCF	Parti Communiste Français
PDG	Président Directeur Générale (equivalent CEO or MD)
PME	Petites et Moyennes Entreprises (equivalent of SME)
Prépa	Post-*baccalauréat* preparatory school and *sine qua non* for entry to *grandes écoles*
Sciences-Po	Institut d'Etudes Politiques (Paris)
X	L'Ecole Polytechnique

Preface

The evidence that France 'must be doing something right' in managerial and/or educational terms is there for all to see: France has undergone a very rapid final stage of industrialization; it is substantially richer than some of its European neighbours including Britain; and it boasts a qualitatively better interface between industry and government.

The fact remains that we tend to think of France in picture postcard terms – it evokes thoughts of *vin de table* and smelly urinals, rather than fast trains and nuclear power. France is misapprehended in a particular, old-fashioned sort of way. This is intriguing in view of the nation's high-profile, high-tech accomplishments. The paradox is explored at length in Chapter 1.

The stereotype extends to management. We would no more think of learning from French management than we would from, say, Greek or Portuguese management. Yet France has obvious strengths, and they are distinctive; they are not like US or West German or Japanese strengths.

The French have a singular vision of what constitutes a suitable management apprenticeship. The emphasis is on formal intellect. Educational credentials prevail over all other influences in career progress. The management education system is hyperselective and geared towards providing large companies with a core of senior managers. High-fliers are thus earmarked for early responsibility and rapid promotion. This facilitates their learning process, but leaves those excluded with the prospect of limited advancement.

Thus France has pursued the academization of management further than other countries. In what ways that makes the French better managers is a *leitmotiv* of this book. The strengths and weaknesses of this fixation on intellect are also considered, as is the impact of socio-cultural factors on the shape of French management. Moreover, the authors draw heavily on anthropology and sociology to fuel their characterization of French management.

It is particularly apt that this preface should be written exactly two hundred years after the Revolution, during the month of the bicentennial celebrations. An underlying theme in the book is the impact of the values of 'liberté, egalité, fraternité' on the style and demeanour of contemporary French managers.

Loughborough

Chapter One

The challenge of France

> 'On ne connaît jamais un être, mais on cesse parfois
> de sentir qu'on l'ignore.' ('One never really knows
> an entity, but one may sometimes reach the point of
> no longer being completely ignorant thereof.')
> (André Malraux, 1946.)

France has a strong image. People have a view of what France is like. Around the world people can tell you what is 'typically French'. France is not one of those wishy-washy countries about which people have difficulty dredging up any tangible fact or presentable impression.

This conviction of familiarity is underpinned for Anglo-Saxons by the fact that France has been our ally in two world wars. And for British people in particular it is sustained by the nearness of France: we have all been there, learned some French at school, and seen their children going round our towns as well every summer.

But this popular consensus has several shortcomings. It is out of date, having more to do with our great-grandfathers' experiences in the First World War than with France in the 1990s. It is over-stereotyped, especially with regard to a comparison with Britain. And although French commentators themselves tend to emphasize the blockages to change in French society, France has shown a certain dynamism in the post-war era which is obscured by the popular view.

Let us start with a literally homely example. Foreigners know that most of the French live in rather nasty terraced tenements whose rents were fixed around the time of the First World War. Not so, according to Theodore Zeldin (1983), who has found that over a third of French workers own their own homes, and that by the time of retirement a half of them do. The French have more than doubled their expenditure on homes from 8 per cent in the 1930s to 20 per cent today. Furthermore, only 7 per cent of the French live in tower blocks while a half live in detached cottages and a third in villages and small towns.

Or consider pets. Everyone knows that Britain is a pet-loving, and especially dog-loving, society. Yet according to Zeldin again the French are importing 400,000 dogs a year (mostly from Britain!) while the British dog population changes little. In fact the French have more dogs than the British, more cats, more caged birds – and this with a smaller (human) population (Zeldin, 1983).

Or think of that traditional British strength – sport. Again there is evidence marshalled by Zeldin that the favourite leisure pursuit of the British is watching television. Not so for the French, more of whom (i.e. higher proportions) go shooting, go fishing, do gymnastics, watch sport and also go dancing, than is the case in Britain (Zeldin, 1983). Voltaire once quipped that there is as much in common between a Dutchman and a Frenchman as between a tortoise and a lively monkey. But what about a Franco-British comparison?

The French economy

Probably the worst British misapprehension of France, however, is in economic matters. Britain has in fact engaged in serialized economic hero-worship of other countries. In the 1940s and 50s it was presumed that the USA was the exemplar of good business organization; later the admiring regard shifted to West Germany, and later still to Japan. Yet the British have now to acknowledge that it is France that is the fourth largest exporter after the USA, Germany and Japan.

Some of the economic relativities are startling. Gross domestic product (GDP) per capita figures, in terms of purchasing power parities (adjusted to take account of price differences), are offered in OECD reports (OECD, July 1987). The relevant figure for France for 1984 was $12,643, not that far behind West Germany at $13,265 and variously ahead of Austria, Belgium, Italy, Japan, the Netherlands and Britain.

The same source gives some indicators of living standards. On car ownership, for example, the French are again ahead of Austria, Belgium, Denmark, Finland, Iceland, Italy, the Netherlands and Britain, and way ahead of Japan (OECD, 1987). On telephone density France is in ninth place in a list of 25 industrialized countries and again ahead of Britain, if only by a small margin. On doctors per head of population France is well up on the OECD league, and the comparison with Britain is stark, with French relativities being closer to the USA than those of her Channel Tunnel neighbour! Similarly, when it comes to infant mortality, only five countries in the OECD list of 25 countries have better records than France, and France is ahead of West Germany, Great Britain and the USA.

When France feels free

It may be argued that these economic comparisons between France and other countries are no more than differences of degree. This is both ostensibly true and misleading at the same time. The difference of degree argument is unhelpful because it fails to illuminate the variety of qualitative differences that underpin the French post-war economic achievement, many of which are explored in subsequent chapters. There is also a diachronic difference, which is not obvious to outsiders.

For most of the continental European countries the Second World War was the economic nadir and the post-war period saw continual improvement, subject only to changes in economic climate. This truism is not inapplicable to France, but it misses out a French subjective reality.

In the summer of 1944 with the liberation from German occupation the worst may have been over for France, but there was still more to come. The chronic ministerial instability of the Fourth French Republic (1946–58) made France a joke among democratic countries. Worse still the failed attempt to regain their colonial empire in Indo-China was followed by an even more harrowing attempt to hold on to Algeria, which also failed.

In the French popular mind, the 'period when things were bad' is much longer than the four years of Nazi occupation. It stretches back from that time to the horrors of the First World War and the insecurity and stagnation which followed it, as well as forward to Algeria. This idea is caught by François Nourissier (1971), who asserts that the post-1962 period, after the settlement of the Algerian question, is novel in French life in the absence of military defeat or adventurism, ministerial instability and economic stagnation. One might add that it is only after the de Gaulle–Konrad Adenauer entente that France is free, for the first time for nearly a century, of fear of Germany.

All this makes France somewhat different from her European neighbours. Economic improvement may have started after the War, but a widespread conviction that things were going well came only later. This also helps to explain the greater French consciousness of national well-being: it is more recent and less taken for granted.

The French focus

Another feature of the French economic achievement is that it is more sharply focused than that of most other rich countries. It is focused in two ways that tend to overlap: on high-tech products, and on government-sponsored projects. Consider some of France's achievements.

Radar was a British invention, but French radar now rivals ours. And in air traffic control systems France is a world leader. In a straight fight with a British firm in the mid-1980s for a field communications system for the American army, the French won the contract.

3

French railways and rolling stock were badly damaged in the War; the French government responded with an imaginative appointment of an enterprising engineer to head the post-war SNCF (Société Nationale des Chemins de Fer). Today the TGV *(train à grande vitesse)* holds the world speed record at 236 mph. By the mid-1980s the TGV had already seen a million miles of operational service: the British equivalent APT (advanced passenger train) never got into service. The French are also leaders in designs for a prototype economy car: they have one which does 100 mpg.

Not only in transport but also in communications: up until the 1970s France had a grotesque, pre-war, electro-mechanical telephone system. Then the government summoned the engineers and gave them the money and the freedom to produce something that would be a credit to France. The engineers dismissed less sophisticated alternatives and went for an electronic switching system, digital, first developed by the Post Office in Britain in the 1960s. Today over 90 per cent of France has been digitalized. In Britain the hope is that with Plessey's development of System X the country will be digitalized by the end of the century.

Again France has not done things by halves. The expansion into digital has meant that France was poised for other computer applications. Already, over a million homes have subscriber-operated electronic directory enquiries. The system was backed by the government, which gave away thousands of the apparatus to aid its uptake on a national scale. These Minitels can receive all sorts of services/information, after the manner of the British Prestel invention. The difference is that, in Britain, Prestel has only 65,000 subscribers to Teletel's million plus subscribers in France.

To complete the picture of the French telecommunications advance, France has also developed a videophone, and 1,500 have been installed as part of a pilot scheme. This development is again based on a British invention, that of fibre optics. It has to be said, however, that the French videophone is expensive, and the evidence in the late 1980s does not suggest a large-scale take-up as yet.

Energy and policy

The quip: *en France on n'a pas de pétrole mais on a des idées*, has now become so much part of national consciousness that no one can remember who coined it. It is true that France has no North Sea oil like Britain and Norway, or for that matter coal like Belgium and Germany, or natural gas like Britain and the Netherlands.

In this instance, the idea was to go nuclear. Following the 1973 oil crisis, France commissioned six pressurized water reactor nuclear power stations a year: by the mid-1980s France had over thirty of these nuclear power stations in operation. The result is cheap electrical power, and the ability to export some 8 per cent of national electricity output, some of it to Britain. Again the comparison with Britain is instructive. Through its nuclear energy policy France has achieved a measure of national independence (from oil): they are saving as much on oil imports as Britain has been making on oil exports.

Not everyone likes the idea of nuclear power generation, for reasons that are well-rehearsed. Yet it is noticeable that there has been a much wider acceptance of nuclear power in France than in, say, Britain, Sweden or West Germany. While there is some disquiet in France about the discharge of nuclear waste into the sea, it is recognized that the danger of the discharge is controlled by sealing the waste in glass. The process is known as vitrification, and is a British invention, though the French are now the leaders in the field. Britain recently bought a vitrification plant from France.

La technologie au service de la vanité nationale

The French formula, apparent in the examples of telecommunications and nuclear energy, of government initiatives plus funds plus research brainpower does not always work. In the 1970s it was common to recount the instance of the French failure with computers. The state-sponsored computer firm Bull received substantial government funding but ultimately failed to generate a rational product range likely to achieve market success. Yet this étatiste approach has had more successes than failures. One area of success has been the aeronautical and space industry.

In 1960 France exploded its own nuclear bomb. By the following year it had its own independent nuclear ballistic missiles. De Gaulle at this time propounded the strategic principle that France should become technologically independent. Again the result can be seen in the mid-1980s where France has a fleet of six ballistic missile carrying submarines. But unlike the British Polaris submarines, France's 96 sea-based missiles are of all French technology.

But France has not neglected conventional weapons. Its Mirage jet is one of the most exported fighter aeroplanes in the world. The French also make five types of helicopter, and claim to be number one in international helicopter sales. French Exocet missiles were shown in the 1982 Falklands War to be the most deadly, hugging the ground to avoid detection. In short, France has become Europe's leading armaments manufacturer.

From Blue Streak to Ariane

In space research France again has overtaken Britain. In the 1950s France was only learning to build rockets, while Britain forged ahead with Blue Streak. This was the most advanced rocket launcher in Europe, and Britain was well placed. In the event, although Blue Streak performed well, the government abandoned it.

France continued to pour money into space research, and started to launch rockets in the 1960s. In the 1970s work began on Ariane, leading to the first launch in Guyana in 1979. Ariane has now become the leading satellite launcher. In the mid-1980s France won a contract to build a communications satellite for the Arabs, to be launched, of course, by Ariane.

The French have also developed an earth resources satellite, with a stereoscopic camera that will look down and photograph in detail any point on earth. Applications for this earth resources satellite include agriculture, mapping, oil exploration and even town planning.

From projects to projections

In the areas outlined in the last few pages – radar and railways, tele-communications and computers, aeronautics and space research – there are several intertwined themes. Most obviously the achievements in these areas demonstrate French technical virtuosity and will to succeed. It is important to push home this point since there is a tendency in the Anglo-Saxon world to regard France as an engaging but rather backward country, something like Spain or Italy with a different accent. This might have been true in the first half of the century, but it is not in the second.

These achievements also show something else. They are very much state initiatives, even where, as is so in some of the cases outlined above, it is private sector companies that are doing the development and manufacture. It is an important feature of the French system that government is more active in what in Anglo-Saxon countries would be called industrial policy and science policy. It is also the case that many firms in France have a relationship with government that is qualitatively different from that obtaining in Britain or America. It further follows that the phrase and fact of 'nationalized industry' has connotations in France that are different from those in Britain. To be a public sector firm in France means to partake of the power and glory of the French state – it is image enhancing, not image demeaning.

The idea is introduced at this juncture to signpost later discussion, but also to make a simple though important point. This is to stress the variability that exists from country to country, underneath apparently homogeneous labels. Government, industry and government relations, and the standing of the public sector, are not the same throughout the western world, and in the case of France in particular it is worth turning over the label to look at the meaning underneath.

Individualism and authority

The leitmotiv of this chapter is that France is not always what it seems, or what we have always imagined. And the process of interpretation is sometimes not helped by the use of traditional labels.

The challenge of understanding France in fact is made much more poignant by some quite refined paradoxes. Take, for example, the little matter of authority and individualism. A German writer, basing his views on the findings of West Germany's famous public opinion survey firm, the Allensbach Institut, has produced the following comparisons (Ackermann, 1988):

Proportion of employees in each country who accept
the proposition: 'Basically, I will carry out instructions
from my superior':

Country	%
Denmark	57
England	49
Ireland	45
Holland	39
Belgium	33
Spain	29
West Germany	28
France	25
Italy	24

Here, one may feel, is the stroppy individualist Frenchman we all know: folk wisdom verified by social science! The next line in Ackermann's table seems to support this view:

Proportion of employees in each country who accept
the proposition: 'I only follow the instructions of
superiors when my reason is convinced':

Country	%
France	57
West Germany	51
Spain	41
Italy	39
England	34
Holland	33
Ireland	26
Denmark	21

A nice consistent picture: France is nearly bottom of the first list and on top of the second, probing the same phenomenon from opposite directions.

Now let us juxtapose another finding from a different source. The Dutch psychologist Geert Hofstede surveyed and tested employees of the same American multinational company in some 50 countries. His broad finding is that there are substantial differences in work-related attitudes and values from country to country, revealed by his extensive and unique sample (Hofstede, 1980). But he further systematizes his findings by ranking the respondent countries on four dimensions, two of which are germane to the French authority paradox.

The first of these is the dimension of power distance, or the willingness of people in different cultures to accept differences in the power possessed by individuals, and remember that in industrial societies power distance refers primarily to differences of power enjoyed by people at different levels in formal organizations. Here are the French, in comparison with a few other countries (Hofstede, 1980, 315):

Country	Power distance
France	68
Italy	50
USA	40
West Germany	35
Great Britain	35
Mean for 40 countries	52

Note that the higher the number, the *greater* the tolerance for *inequalities of power*. Is it not intriguing that the French, who are less willing to take orders, are more willing to accept that some people have much more power than others?

There is another bit of this jigsaw in the form of Hofstede's second principal dimension. This is uncertainty avoidance, or the desire to eliminate ambiguity and doubt, to know where you stand, to leave little to chance. This uncertainty avoidance is not constant throughout the world, but again varies from country to country, and France is distinctive (Hofstede, 1980, 315):

Country	Uncertainty avoidance
France	86
Italy	75
West Germany	65
USA	46
Great Britain	35
Mean for 40 countries	64

As with the previous table on power distance, the higher the figure in the uncertainty avoidance column the *stronger* the desire to avoid uncertainty. This finding is again intriguing, since a standard remedy for reducing uncertainty is to accept orders – but the French are reluctant to do this. So we have an apparent contradiction between French attitudes to orders (negative) and power differences (positive), and between desire to avoid uncertainty (positive) and uncritical acceptance of orders as the means to this end (negative).

We have demonstrated these contradictions not in order to give a full and lucid explanation at this stage – though they are explained in the body of the book – but to signal the subtlety and complexity of the issue. Where the French are concerned, stereotypes will get us to the starting line but not to the finishing post.

The idea can be expressed differently. Some societies are seamless garments, so that management and behaviour in work organizations are not compartmentalized. In the USA, for example, management style is like everyday life; it has the same features, expresses the same convictions. But not in France, where behaviours are more compartmentalized. One can deduce little about management style or organizational behaviour in France from everyday life. One can go to France a hundred times as a tourist and know relatively less than one would about Canada or the Netherlands, Germany or Israel. And one has to recognize that compartmentalization is in the eye of the perpetrator.

Paradoxes

This France, with its Minitel and its Exocets, its nuclear power and its TGV, is not a 'modern society' in every way. In its attachment to values and tradition it has more in common with Britain than with America. There is a remarkable continuity in the expression of their values. The state building and centralization of the seventeenth century is re-enacted in the later twentieth century – de Gaulle's conception of the glory of France is not too removed from that of Louis XIV. And there are interesting transmogrifications: from Colbert's fortifications to the Maginot Line, from leadership in style to leadership in space, from the cult of nobility to the noble product.

There is also a tension between nationalism and internationalism. The best of the French past seems to transcend national frontiers. Cartesianism is a logical system on offer to the world, not just to France. The Rights of Man, formulated in the early stages of the French Revolution, are a charter for humanity, not special pleading for the French. The metric system conquered most of the world, as has the Napoleonic Code, in the form of codified law rather than case law.

At the same time, post-war France has given national self-interest a clear focus not witnessed since the days of Palmerston in Victorian

Britain. France's aid to the Third World is mostly tied aid – the beneficiaries buy French goods with it. Within the EEC the common agricultural policy has bolstered French farmers. Oil crises come and go, yet France always knows how to 'soigner les relations' with the Middle Eastern states that matter. And when the Channel Tunnel comes, it will be French railways that gain.

French industry too is torn between a backwards and a forwards orientation. In the previous pages we have emphasized the forwards: the successes, noble products, triumphs of state initiative crossed with technological virtuosity. But there is also an old-fashioned side. A grudging, incremental acceptance of industrial democracy (surpassed only by Britain), the low profile of firms such as Michelin, corporate paternalism, workplace discipline and the rewarding of seniority.

One might indeed encapsulate some of these tensions by postulating a 'diabolic hexagon'. L'Hexagone is a popular term for France, whose geographical shape is roughly hexagonal. Were we to ascribe values to the six sides constituting the hexagon, then the upper lines must bear witness to the classic values of the French Revolution that still adorn every town hall. Yet these need to be counterbalanced by other predilections that illuminate French behaviour in organizations. So our hexagon might look something like Figure 1.1.

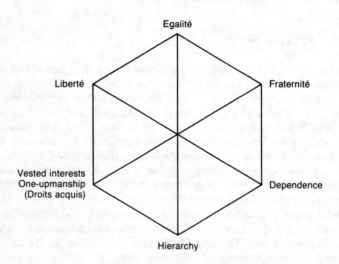

Figure 1.1 Schematic diagram of the 'hexagon' that constitutes France.

Much of what follows will constitute an unpacking of these tensions.

Chapter Two

Cadres, qui etes-vous?

> 'Les' cadres, grammaticalement, passent encore.
> Mais 'le' cadre, c'est plus intriguant. Cette person-
> alisation, cette singularisation du terme, et puis des
> expressions telles que 'cadre moyen, supérieur',
> 'petit cadre', 'il est passé cadre', correspond au
> besoin de désigner une catégorie sociale nouvelle.
> (The plural cadres is just about acceptable
> grammatically. But in the singular, it is far more
> intriguing since the term is personalized. Moreover,
> the emergence of phrases like 'middle manager',
> 'senior manager', 'junior manager', 'he has been
> named cadre' indicate the need to identify a new
> social group.)
>
> (Jean-François Revel, L'Express, 12 June 1967.)

Literally speaking, cadre is a noun meaning 'frame' (of a painting or mirror). In the industrial setting, Harrap's gives the definition, 'salaried staff'; Larousse suggests, 'officials'; whilst Collins opts for 'executives, managers and managerial staff'. Over time the noun has extended its application and can now be employed as an adjective. For instance, un emploi cadre (a management level job), une femme cadre (a woman manager).

What is a cadre?

This term cadre is one which has no equivalent in other languages (other than Italian where the word quadri was adopted by business in the 1970s). Basically, it corresponds to 'manager' in English, though with rather different legal and sociological connotations.

The origins of the term in a business setting date back only to the 1930s. Prior to that, the word cadre is only used in a military context, where it denoted the ensemble of commissioned and non-commissioned officers. But in 1937 the word made its first appearance in the title of a professional organization – la Confédération Générale des Cadres de l'Economie (Grunberg et Mouriaux, 1979, 11).

The emergence of the term coincided with the industrial unrest of the mid-1930s (le Front Populaire and the 1936 strikes) and the consequent desire on the part of graduate engineers to distinguish themselves from the employers on the one hand, and the workers on the other. Initially, then, this new socio-professional category was composed essentially of graduate engineers, and was meant to assert their position and status in negotiations. But, over time, it has attracted disparate groups (Boltanski, 1982, 52) in search of status and representation, and has extended its boundaries to include 'others enjoying some level of authority' (NEDO, 1987, 63).

The thirties therefore represent a critical stage in France's managerial evolution. This is the point at which historical forces pushed France into creating a buffer group between workers and employers, rather than attempting to reduce the fissure between the two factions and treating them as mere strata within a unit. Studies at LEST, a famous French research institute at Aix-en-Provence, point to the German model as an expression of the unitary approach (Benguigui *et al.*, 1975, 466). The West Germans distinguish only between *Angestellter* (white-collar) and *Arbeiter* (blue collar), and endeavour to minimize organizational hierarchies and to reconcile differences through consultation (Lawrence, 1980, 42–49). The French on the other hand seem to have opted for a tripartite solution which includes this fleshy intermediary class: *les cadres*.

How to become one

There are basically two ways of achieving *cadre* status: by virtue of educational credentials, or through loyalty to a given company.

Those fortunate enough to graduate from one of the 'super-universities' or *grandes écoles (baccalauréat* = 'A' level plus five years of full-time study in higher education[1] can look forward to immediate *cadre* status on entering professional life, whereas a person with only two years' post-*baccalauréat* education (a vocational course such as DUT or BTS as described in the next chapter is likely to have to wait five or ten years to *passer cadre*. As for an *autodidacte* (self-taught person), the only real chance of turning *cadre* is to prove himself over several years[2] in a company and hope to be named an *ingénieur-maison* – a title which is company specific. In other words, by changing companies the *cadre* of this latter type is likely to have to relinquish his status.

Qualifications are clearly the favoured currency, and time is the price paid for those who are in short supply of this currency. This trade-off between time and qualifications gives rise to a remarkably

---

1 Higher qualifications are generally designated by the number of years the course lasts after the *baccalauréat*, e.g. *Bac* + 2 for DUT, BTS, DEUG and DEUST, *Bac* + 4 for a *maîtrise* or some business school diplomas and *Bac* + 5 for engineering schools and DESS.

2 Decades even, since it is often a nominal, end-of-career gesture to reward *bons et loyaux services*.

stable continuum, with particular qualifications corresponding to an implicit 'apprenticeship' (socialization and selection) period before one can have pretensions to *cadre* status.

Needless to say, this produces two distinct populations of *cadres* – those with educational legitimation, and those without. This divergence gives rise to mild disdain on both sides: those 'with' will secretly deplore *le manque de culture générale* (that is, the lack of intellectual refinement based on superior education of those without), whilst those without bemoan the automatic handing out of *cadre* status. One *autodidacte* half-jokingly confided, 'Soon they'll be naming them *cadre* on admission to the *grandes écoles*.'

Defining the population

Exactly what defines a *cadre*, rather like what constitutes a *grande école*, is a subject of some debate. No account of the French managerial class seems to be complete unless it opens with a long and confusing synthesis of the alternative definitions. Most authors seek support from the official texts, but even these offer no standard definition (Grunberg and Moriaux, 1979, 212) – a most unsatisfactory situation from the stance of Cartesian logic. What is more, the static nature of the texts makes them particularly inappropriate for defining what has always been a changing category. The only practical solution is to take an evolutionary perspective.

In attempting to single out the *cadre* population, we can immediately set aside the categories of shopfloor (*ouvriers*) and office workers (*employés*[1]). However, a more contentious issue is whether the foremen (la maîtrise) and directors (les dirigeants) belong to the class. This depends on different industrial sectors and even individual firms – some choose to distinguish these categories even though the nature of their work is comparable to that of the *cadres*. Certainly it is more or less impossible to identify the *differentia specifica* of their work as distinct from the foreman or director – and any differences in activity are differences of degree rather than kind.

Attempts in our own study to get *cadres* to engage in self-definition elicited various responses. Some *cadres* saw their collective identity in terms of general responsibility – *vis-à-vis* the personnel or in terms of completing a task. Others felt that the common denominator was a state of mind rather than a type of activity – as one *cadre* put it, 'a blend of adaptability, *esprit de synthèse* and initiative'. However valid these answers, they proved rather unsatisfactory criteria for distinguishing

---

1 The term *employé* only includes office workers, not *cadres*. Fifty years ago a *cadre* would have been *un employé supérieur* but they have managed to discard that association and distinguish themselves from the rest of the office personnel.

cadre from *non-cadre*. So the term *cadre* starts to look like a status and a state of mind rather than a set of distinctive and usefully identifiable tasks.

Collectively, the various stabs at definition by French authors are perhaps more interesting for what they tell us about the writers themselves than what they reveal about the *cadre*. In effect, this preoccupation with delimiting the contours is perhaps a manifestation of, 'the French obsession with labels, and the mania for confining people to airtight social categories'[1]. In fact, this national propensity to dissect, compartmentalize and classify is something which Zeldin (1983, 336) also observes: 'The government's sociologists, not frightened of being schematic, have divided French people up into five different species.' Reynaud and Grafmeyer (1982, 13) too, comment on this penchant for taxonomies: '*On célèbre volontiers le culte d'une raison déductive et classificatoire plutôt que le respect de l'expérience et de ses diversités*' (We are far more impressed by deductive reasoning than empirical evidence).

There can be no formal definition since the precise frontiers of the group are vague. Everyone knows where it starts, but no one can tell where it ends. One is reminded of Lord Denning's celebrated judgement: 'Like many other beings, a banker is easier to recognize than to define' (*Dominions Trust* v. *Kirkwood*, House of Lords, 1966). Thus, the scope of the term *cadre* must be ascertained through its connotations – by examining the meaning it has acquired over time.

Homogeneous body?

Given the varying backgrounds of the *cadre* population and the confusion over requirements for eligibility, it would seem fair to say that they are a heterogeneous mass. Certainly this is the verdict most French authors seem to return (Doublet and Passelecq, 1973, 121). They point out, for instance, that the national statistical service (INSEE)[2], places *cadres supérieurs* in the same socio-professional category as *professions libérales*, while *cadres moyens* are alloted a separate category, alongside schoolteachers and qualified nurses.

The diversity of the *cadre* population is largely the result of a massive increase in the number of *autodidactes* (self-taught *cadres*) throughout the 1960s (Boltanski, 1982, 48) – and the consequent drift away from any neatly defined population of *grandes écoles* graduates. This in turn has provoked an inevitable *vulgarisation* (devaluation) of the title.

---

1 Fabienne Pascaud reviewing Françoise Dorin's play *l'Etiquette*.
2 INSEE – Institut National des Statistiques et des Etudes Economiques.

But, by drawing attention to the internal subdivisions between, for instance, commercial and engineering graduates, between 'divine right' *cadres* and non-graduate *cadres*, indigenous observers give a one-sided view of the situation. Like Chinamen boasting Chinese heterogeneity, their case sounds doubtful to the outsider who perceives a unity not apparent from within.

When we asked plant managers about the meaning of *cadre* status they were able to provide an exact list of their *cadres*. Thus the definitional problem is largely academic.

At the same time there is a complication in the fact that all companies do not use the same criteria for admittance to the *cadre* group. But this should not detract from the strong sense of belonging, associated with the category – as well as the difficulties involved in gaining access. The barriers to entry mean that for many employees *passer cadre* is a real aspiration or achievement. To cross the threshold involves sacrifice and enhances status.

The *cadre* title therefore has a motivational aspect – and for employers, it represents a means of duplicating available rewards/reprimands. The system of material rewards and sanctions doubles up with a system of symbolic rewards and sanctions. In effect, the *passage-cadre* (transition) is the critical transition in the French hierarchy since it represents a change of status (unlike UK where the manager has no legal status) and allegiances – from trade union to employing company (Maurice *et al.* 1977, 770–771).

This notion of *cadres* as an entity is very much endorsed by French newspapers, which are quick to bestow a collective identity upon the group: 'Les cadres sont...', 'Les cadres font...', 'Les cadres veulent...' (Boltanski, 1982, 407). A selection of recent headlines may help convey this idea of a presumptive homogeneity:

'Ce qui fait marcher les cadres?' (The *cadres*, what makes them tick?)

Le Point, 18 May 1987, 32.

'Pouvoir d'achat: oui, les cadres ont perdu'. (Purchasing power: yes, the *cadres* have lost out.)

Le Point, 13 April 1987, 60.

'Les cadres français? Des autocrates!' (The *cadres*? True autocrats!)

L'Expansion, 20 September 1979, 81.

'La vérité sur la retraite des cadres'. (The real retirement prospects of *cadres*.)

Le Nouvel Economiste, 7 November 1986, 48.

'*Cadres: comment réussir sa carrière*'. (*Cadres*: tips for career success.)
Le Nouvel Economiste, 29 May 1987, 81.

'*La grande tentation des cadres: décrocher*'. (The great temptation – opting out.)
L'Expansion, 18 October 1979, 121.

'*Un allègement de la fiscalité pour les cadres*'. (A lightening of their tax burden.)
Le Monde, 22 June 1987, 13.

These quotes clearly suggest a degree of homogeneity unparalleled in the Anglo-Saxon context. The word 'manager' would be an uneasy substitute for *cadre* in the chosen headlines. This suggests that French *cadres* have a much more focused identity than their Anglo-Saxon counterparts. Newspapers talk of them in a way more befitting of a far more restricted group – executives, for instance.

It appears that in spite of their dispersal in terms of social and educational backgrounds and revenue, *cadres* do share a number of core characteristics which unite them – in much the same way as the modern agribusinessman shares an underlying cohesiveness with the small-time farmer. These distinguishing features are primarily legalistic – their own status, retirement scheme and placement service (APEC[1]), different probationary periods and fixed monthly income as opposed to variable weekly wage. But there is also an intangible element – the much-vaunted, yet indefinable, *état d'esprit*, as well as an undeniable sense of pride and belonging.

Consumer group

Seen from outside, *cadres* are certainly perceived as a homogeneous group, and referring to them as such enhances their unity. Politicians, for instance, will angle for the *cadre* vote *en masse*, in a way which would be totally ineffectual in Britain. A British politician would never look upon managers as some sort of 'block vote'. Indeed, if the *cadre* has a British equivalent, it is more likely to be the 'yuppie', and British politicians might well try to attract the yuppie vote.

The notion of the *cadre* as the original yuppie is also not without interest. Both, after all, are manufactured social groups, with their own particular identity and values. It was the *cadres*, in the mid-50s, who helped introduce and legitimize acquisitive American values in France:

---

1 APEC – Association pour l'emploi des cadres, a placement service for unemployed *cadres*.

16

L'attachement au biens matériels qui s'exprimait
chez le bourgeois par le désir de la conservation, se
manifeste chez lui par le plaisir de la consommation.
(The bourgeois demonstrated his fascination for
material possessions by his eagerness to save; the
cadre shows his by his desire to spend.)

(Bléton, 1956, 200.)

Cadres became a prime target for advertisers, who have created an image and ascribed a specific lifestyle to them: '*le mode de vie des cadres*' ('their way of life') has become a stock phrase which conjures up visions of a voracious and discerning consumer of goods and services:

La logique du système de consommation tend à lui
faire croire qu'il existe un style de vie, un 'standing'
qui lui est propre, et que ce serait le déchoir que de
ne pas l'atteindre. (The *cadre* has been hyped up
into thinking that there is a certain lifestyle and
standing which befits him and which must be
attained at all costs.)

(Doublet and Passelecq, 1973, 111.)

The socio-professional identity of this group was shaped and re-inforced by specialist magazines inspired by the American journal *Fortune*. Thus, *l'Express* (1957) dubbed itself '*le journal des cadres*' (the magazine for *cadres*) – and was followed in 1967 by *l'Expansion* which also specified the *cadre* as its target reader. These journals signalled a change of tack for the French economic press, which until then had provided financial information for owners and shareholders. But from the late 50s onwards it focused on the *cadre*, and on en-couraging a new business-literate generation of managers (Boltanski, 1982, 184). There is no sign of this tide of management magazines ebbing – 1987 saw yet another new one, '*C comme Cadre*' ('M' as in Manager).

A latent malaise?

Ironically, the unity of the *cadre* group is further enhanced by the existence of a much-vaunted 'malaise'. Virtually every French text dealing with the managerial population devotes a section to this notion – indeed, the phrase '*le malaise des cadres*' has become some-thing of a cliché.

Ever since their first appearance in 1936, *cadres* have been represented as a population that is 'misunderstood, humiliated, unpopular... caught in a pincers between *patronat* and proletariat' (Boltanski, 1982, 244

17

(Eng. trans.)). Obviously, this has a lot to do with the nature of the group which is, by definition, a buffer group. It was precisely because these graduate engineers did not fully identify with either employers or workers that the notion of the *cadre* emerged. The sense of being shut out, experienced by graduate engineers at that time, was described by Georges Lamirand:

> Abandoned by both sides, engineers discovered that they were neither fish nor fowl, that they constituted a third party imperilled on two fronts, in the sad position of an iron caught between hammer and anvil.
> (Boltanski, 1987, 40 (Eng. trans.).)

To some extent, the situation has still not been resolved. The ambiguity of the *cadre's* position manifested itself most clearly in 'the events' of 1968. Some *cadres* sided with the workers by striking while others were held 'hostage' by angry workers. This simple antithesis reveals the rival pressures exerted on *cadres* – their divided loyalties were a sign that they still did not know where they stood. The same predicament continues to haunt the *cadre* today – and in a roundabout way, it is this uncertainty which defines membership of the group (see Figure 2.1).

Besides this rather abstract reason for unease, concrete reasons relating to the prevailing economic environment were also invoked by the managers we interviewed. Some referred to the loss of purchasing power, the loss of job security and, more particular to the French context, the loss of social standing of the *cadre*.

It appears, however, that the problem may be overstated. One *cadre* from our interview sample suggested that the *cadre* has little to grumble about in relation, say, to the foreman. After all, the *cadre* still enjoys a privileged social position, albeit slightly tarnished by the 'proletarization' of the group ('*privilège*' is a word which appears frequently in advertising directed at *cadres*). This leads one to wonder whether we should pay heed to this alleged malaise – is it not stronger in some people's imagination than in reality? There is a case for speculating that the said malaise is little more than a defensive mechanism aimed at shielding the group from potential intruders who would swell the numbers, leading to further 'proletarization' – or perhaps a means of promoting group solidarity among a fairly disparate mass of salaried workers.

Social esteem

Notwithstanding these existential uncertainties which have led many commentators to speak of a 'malaise', at a more straightforward level the term *cadre* has been viewed as status-enhancing.

Figure 2.1 The *cadre* as 'pig in the middle'. (Extract from Lauzier's album *Les cadres* (© Dargaud, Editeur Paris, 1981, by Lauzier.)

The collective identity of the *cadres* has spilt over from its professional confines and taken up a social position. The *cadres* have become the social group to emulate, French society's trend-setters. The creation of the category offered an unprecedented degree of social mobility in France. Previously, the only bridges between the *petite* and the *grande bourgeoisie* had been via *l'artisanat* and commerce. The new category offered possibilities of upward mobility on a massive scale, in what remains a notoriously viscous social environment (Santoni, 1981, 134).

At the top end of the scale the *cadres supérieurs* enjoy a social status which is on a par with the professions – doctors, lawyers, architects. This can be attributed to their education levels which are usually not very far removed from that of their professional counterparts. The *cadre* is the latter-day bourgeois – well-off, known and respected in his neighbourhood:

> *Héritier du bourgeois, le cadre recherche la*
> *distinction, il aime le luxe, il est obsédé par le*
> *'standing', et il recherche le classicisme. Un certain*
> *snobisme caractérise son comportement.* (As a
> descendant of the bourgeois, the *cadre* is obsessed
> by distinction, luxury, standing and he yearns for
> refinement. His behaviour is typically snobbish.)
> (Blazot, 1983, 157.)

19

Of course, the social esteem enjoyed by *cadres* is also a product of the education system and the general standing of management. The *grandes écoles*, which supply graduates to the blue chip companies, are able to attract the brightest students, since their label is virtually an 'open-sesame' to all careers. But this requires the collusion of French companies which tacitly guarantee immediate *cadre* status and early responsibility. As long as this complicity works, 'we'll select them, you buy them', the *grandes écoles* will continue to attract a very high calibre of undergraduate recruit – thereby contributing to a virtuous circle in the status of the *cadre* (Ardagh, 1982, 43).

Role of the *cadre*

Just as the manager must manage, so the cadre is there to *encadrer*. Yet the accepted translation of 'to manage' is 'gérer'. Benguigui *et al.* (1975), refer to '*une mission spécifique: gérer – et plus précisément encore* **encadrer**' ('a specific mission: gérer – but even more precisely *encadrer*'). It is possible to infer from this nuance that there is a difference in the conception of French and Anglo-Saxon managers.

The fact that the French term was borrowed from military circles is not without significance in this respect. The verb *encadrer* has a notion of policing, which Horovitz (1980, 86) suggests is reflected in the French approach to management control. And if we trace back the word, its literal meaning (as a frame) also reflects the constraining role of the *cadre* which is implicit in the following quotation from a practising manager:

> *Nous avons beaucoup de mal à nous faire à l'idée*
> *que la résolution de conflits, la conduite, la*
> *correction, voire la contrainte des autres, font partie*
> *intégrante de la fonction de cadre.* (We have great
> difficulty in coming to terms with the less savoury
> aspects of our work – namely, conflict resolution,
> leadership, punishment and even constraint.)
> (Emilio Fontana, *Points de Vente*,
> 1 February 1987.)

But setting semantics aside, the role of the French *cadre* has always been different from that of the Anglo-Saxon manager. From the outset *cadres* have had a specific mission which went beyond corporate expectations. Initially, in 1936, their role was to act as a stabilizing force in the increasingly confrontational worker/employer discussions. Then, when de Gaulle returned to power in 1958, he put the onus squarely on *les cadres de la nation* to rebuild the French economy, thereby restoring France to her former glory. Justifiably, the *cadres* have come to be regarded as the prime architects (and beneficiaries) of France's economic success and the rise in living standards over the three decades known as *les Trentes Glorieuses* (the thirty years of glory – 1945–75).

Of late the national socio-economic responsibility of the *cadre* is less explicit, but lives on:

> *La vocation des cadres est de guider la classe*
> *ouvrière dans la voie du progrès.* (The cadres'
> vocation is to act as a beacon for the working classes
> in their journey down the road of progress.)
> (Blazot, 1983, 12.)

> *C'est lui qui fait le niveau de vie de la nation.* (It is
> they who maintain the nation's standard of living.)
> (Blazot, 1983, 13.)

> *Les cadres sont les artisans de la mutation sociale*
> *en cours.* (The cadres are the facilitators of on-going
> social change.)
> (*Le Monde*, 23 June 1987, 44.)

The *cadres* see themselves as privileged partners of the economic and political powers that be. Their union (CFE-CGC) prides itself on its clout in high circles and recently stated that:

> *La confédération s'est toujours fait entendre et, dans*
> *bien des cas, a obligé patronat et gouvernement à*
> *tenir compte de ses options.* (One way or another,
> the employers and the state are forced to take
> account of the preferences of this management
> confederation.)
> (*Le Monde*, 23 June 1987, 44.)

An even more explicit description of the *cadre*'s socio-economic mission is encountered in a report by the Fédération Nationale des Syndicats d'Ingénieurs et Cadres (National Federation of Managers' Unions):

> *Il ne suffit pas d'exister; il faut vivre et plus encore*
> *avoir des raisons de vivre. Ce sera demain le rôle*
> *des ingénieurs et cadres de fournir ces raisons, de*
> *participer à leur mise en place dans la société,*
> *d'animer et d'entraîner les autres, de transmettre*
> *connaissance et idéal, de s'engager résolument dans*
> *l'action civique et sociale afin que le progrès se*

21

> confonde avec la civilisation dans le coeur des
> hommes. (Mere existence is not enough. We must
> live and have a reason for living. And the onus falls
> upon the cadres to provide these reasons, to
> implement them, to motivate others and show them
> the way, to communicate, and to take an active part
> in society, so that progress and civilization may
> become one in the hearts of men.)
>
> (Blazot, 1983, 94.)

This mixture of management role and philosophy might appear excessive by Anglo-Saxon standards, but corresponds to the quasi-divine mission with which the cadre has been entrusted in France. The French seem to regard their managers as the moral, as well as economic, saviours of the nation. They have a responsibility as rôle models, which others seek to emulate. It is difficult to know to what extent this is merely rhetoric, but there does seem to be a distinct awareness of their social responsibility as an example to the workforce, and their contribution to the nation's wealth. This was clearly expressed at the Confédération Française de l'Encadrement (formerly the CGC) conference, which described its members as:

> Le moteur économique, le promoteur social et le
> garant de l'avenir du pays. (The social and economic
> force which guarantees France's future.)
>
> (Le Monde, 23 June 1987, 44.)

The likelihood is that their future rôle will be boosted by the need to prepare for the unified European market planned for 1992. The same article in Le Monde refers to:

> Une convergence sur certaines préoccupations
> essentielles, comme l'échéance de 1992 et le rôle et
> la place de l'encadrement. (The role of the cadre in
> the success of a unified European market.)

Masculine aura

There are also a number of factors which contrive to give the term cadre a masculine connotation. Historically of course, the term was borrowed from the military – the male preserve par excellence. Inevitably, this has had repercussions on popular perception of the cadre. The macho a priori was reinforced by the fact that the category was initially composed almost exclusively of graduate engineers, and with even the most prestigious engineering school (l'Ecole Polytechnique) remaining single-sex until 1972, male engineers have left their 'virile' imprint on it. Finally, the term is lumbered with a masculine tag – **le** *cadre* – which merely exacerbates the problem, acting as a perceptual barrier to the inclusion of both male and female in that category. Incidentally, this is a problem not encountered in Anglo-Saxon countries where the neuter gender has swept all before it.

Many books and journals are now addressing the issue with a token section rather clumsily entitled *cadre au féminin*. In addition, as noted earlier, the noun *cadre* has actually been deformed so that it can now be employed as an adjective. This makes it marginally easier to include women in the appellation – *une femme cadre*. However, it will be some time before the historical preconceptions surrounding the term are overcome.

Chapter Three

The making of French managers

'*Les grandes écoles sont rendues abusivement responsables de tous les maux dont la France est affectée et en même temps créditées tout aussi abusivement de tous ses succès.*' ('The grandes écoles are falsely blamed for all France's vices and, just as wrongly, credited with all its virtues.')
(Conversation with Roger Fauroux, former head of l'Ecole Nationale d'Aministration.)

The French education system

Much of the best and the worst in the French national spirit can be imputed to the concept of education as inspired academic pedagogy confined to the classroom walls: its role is to transmit knowledge and to train intellects, not – as in Britain – to develop the full individual.

(Ardagh, 1987, 453.)

Any understanding of French management necessarily implies a knowledge of the French education system since there can be few nations in the world which take education quite so seriously. This brief descriptive section sets out to fill in the basic details for readers who may be unfamiliar with the French education system (see Table 3.1).

The French equivalent of the old eleven plus having been abolished in 1957, French school children enter common or comprehensive schools at the age of eleven. The issue of public or private education does not arise in the same way as it would in Britain since the state education system absorbs 90 per cent of the school population, regardless of social and income level. In France, private school means church school and many children would be embarrassed to admit going there – and not just because of predominantly atheistic attitudes. With tougher discipline and old-fashioned teaching methods, the private school is usually a refuge for the *cancres* (dullards) – children who cannot keep pace with the relentless state school system.

Table 3.1   The French educational system

Primary: 5 years		[Age]
● CP	(cours préparatoire)	6/7
● CE 1	(cours élémentaire 1)	7/8
● CE 2	(cours élémentaire 2)	8/9
● CM 1	(cours moyen 1)	9/10
● CM 2	(cours moyen 2)	10/11

Secondary: 7 years

- ● Collège: 4 years
  - — 6ème (first foreign language) 11/12
  - — 5ème 12/13
  - — 4ème (second foreign language) 13/14
  - — 3ème 14/15

- ● Lycée: 3 years
  - — 2de 15/16
  - — 1ère 16/17
    (choice of *baccalauréat* options)
  - — Terminale 17/18
    (*baccalauréat* exam)

Higher Education

- ● University:
  - — 1st cycle: DEUG Bac + 2
    (*Diplôme d'études universitaires générales*)
  - — 2nd cycle: Licence Bac + 3
    Maîtrise Bac + 4
  - — 3rd cycle: DEA Bac + 5
    (*Diplôme d'études appliquées*)
    Thèse d'Etat Bac + 8
    (Doctorate)

- ● Grande Ecole:
  - — *Ecole préparatoire* 18/19
    (minimum of 1 year for top commercial schools,
    and 2 for the top engineering schools)
    Entrance exam
  - — Admission to *grande école* 20–22
  - — Graduation 23–25

Secondary education in France has two cycles: the first cycle is compulsory and is given in comprehensive schools called *collèges*. This lasts from 11 to 15, but at the age of 13 some 12 per cent transfer to a *lycée d'enseignement professionnel*, LEP or technical school, to take the three-year craft course leading to the Certificat d'Aptitude Professionnelle (CAP). At the start of the second cycle, some 23 per cent, aged 15, join these vocational *lycées*, some to do the CAP, others the shorter and more broadly-based Brevet d'Etudes Professionnelles (BEP). It needs courage, however, in white middle-class suburbia to get off at this stage, enter an LEP and learn a blue-collar skill. It is taken as a sign of premature failure in an academically obsessed country.

This second cycle of secondary education lasts three years and caters for those deemed capable of passing the *baccalauréat* (university entrance exam). Although all the *lycées* have theoretically standardized intakes, they do in fact have different clienteles. The best *lycées classiques* are still largely a preserve of the bourgeoisie while the others, because of geographical distribution and lack of prestige, receive more working-class and fewer bright children. One only has to look at the *baccalauréat* results of schools for confirmation. While an average *lycée* might be satisfied with a 70 per cent success rate, the top high schools (such as Louis-le-Grand, Henri IV or Saint Louis) would be uncomfortable with less than 90 per cent.

There are nearly thirty *baccalauréat* options, which are sets of pre-packaged subject combinations. For instance, the *bac C* is the highly rated maths and physical sciences option, the *bac D* the maths and natural sciences option, the *bac G* the management option, the *bac H* the computing option. Whilst each option has a particular focus, each also carries traces of all the other subjects (French, history, geography, mathematics, sciences and modern languages) – the aim of the *baccalauréat* being to provide a high level of *culture générale*. For instance, the main arts option (*bac A*) includes maths but the subject is given a lower weighting.

The formalized grouping of subjects has made it easy to make comparisons – and a hierarchy of prestige has emerged which is essentially determined by the maths content of each option with the *bac C* ruling the roost. Such is the importance attached to some combinations of subjects that parents may prefer to see their children repeat a year, or pay for private tuition in their weaker subjects, rather than encourage them to follow less demanding courses, for which they may be better suited.

Taken at eighteen or so, *le bac* is far more rigorous and brain-taxing an exam than its English equivalent, A-level GCE, and even more essential as a passport to higher education. Thirty-eight per cent of an age group reach *baccalauréat* level with thirty per cent succeeding. Overall, some 54 per cent of the 16 to 18 age group stay on for some form of general or vocational education.

The stated intent of the Socialist government (1981–86) was to increase the number of pupils gaining the *baccalauréat* to 80 per cent of an age group (currently 30 per cent) by the year 2000. This desire to improve education and academic standards reflects the twin determinations to prepare young people more effectively for a high-tech future and to reinforce rather old-fashioned republican virtues. Both may be intimately related to France's concern to maintain its status and identity in a world dominated by superpower rivalry and Anglo-American mass culture.

Higher education

Higher education is provided in institutes of advanced technology, universities and grandes écoles (see Figure 3.1). A baccalauréat gives automatic entry to university, where courses comprise three cycles. The first, lasting two years, leads to a general university studies diploma, the Diplôme d'Etudes Universitaires Générales (DEUG) which covers both compulsory and optional subjects. After this students may leave or stay on for the second cycle. This also lasts two years, the first year of which leads to the licence (equivalent of a BA) and the second to the maîtrise (MA). The third cycle involves either three years leading to a doctorate or a one-year Diplôme d'Etudes Supérieures Spécialisées (DESS) in a highly specialized area.

In an attempt to ease the overcrowding and remedy the absence of vocational training in the universities, the government created Instituts Universitaires de Technologie (IUT) in 1966. These were intended to provide a more practical grounding and fill a manpower gap at middle management level. Like the universities, the IUTs recruit baccalauréat holders, but unlike the universities, they offer intensive vocational training (in management, commercial and technical subjects) over a two year period. They include industrial placements and the failure rates are lower than at the traditional universities.

For many years industry did not recognize the qualifications gained in the IUTs because of a traditional bias against semi-vocational education, still considered the poor relation in the French educational system. After initial prejudice against courses of this type, the IUT diploma has now gained recognition in industry. Many employers now prefer it to a DEUG or even a licence, the teaching of which, even in science subjects, is perceived as too theoretical.

The grandes écoles are a feature of the French educational landscape which has no equivalent in any comparable Western country. Students are selected by competitive entrance examinations, having been subjected to two or three years of intense preparation in special post-baccalauréat classes. Some of the grandes écoles are under the control of the Ministry of Education, for example the Ecole Nationale d'Administration (ENA). Others are sponsored by bodies such as the chambers of commerce, for example the Ecole des Hautes Etudes Commerciales (HEC), while others are controlled by different ministries, for example the Ecole Polytechnique by the Ministry of Armed Forces.

27

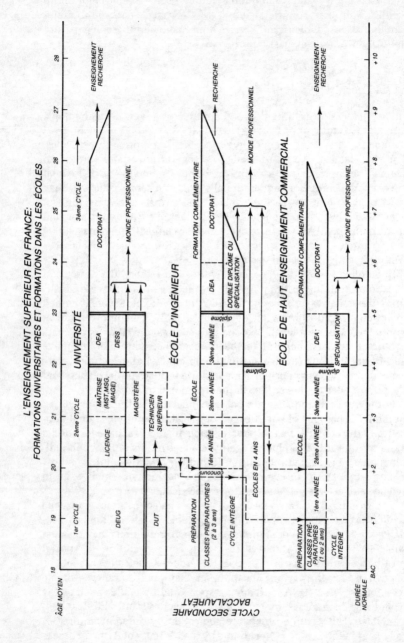

L'ENSEIGNEMENT SUPÉRIEUR EN FRANCE:
FORMATIONS UNIVERSITAIRES ET FORMATIONS DANS LES ÉCOLES

Management in France   Fig. 3 - 1

SIGNIFICATION DES SIGLES

DEUG   : *Diplôme d'Etudes Universitaires*
               Générales
DUT   : *Diplôme Universitaire de Technologie*
DEA   : *Diplôme d'Etudes Approfondies*
DESS   : *Diplôme d'Etudes Supérieurs*
               Spécialisées
MST   : *Maîtrise de Sciences et Techniques*
MSG   : *Maîtrise de Sciences de Gestion*
MIAGE   : *Maîtrise d'Information Appliquée à*
               la Gestion des Entreprises

Figure 3.1 The higher education system in France.

Not all the *grandes écoles* enjoy the same prestige. Perhaps the most sought after places are at l'ENA which is neither an engineering nor a business school, but a civil service training college. Entrance to l'ENA is extremely competitive, and most candidates have undergone training at the Paris Institut d'Etudes Politiques (commonly known as Sciences-Po), a private institution created in 1871 and superseded in practice by l'ENA. The position achieved in the final examination at l'ENA determines the choice of appointment, and the spirit of rivalry is maintained throughout the course, as an individual's whole career may be determined by a quarter of a mark in the final assessment.

While the number of students at the universities has been increasing in an uncontrollable way since the war, the intakes of the *grandes écoles* have remained almost static, and their students have continued, albeit perhaps not so easily as in the past, to find satisfying employment.

The role of education

A long-standing feature of French society is the high premium it places on intellect. Where America extols money, West Germany work and Great Britain blood, France has nailed its flag to the post of cleverness. It is achievement in the educational field which determines inclusion among the decision-makers of French society. The nation is governed by its star pupils, and the higher reaches of management are no exception. Brains are deemed an acceptable means of procuring social eminence – and as Vaughan *et al*, point out, they are certainly 'a less invidious ground to invoke in a democracy than either hereditary privilege or the acquisition of wealth' (1980, 99).

Educational credentials are ideal props for authority since they are verifiable discriminators of the organizational hierarchy. In France, they indicate status and competence in much the same way as an individual's salary situates a person in the US. The graduate of a prestigious *grande école* is demonstrably 'better' than his organizational subordinates and this justifies inequalities of power (remember the conundrum posed in Chapter 1!). Thus, élitism and the French preoccupation with egalitarianism are reconciled, since the systematic testing of intellectual merit gives everyone (in theory) the same opportunity of access to the élite.

In keeping with this desire for objectivity, mathematics is the central feature of French selection methods in education. From secondary school onwards, a priority is given to the mastery of mathematical tools and to the quality of logical inference. The maths input provides the basis for the pecking order in *baccalauréat* options and determines admission to the top flight *grandes écoles* – both in engineering . . . and management.

French higher education is thus based on a two-tier system which is rooted in France's history and distinguishes the exclusive *grandes écoles* and the sprawling universities.

The appellation, *grande école*, is a general and not an official term. The *grandes écoles* are a diversified ensemble of small or medium-sized autonomous establishments which were created outside the traditional university stream in response to precise sectoral needs – notably in engineering, applied science and management studies. The precise criteria for acquiring the precious label are not at all clear. For the same reasons, it is hard to specify the exact number of these schools, though about 160 lay claim to the rank, with an average of a mere 400 students each.

In comparison to the *grandes écoles*, the universities have a distinctly lacklustre image. Part of the reason for this lies in the need to cater for too many students of differing abilities. This is primarily due to the fact that universities have no control over the quality of intakes. A *baccalauréat* gives automatic entry to university – as opposed to the highly selective regime operated by the *grandes écoles*. The contrasting systems will be discussed more extensively in the following section.

Management education in France

Paradoxically, while education in general has been exalted, management education has had some trouble in gaining legitimacy. The universities, which specialized in classical education were, until recently (1955), particularly reluctant to embrace this vocational discipline. The 1980s, however, have witnessed the belated emergence of an enterprise culture, in a society which has traditionally been hostile to the ethos of wealth creation – and nowhere is this turnaround more apparent than in the attitudes of students. In 1968, they were busy trying to burn down the Bourse (French stock exchange); today, every self-respecting business school has its own investment club. There is a new-found willingness to treat business as socially acceptable, and essential to the life of the country.

Pre-career management education: games people play

There is something distinctly mercenary about pre-experience management education. Each party involved seems more concerned with beating the system than achieving a common end. Students seem to repress their sense of vocation, schools are obsessed with pecking orders and companies pay inflated salaries for raw graduates from the right places. The whole edifice seems founded on abstract values which are only tenuously linked to the production of well-adjusted managers.

The extent to which the system has assumed a logic of its own is perhaps best illustrated by the saga of lengthening scholarity. In order to ward off fears of unemployment, there is a student demand, which schools and universities are meeting, for longer courses. But the value of protracted studies is relative, and because the tendency is generalized, companies have merely responded by adding two years to their recruitment bench–mark. Posts which were filled by *baccalauréat* entrants are now reserved for people with two years higher education, typically from an institute of advanced technology (IUT). Consequently, students delay their entry into active life and companies recruit individuals who have no desire to undergo a further period of induction training – it seems like a no-win situation.

Yet the games in which they engage have a sense of coherence and compatibility – the system works because the parties complement one another and play by the same rules.

Games students play

Devil take the hindmost
Effectively, management education begins when pupils choose their *baccalauréat* options. Although there is a management option, pupils with real managerial aspirations will steer clear of it! They will choose instead the maths and physical sciences option (commonly termed *le bac C*) which affords the best chances of admission (entrance exam permitting), two years after *baccalauréat*, into both engineering and commercial *grandes écoles*. The irony that the management option leads to anything but a high–powered managerial position is compounded by the fact that there are over 20 *baccalauréat* options but only one which really counts. This situation has been condemned as the dictatorship of the *bac C*.

On completing the *baccalauréat*, it is accepted that those who can, will proceed to the *prépas* (preparatory schools) to be coached through the *concours* (entrance exam) to the *grandes écoles*. Competition to enter the most successful Parisian *prépa* (Louis-le-Grand) is said to be tougher than the subsequent entry into one of the prestigious trio of management schools (HEC/ESSEC/ESCP), collectively known as *les grandes parisiennes*. Students are kept informed of the relative success rates of the various *prépas* by annual 'hit parades' published by the journals *l'Etudiant* and *Le Monde de l'Education*, thereby instilling an early notion of career strategy.

In the preparatory schools, the students are subjected to an intense work rate, based essentially on maths, which can make the subsequent pace at the *grande école* seem decidedly slack.[1] For most students

---

1 In fact, the high pressure experienced during this training period prompted *The Guardian* to dub preparatory schooling, 'the cram de la crème' (Ardagh, 1982, 511).

l'enfer préparationnaire (the hell of the preparatory school) represents the peak effort since, having reached the inner sanctum of the *grande école*, the diploma is *de facto* guaranteed.[1]

As one 'Polytechnique' student put it:

> 'De toute façon, il faut avoir tué père et mère pour sortir sans diplôme.' ('Anyhow, in order to fail one would have to commit patricide.')
> (*L'Expansion*, 11 November 1982, 121).

In other words, the gains stemming from admission to a *grande école* are so automatic that students are wont to perceive entry as a landing point rather than a launch pad.

The notion of career strategy manifests itself again in the choice of *grande école*. Students display precocious awareness of their own limitations, so they will only enter exams they feel capable of passing. Evidence of this can be seen in the fact that it is not necessarily the top *grandes écoles* which attract the most candidates. The students engage in a large measure of self-selection to avoid paying costly exam fees where there is a low likelihood of success. They are sensitized early into optimizing their chances and cutting their losses.

Charades

What is more, students will renounce vocational preferences in favour of instrumental disciplines. In order to keep their options open, students are best advised to pursue maths to the limits of their potential. The route to the top is clearly signposted which minimizes the risks of losing potential talent through misinformation. But the price paid is a snubbing of vocational courses and a sheeplike procession towards the same *grandes écoles* because of the tremendous career advantages they confer. This reaffirms a calculating approach to education which seems especially pronounced among French students. Indeed, the student magazine *l'Etudiant* constantly reinforces this notion – with references to tips, short-cuts, success rates and tactics in gaining access to the various establishments (for instance, the December 1986 issue, p. 120).

Games educational establishments play

For nigh on two centuries, the top engineering *grandes écoles*, spearheaded by l'Ecole Polytechnique, have groomed their alumni to take up positions as *les cadres de la nation* (the nation's organizers), in spheres as diverse as business, politics and public service. Not surprisingly, the schools' legitimacy as suppliers of the nation's business élite

---

1 It is worth pointing out the contrasting situation of the universities which have to carry out substantial reductions at the the end of the first and second years to compensate for the impossibility of selection at entry. At some universities, less than 50 per cent of those admitted will actually graduate (*L'Expansion*, 7 March 1985, 81).

does not rest on the curriculum (albeit generalist in content) but on the type of education they impart. The French graduate engineer is not only knowledgeable or well versed in engineering; he is, first and foremost, the product of a mind-stretching system which has nurtured him for leadership positions in industry. More than in other countries, French engineers enjoy a privileged social status, which can be seen by their widespread presence in upper management.

The seal of approval from a prestigious engineering school endorses its holder's capacity for rapid learning and intellectual virtuosity. The quality of the raw material is guaranteed by a highly selective recruitment process, which requires two years' additional schooling beyond secondary education – and the finished product has the added feature of three years of intensive study. In short, the graduate engineer is endowed with the necessary resolve and analytical ability to tackle any problem.

On top of this, the schools bestow on their students the social wherewithal and an influential old-boy network to enhance their career chances (the institutionalization of school links is discussed in more detail in Chapter 4). For instance, by the time he graduates, a *polytechnicien* (student of l'Ecole Polytechnique), has assembled a battery of real or assumed advantages that ensure speedy professional ascent. To add to that, he will have inherited a network of contacts which transcends all sectors. Indeed, the engineering schools have been so convincing in promoting themselves as 'surrogate management schools' that one can understand in part the belated emergence of American-style business schools in France. The success of the engineering schools also explains the tendency for commercial *grandes écoles* to emulate them.

Follow the leader

The first signs of emulation were seen in the explicit attempts by l'Ecole des Hautes Etudes Commerciales (HEC), the foremost commercial school, to don the apparel of the engineering schools at its inception. The school was set up in 1881 with the express intention of breaking the engineers' stranglehold over large sectors of business in the expanding industrial climate of the late nineteenth century. From the outset, HEC espoused what were considered the most prestigious aspects of the state-sponsored engineering schools, notably a socially biased, post-*baccalauréat* recruitment policy. Furthermore, HEC's curriculum rested firmly on the cornerstone of law, a noble discipline which lent commercial education a veneer of academic respectability. In terms of image it looked to l'Ecole Centrale for guidance since this was the only private engineering school which had managed to stamp its identity among the state *grandes écoles* (the very first head of HEC was in fact a *centralien*).

Naturally enough, HEC spawned its own imitators, a network of provincial commercial schools (ESCAE[1]) which, by association, tended towards the *nec plus ultra*, l'Ecole Polytechnique. Perhaps the most striking legacy from the engineering schools was the widespread adoption of maths as the critical entry determinant. This tribute to engineering influence is justifiable as an objective measure of merit for selection, but it would appear that the elements of scholastic success are poorly matched with those of professional success.

The less prestigious commercial schools (mostly private rather than sponsored by the Chambers of Commerce like HEC and the ESCAE network) are also faithful to the HEC model. These lesser schools are forced into reducing the maths input (concession) in order to recuperate those who fail the *concours* (entrance exam) owing to a weakness in maths. But, in other respects they do their best to imitate the more prestigious establishments.

The prime manifestation of this lies in their names, which are reminiscent, not to say replicas, of the more venerable establishments. They are abetted in this by the French penchant for acronyms, which lends itself to abuse. Lesser schools capitalize on the confusion in order to imply similar status to the provincial commercial schools (ESCAE). One personnel manager we interviewed speculated that new commercial schools were named by picking out three of the following at random: '*école, institut, supérieur, hautes études, gestion, finance, direction des entreprises, affaires*', and translating the result into English if need be. There is undoubtedly an element of deliberate *trompe l'œil* in many appellations – to dupe potential students, their parents and employers alike. The profusion of acronyms can prove quite bewildering, even to the initiated.

The same goes for the popular confusion surrounding the various degrees of state accreditation. Some of the less scrupulous schools shrewdly exploit the billing *homologué par l'état* (state registered), knowing that the uninitiated will equate it with the more exclusive *diplôme reconnu par l'état* (state approved qualification). The former merely indicates the level of the qualification, whilst the latter is an attestation of quality. It implies that the Ministry of Education has some say in the syllabus and teaching methods as well as naming the Chairman of the Admissions and Examiners' Board.

Further evidence of mimicry can be seen in the necessity for the most embryonic business school, whose future still hangs in the balance, to set an entrance exam. This is intended to set them apart from the universities and, by implication, identify them with the *grandes écoles*. Generally, the said exam is more than a touch symbolic since meeting entrance requirements has less to do with exam marks than

---

1 ESCAE – Ecole(s) Supérieure(s) de Commerce et d'Administration des Entreprises, more prosaically referred to as the *Sup-de-Co*.

parental funds. The schools demand high tuition fees since they do not have the same ability as the *grandes écoles* to attract financial support from companies *(taxe professionnelle[1])*. These private schools have also some difficulty in attracting permanent academic staff and generally resort to a mixture of part-time teachers and visiting staff. But that is not to say they do not know how to market themselves. On the contrary, their less prestigious position makes it essential to maintain a high profile. Guaranteed selling points like an international perspective, old–boy networks, sporting associations and *junior-entreprise* (student-run consultancy) invariably feature prominently in their seductive literature.

Universities are limited as to the extent they can copy the *grandes écoles*. For instance, the universities must operate an open-door policy whereby any holder of the *baccalauréat* is eligible for admission. The fact remains that the most successful universities are precisely those which have found a way round these constraints. Foremost among these universities is the management university of Paris IX-Dauphine created in 1968 in response to student discontent and housed in the recently vacated NATO headquarters.

Dauphine's selection, competition and professionalism give it all the hallmarks of a *grande école*. By law it should not practise selection – yet, in reality, only people with a *bac C* (maths) need apply and 95 per cent of the intake in fact obtained a distinction in their *baccalauréat*. This is deemed preferable to selection '*par la file d'attente*' or '*par la règle de l'autobus*' ('first come, first served'). As a result Dauphine's reputation among employers is enhanced and its students can expect increasing numbers of unsolicited job offers. Although the university clearly flouts the principle of non-selection, the state is prepared to turn a blind eye to uphold the reputation of this jewel in a lacklustre university system.

Dauphine also pays the same attention as the *grandes écoles* to industrial placements – demonstrating full awareness of the importance of these initial contacts between students and companies. In the same vein, Dauphine has followed the example of the *grandes écoles* and organized annual job fairs, as well as a yacht race whose teams are composed of students and executives, and which amounts to a floating job fair. The teaching methods, too, are reminiscent of the *grandes écoles* in that they are based on group work rather than the staple university diet of lectures. Thus, it has taken on many of the accoutrements of a *grande école* education as regards length and format of studies, but most importantly in terms of recruitment. It would seem that any

---

1 Established in 1925, *taxe professionelle* is a levy on companies (0.6 per cent of the payroll) which they may donate to any pre-entry training establishment. Responsibility for prospection and collection of the funds is left to the students themselves who act on behalf of their institute.

university which seeks to emulate this success is destined to follow Dauphine's lead and renounce its university origins in order to gain credibility in the business community.

What appears to be universal convergence towards the Polytechnique blueprint even extends to the Institutes of Technology (IUT) which were destined to replenish the ranks of middle managers by providing a shorter and practical apprenticeship to management. Like certain universities, the institutes have resorted to selection by introducing a mini-'concours' which, according to a headteacher interviewed, has turned them into scaled down grandes écoles.

Moreover, with the top commercial schools extending the period of preparatory schooling to an obligatory two years in order to align themselves with engineering studies, the institutes have found their vocational two-year courses devalued in relative terms. Once again the influence of the top engineering schools has prompted emulation with each educational establishment lengthening its curriculum – partly for image purposes and partly to attenuate student fears of unemployment.

Rather than trying to respond to demand in a pluralist fashion, each establishment strives more or less consciously to attain the Poly-technique ideal. They seem undeterred by its relation to a bygone age and its oblique approach to the acquisition of management skills. L'Ecole Polytechnique remains the archetypal model, the universal point de repère which renders comparison between the various estab-lishments easy and apparently legitimate. This gives rise to another game.

King of the castle

The predilection for hierarchies is a familiar feature of French culture and the facile ranking of educational establishments provides the press with an eager readership (incorporating students and their parents, teachers and employers). Each category of establishment is regularly scrutinized and classified in league tables compiled by l'Etudiant or Le Monde de l'Education. There are even cross-category (all-comers) surveys conducted by l'Expansion based on starting salaries offered to graduates. The higher the league position, the higher the signing-on fee commanded by its graduates. Irrespective of their initial accuracy, these comparisons tend to prove self-fulfilling since employers use them to align their salaries on market trends thereby reinforcing findings presented as neutral.

Of course, conventional bases of comparison always favour the same schools, so the lesser schools endeavour to find new criteria which will upset the traditional pecking order and put them to the fore. Certain schools will point to the number of times they are oversub-scribed as an indication of exclusiveness. They will publicize the low chances of admission and on this basis will claim to rival the top schools – carefully neglecting to acknowledge the perspicacious self-selection in which prospective students engage.

However spurious, such comparisons fuel intense rivalry among the various establishments. Some student interviewees suggested that the heads of the schools were actually more attentive to the starting salaries of their students (as quoted, for instance, in *l'Expansion's*, *'Combien gagnent les débutants'*, 18 June 1987) than to the contents of the curriculum. Indeed, one observer of the system was of the opinion that:

> Les responsables de l'école surveillent la moyenne
> des salaires d'embauche avec une passion comparable
> à celle du petit porteur sur les cours de la Bourse.
> (Those who run the school scrutinize the going rate
> for new graduates with the zest of a small shareholder
> checking the prices of stocks and shares.)
> *(Le Nouvel Observateur*, 21 January 1983, 16.)

This concern for image has implications for the extent to which schools can afford to err from the path cut by HEC/Polytechnique. Schools are reluctant to take initiatives which diverge excessively from the accepted norms. In short, form outweighs substance.

In spite of the jockeying for position, the level of consensus surrounding the intricate pecking order is high and counter-jumping is minimal. Some measure of the immutable nature of the hierarchy can be illustrated by the fact that, when the Raymond Barre government (1976–81) decided to upgrade French technical education, the only policy it could come up with was to make it easier for the best pupils on vocational courses to enter the *grandes écoles*. The point is that there is only one hierarchy in France.

The leading three commercial *grandes écoles*, HEC/ESSEC/ESCP, are closely followed by the regional *Ecoles Supérieures de Commerce* (led by Lyon) mingled with a few of the private schools mentioned earlier. The attraction of these prestigious schools is that their label is a guarantee for life. In particular, the stamp HEC/ESSEC/ESCP is a passport to a prosperous career. But the stakes are not negligible. The failure rates in reaching these schools is high and the preparatory system leaves many people bitter or demotivated after two years of sustained effort and not even a concrete qualification to show for it – their only consolation being direct access to the second year of university courses.

Furthermore, the schools are not only intellectually élitist, they are also socially discriminating. Based on a trad'tionally hierarchic society, management education in France is a distinctly class-bound affair. The pattern of socially biased recruitment was set by the engineering schools in the eighteenth century using Latin as a social filter. The discipline has since changed, but the mechanism lingers on even in the business schools.

Marceau's analysis of the socio-professional origins of the alumni at the business school INSEAD revealed that the higher social strata are strongly over-represented, suggesting 'a high degree of inheritance of occupational aspirations' (Whitley et al., 1984, 86). This concurs with Claude Vincent's view of France as a 'high-viscosity' society, where upward mobility is a generally slow process – notwithstanding the much publicized rise of exceptional individuals like Pompidou whose humble backgrounds serve to defuse criticism of élitism.

Certainly the top schools are reluctant to divulge statistics on the socio-professional composition of intakes. At HEC, the offspring of employers, senior executives and the liberal professions account for 70 per cent of those admitted (L'Etudiant, December 1986, 112). A number of sociologists maintain that the educational achievements (power merited) of the classe dirigeante (ruling class) simply serve as a smokescreen to mask its origins (power inherited). Bourdieu and Passeron (1964), in particular, contend that by requiring managers to be supernumerate, access is biased towards well-to-do students who benefit from an earlier and easier apprenticeship to abstraction.

Whatever the exact mechanism, management education remains heavily biased towards the higher social classes and does not appear to be making any great contribution to the democratization of management. Nor are there any signs of change, with the grandes écoles jealously guarding their prestige by limiting the growth of successive intakes[1]. The barely perceptible rise in output of grande école graduates is in stark contrast to the continual increases in university subscriptions. The élitist tradition shows no real signs of weakening.

Games employers play

Baiting
On the face of it, employers would appear to be the prime victims of the 'trivial pursuits' of schools and students alike. But they appear willing victims since they pull out all the stops to lure in the top candidates. IBM-France for instance has a section specifically concerned with the schools, 'Relations grandes écoles' (a title which consciously omits the universities). The blue chip companies will start their pursuit of the best talents early by visiting the schools and conducting 'dog and pony shows' – presentations by senior people who outline career path opportunities. It is not uncommon for the best graduates to receive more than ten offers of employment which enables them to play hard to get (and raise the bids).

Whilst the salaries demanded are often exorbitant, companies tend to play along, dangling gilt-edged carrots to attract the brightest

---

1 The total numbers in the grandes écoles are less than 5 per cent of all those in higher education, but their influence is large out of all proportion.

available talent. Companies are apt to look upon the *grandes ecoles* as elaborate sifting systems rather than purveyors of knowledge – and some make no secret of the fact that they are primarily purchasing the *'concours'* (entrance exam):

> La qualité des élèves n'est pas un produit de l'enseigne-
> ment mais de la sélection. (The quality of the graduates
> is due to the selection process not the teaching.)
> (*L'Expansion*, 11 November 1982, 121.)

Although the salary gap between commercial and engineering graduates is constantly being eroded, companies still continue to favour the engineering schools which are entrusted with the making of French managers, even if they no longer hold a monopoly. There is no shortage of companies ready to pay back (to the state) the fees of a *'polytechnicien'* in order to capture him immediately on graduation and spare him ten years' forced labour in state service.

Company indifference regarding the transmission of occupationally relevant management skills merely endorses the view of qualifications as 'entry tickets'. Access to business is not associated with qualifications embodying a job-specific content, in the same way as access to architecture, medicine or law.[1] But French companies seem to push this argument to excess. Most employers would still prefer products of Polytechnique (engineers) or l'ENA (civil servants) to their HEC counter-parts (managers). Strictly speaking, the former were not designed to train managers for private enterprise, but both students and employers treat them as such. Students intent on a career in industry will have no qualms about heading for these schools, whose label is an open sesame to all careers. Moreover, their legitimacy is enhanced by the philoso-phical viewpoint that the practice of management (as opposed to its theoretical concepts) cannot be taught.

To develop this last idea, there is a deep-rooted belief in France that managers are born, not made. As Dominique Xardel, the head of l'ESSEC (one of the top trio of management schools), put it:

> Let's be clear; in a school one acquires information,
> one can develop aptitudes already existing in an
> embryonic state, but one can hardly create them.
> (Whitley *et al.*, 1984, 67.)

Training can only bring out innate talent, it cannot generate it spon-taneously. A *grande école* education of any sort is regarded as a useful

---

1 The importance and relevance of management qualifications was neatly summed up in the epigram, 'With one you can do nothing, without one you can get nowhere' (L'Expansion, July/August 1977 p.66).

apprenticeship to management. What the products lack in technique they make up for in intellect and application. In spite of a slight erosion of the gap between engineering and commercial schools, the former remain dominant on employers' hit lists–and have shown their intentions of retaining pole position by including business options in their curricula.

It has already been noted that universities, with the notable exception of Dauphine, suffer the brunt of company mistrust because of the alleged inapplicability of their teaching or research. In spite of attempts to become more vocationally relevant, the university system is still tainted by a reputation for authoritarian, non-interactive teaching, which does not lend itself to the teaching exigencies of management education. As far as many employers are concerned, the products of the universities are still synonymous with the teaching profession and the dole queues.

There is a slightly brighter picture for the IUTs (Instituts Universitaires de Technologie) with their vocational two–year technical or management courses. Their reputations are rising as witnessed by shortening lead times for their students to reach *cadre* status. Yet, the IUTs remain 'Cinderella' establishments. This makes them a favourite hunting ground for the large retail stores (like Auchan or Carrefour) which are themselves snubbed as *'vendeurs de sardines'* ('sardine sellers') by *grande école* graduates. One might say that the large retailers get their recruits at a discount.

Post-experience management education

Next we will first consider the state influence on the demand for management education and then explore the supply and demand aspects of the equation.

State influence

State intervention in the field of management education was fairly limited until, in typical French style, it was decided that management training warranted formal national commitment. A levy was imposed on companies with more than ten employees, whereby expenditure on training had to be equivalent to 1.1 per cent of the payroll. Companies were left with entire discretion as to how, and on whom, the money should be spent (*cadres* are typically allocated 30 per cent of the budget). Setting compulsory spending levels has underlined state enthusiasm for training, as well as providing it with annual statements of progress and a database to fuel the long-term thinking of government, corporations and educational institutions. However, creating a legal requirement to spend was hardly a declaration of faith *vis-à-vis* the companies, since it implied that they would not undertake training on a voluntary basis.

Companies have been forced to pay more attention to training since they have to draw up a training plan to be submitted to and discussed with the *comité d'entreprise* (works council). If a company falls short of the statutory requirement, the balance is forfeited to the Treasury. For this reason, the levy was initially perceived as an extension of the tax burden. But gradually firms have started to look upon it as an investment that can be integrated into the firm's strategy. Needless to say this legislation provoked an immediate rash of consultancy firms hoping to cash in on obligatory spending.

Company approach

National commitment to adult education inaugurated in 1971 is starting to bear fruit. Initially, companies were prone to treat this as an unwelcome chore because of the difficulties associated with application, not least the compilation of statistics for the government. Small firms, in particular, are unable to spare someone full-time to deal with the administration, so the PDG (MD or CEO who is also the general dogsbody in many small companies) is obliged to take the task upon himself.

Deciding who should attend which course and when is quite onerous as well as politically explosive, and must be reconciled with conflicting pressures on the PDG's time. Trying to please everyone is not easy especially without full information about available courses. Consequently, in one of the small companies visited, the training budget had become a slush fund used to indulge meritorious or restless *cadres* by sending them off on courses. A provincial *cadre* will look upon a few days in Paris as a perk and notification that he is on the fast track. Alternatively, the training budget may be used as a solution for a long-standing problem – an individual may be sent off on what is termed un *stage alibi*, whereby subsequent foul-ups will not be attributable to inadequate training. So training becomes a piecemeal affair destined to keep individuals and the works council happy.

The problem is compounded for smaller companies by the fact that they can ill afford to be deprived of their top *cadres* for lengthy spells. What is more, training represents a danger for the company since it puts its prime talent on display and at the mercy of potential poachers. The reaction of one PDG interviewed was, why release a *cadre* into a tempting environment where he will sound out opportunities and, more importantly, gain a qualification negotiable on the open market? Worse still, those sent on courses might return in a position to challenge existing practices and either cause upheaval or feel frustrated at not being given free reign to apply what they have learnt. For sound practical reasons, therefore, many small companies have dispensed with the burden in the most expeditious way, by paying the balance to a recognized training body or, as a last resort, to the Treasury.

Increasingly though, even small companies are beginning to come to grips with the training levy. Gone is the era of folkloric courses (improve your memory or faster reading) which conveniently satisfied the legal obligation. Companies are starting to realize that practical gain can be derived from incorporating training into their long-term strategies. This is corroborated by the appointment of training personnel to prepare statements of intent (submitted for works council approval) and make more efficient use of the budget through better information of training opportunities.

A professional association (Groupement des Agents Responsables de la Formation) has even been created to lend weight to the function. Nonetheless, the title *responsable* (as opposed to *directeur*) betrays the fact that this remains a low prestige function – one to be avoided by budding directors.

Provision of post-experience courses

It had been anticipated that the MBA would become as big in Europe as it is in America. In fact, its popularity was overestimated, and the business school INSEAD has had to diversify in order to subsidize its ailing MBA programme. Originally set up in 1958 specifically to provide MBA courses, INSEAD now devotes two-thirds of its faculty time to short courses for in-service managers. INSEAD has had to respond to company demand for more specialized programmes. It has done so by offering a wide range of short courses for actual or prospective senior managers. Increasingly, INSEAD is liaising with the companies which support it, and designing tailor-made programmes destined to sort out specific corporate problems – presumably a reflection of the desire to use the compulsory expenditure more strategically.

This is a general trend in French management development programmes. More and more establishments are finding they have to move closer to the work place, both intellectually and physically – not least because customized courses are highly profitable. The tailor-made course is a booming business. Even the large consultancy organizations (CEGOS, CNOF) have been forced into providing intra-company programmes since demand for standardized programmes is waning. Needless to say, this fast-developing activity has engendered a new rash of small firms whose speed and versatility is well suited to tackling company-specific problems.

The schools too, are keeping up with fashion, by being more attentive to the needs of their customers, the companies. They are developing more creative links with local companies, primarily through well-honed executive development programmes and by encouraging staff to engage in consultancy work. Most of the leading *grandes écoles* boast some sort of centre for management development. For the schools this is a lucrative activity which helps to supplement income from undergraduate fees and the *taxe professionnelle* from the companies. It only represents a marginal cost since they have the facilities and staff at their disposal, not to mention a ready-made reputation. The school's renown will be exploited to attract executives to it – sometimes in search of a label they missed out on earlier in their education.

Well-prepared managers?

Does the French system manufacture a good product? In answer to that question, it is worth reviewing a number of the points touched upon in the preceding discussion.

First, we must consider the basis for selection, Maths, as a culturally neutral and precisely quantifiable criterion, is used as an objective measure of merit for entry into the *grandes écoles* – including the top flight business schools.[1] This raises questions about compatibility of means and ends. Does France really need supernumerate managers? In terms of subject matter the answer is probably no. But if we consider the depth and rigour of the study process, the apprenticeship looks more appropriate.

To start with, maths is deemed a faithful indicator of the ability to synthesize and to engage in complex abstract reasoning, qualities which are highly prized in all spheres of professional life. The mind has been trained to grasp complex problems and assimilate new knowledge quickly. Thus, employers are confident that the specific expertise needed for the job and the graduate's potential as a manager can be brought out by the company's own training and development programme.

In addition to this, the intensity and duration of the *grande école* training equips the would-be manager with essential mental and physical capacities: the ability to cope with pressure and to work long hours, a lengthy span of concentration, an analytical mind and a tried and tested work method. To fully appreciate the qualities and mentality of the *grande école* graduates, one must consider the obstacles they have overcome, the uncertainty and competition they have faced, and the sacrifices they have made. Their odyssey will also have brought out their tactical awareness and their single-mindedness which will serve them well in the cut and thrust of the business world.

But perhaps the most important psychological asset which the *grandes écoles* confer upon their students is confidence. The atmosphere within the schools prepares its incumbents for leadership. Secure in the knowledge of where they are heading, anticipatory socialization tends to operate. Individuals assume the values, outlook and poise of the 'ruling class' from an early age. They may not be *au fait* with the technicalities and jargon of management, but they have the social wherewithal and psychological authority to take up positions of power.

---

1 In 1985, only 4 per cent of the ESSEC (business school) intake had taken a non-maths *baccalauréat* option.

In terms of concrete advantages, the schools provide their protégés with a ready-made network of contacts which can prove especially supportive in times of trouble (i.e., unemployment). Career-minded students can start to establish links before even entering the fray of the business world, safe in the knowledge that their cohorts are also bound for the nation's executive suites. To a greater extent than most nations, France pools its élite from an early age which fosters the solidarity born of a common educational experience.

It would seem that despite the fact that the grandes écoles were not specifically designed to train managers, that is the role they have assumed. Indeed, it is a role they have successfully fulfilled, though this success is largely a product of their unique evolution in parallel to the great economic surge of the nineteenth century. The likelihood is that they could not be replicated outside the peculiar French context. For instance, if the schools did not benefit from such historically based esteem, they would no longer attract their proper proportion of the cleverest people in each age group.

Perhaps the best testimony to the quality of their products is that employers will frantically outbid each other to secure the services of a grande école graduate. It could of course be argued that a popular product is not necessarily a good product and that the influence of networks might be artificially boosting the continued demand. However, if the schools really were failing to enhance the raw material then employers could easily acquire the same talent by recruiting at the preparatory stage. The fact that this is unheard of suggests that the schools do provide added value of some sort.

The real problem is that the supply does not satisfy the demand. One interviewee from the sample likened it to the picking of wild fruits which, though tastier, could not satisfy universal demand in the same way as large-scale agriculture. Consequently the top firms have no recruitment difficulties, but the smaller ones which offer less well mapped out career opportunities are deprived of what is presumed to be the top talent.

Of course, by keeping supply low, the grandes écoles are ensuring the marketability of their products. But this can prove detrimental to the graduates themselves who are guaranteed preferential career advancements and can, if they choose, treat their diploma as une rente éducative (an educational annuity). For this reason, there is a tendency to look upon admission to the grande école as a swan song rather than a point de départ. The net result is that grande école graduates are generally not inclined to risk their talents in an entrepreneurial way to stimulate new business, but exploit them instead to gain authority in bureaucratic hierarchies (the theme is treated in more detail in the following chapter).

Needless to say, if the system puts a brake on the motivation of the sucessful, this is doubly the case for those it rejects. The nation is deprived of the individuals whose talents or disposition are not suited to the strict régime of preparatory schools, notably the late developers, the pragmatic or the artistically inclined who are eliminated from the running at an early stage. Later, they are joined by all those embittered by their failure to meet the exacting requirements of the *concours* (entrance exam for the *grandes écoles*). This combined population of potentially excellent managers must resign itelf to impoverished salary and promotional expectations since the top places are virtually reserved to *grande école* graduates – and sometimes to graduates from a particular school.

It is presumably to counteract the negative effects of this 'irreversible' selection system that the state chose to instigate compulsory expenditure on training. However, it will take more than that to seriously open up access to the nation's boardrooms.

Chapter Four

Destiny

> 'La concurrence ne joue qu'une fois, au moment des concours, à l'entrée des grandes écoles, vers 22 ans.'
> ('Competition occurs just once, when students take the entrance exam which determines admission to the grandes écoles, at about 22 years of age.')
> (Conversation with Nicole Bastrentaz, Fondation Nationale pour l'Enseignement de la Gestion des Entreprises.)

Careers are a subject of tremendous interest for *cadres*, as witnessed by the popularity of salary surveys and 'career pull-outs' published by the likes of *l'Expansion*, *l'Express* and *Le Point*. This chapter sets out to examine the various influences on a managerial career in France. Of course, the differences which exist between France and, say, Britain are of degree rather than kind. Themes like education, performance and functional choice automatically affect an individual's career, but their relative weightings vary between corporate and national cultures.

Recruitment procedures

By way of introduction, it may be worth taking a look at the French recruitment process, which contains a number of tell-tale signs regarding ways to the top in France. The form and substance of career advertisements, *curricula vitae* and covering letters all provide insights into the critical influences on career success.

A cursory glance at managerial job advertisements reveals a low emphasis on drive or initiative, by Anglo-Saxon standards at least. On the other hand, advertisements typically refer to more cerebral qualities, *l'esprit critique, la rigueur, la capacité de synthèse* (analytical mind, intellectual rigour, ability to synthesize). To caricature the situation, the French seem to focus on qualities of reception (analysis, synthesis, agility of the mind) at the expense of qualities of emission (charisma, pugnacity, capacity to communicate and motivate).

The advertisement is also likely to specify a particular type of education identified by the number of years the course lasts after the *baccalauréat*: for instance, *bac + 2* for DUT, BTS (short vocational courses) or DEUG; *bac + 4* for a *maitrîse* (masters) or some business school diplomas (increasingly *bac* + 5); and *bac* + 5 for *grandes écoles* (engineering schools) and the university-based Diplôme d'Etudes Supérieures Spécialisées. All this is in stark contrast to the rather vague call for 'graduates' which prevails in the UK. French companies are precise in their requirements and at least give the impression that they will get what they are asking for, typically demanding 'a degree in ...' not simply, 'a degree'.

Sometimes the advertisement even goes as far as to mention a particular set of schools[1] (see Figure 4.1). This is associated with the fact that each school is regarded as producing a very identifiable product with stereotypical qualities and defects. *L'Expansion* (August 1977, 66) actually published a list of the spontaneous impressions of businessmen about the graduates of individual schools. Among the shortcomings, graduates of Polytechnique were deemed too élitist, those of Centrale unimaginative, those of HEC overambitious, those of Sciences-Po superficial and those of l'ENA too theoretical. Clearly, the French indulge in a high degree of typecasting.

The tone of the advertisements is generally subdued by Anglo-Saxon standards. Salaries are rarely quoted or perks brandished as part of the headline (see Figure 4.2). Rather the advertisement will speak coyly of 'appropriate salary' and, although there may be general references to fringe benefits, they are not likely to be itemized. Possibly this is a manifestation of the Catholic reticence to talk about money or may reflect the fact that the salary depends on the incumbent rather than the post. In effect, remuneration tends to be based on criteria which relate to the person – age, training, experience, contacts even – rather than the functions assigned or the results obtained, a very French, and significantly un-American approach.

The advertisements generally close with a request for, '*lettre manuscrite, CV, photo*'. These, too, are highly revealing on closer inspection. The fact that a handwritten letter is often requested implies that it will probably be subjected to the scrutiny of a graphologist. This is surprisingly commonplace and even one of the small firms visited had recourse to such an expert. The implement used, the style and spontaneity of the writing are all analysed to determine the suitability of a candidate – and as one graphologist explained to the authors, neatness, application and conformity are not always interpreted favourably. The handwritten letter also indicates moderate commitment to the company in question since it precludes the 'leaflet drop' approach to job hunting.

The style of the covering letter is generally more deferential and indirect than is the case in Anglo-Saxon countries. According to Tixier in an article in *La Revue Française de Gestion* (October 87, 63),

---

1 *Challenges* (March 87, 32) reports the chief of a large company telling a headhunter, 'This post is wide open... any candidate is eligible... provided he is a Polytechnicien.'

JEUNE DIPLOME

Grande école de gestion

La Société Française EXXON CHEMICAL qui emploie 1250 personnes et réalise un CA de 5,5 milliards de F dont 50 % à l'export fabrique et commercialise des produits chimiques de base et des spécialités pétrochimiques. Elle recherche pour son siège à la Défense un jeune contrôleur de gestion.

Au sein de la Division Chimie de spécialités, il sera chargé de la préparation et de l'analyse des résultats financiers et commerciaux et assurera la liaison dans ce domaine avec EXXON CHEMICAL INTERNATIONAL à Bruxelles. Il effectuera aussi diverses études économiques et statistiques en collaboration avec l'administration des ventes. A terme, il pourra poursuivre une carrière dans le groupe en France ou à l'étranger.

Nous souhaitons rencontrer un diplômé d'une grande Ecole de Gestion (HEC, ESSEC, ESCP, Dauphine) débutant, ayant de solides connaissances en informatique et maîtrisant parfaitement la langue anglaise.

Merci d'adresser lettre de candidature, C.V. complet photo et rémunération actuelle sous référence M 11/507 CY à :

EGOR GESTION ET FINANCE
8, rue de Berri - 75008 PARIS

EGOR

PARIS BORDEAUX LYON NANTES STRASBOURG TOULOUSE
BELGIQUE DEUTSCHLAND ESPANA GREAT-BRITAIN ITALIA PORTUGAL BRASIL CANADA

Graduates
Optimise your marketing flair

| c.£15,000 | *Oil Industry* |

If you are a high calibre, commercially orientated graduate determined to succeed in a highly competitive marketing environment, our client is offering the challenge to match your ambition.

A subsidiary of a leading multi-national oil company, they have openings for a number of young and highly numerate graduates. Those appointed, initially to undertake a broad range of marketing-related roles, will be expected to possess the outstanding ability that is a pre-requisite of progress into key managerial positions.

Your degree discipline will have a business or scientific bias and you will already have gained 2-3 years' commercial experience. A high level of computer literacy is essential, as are well developed analytical and communication skills.

The rewards begin with a salary of c.£15,000, together with excellent company benefits. The future? Your own drive and determination will set the pace and direction of your progress.

If you believe you have the potential to meet the challenge of this demanding environment, please write with full career details, quoting reference 632/NJB/88, to: Nigel Bastow, Consultant, Austin Knight Selection, 17 St. Helen's Place, London EC3A 6AS. Alternatively you can telephone for an application form on 01-437 9261 (01-256 6925 evenings/weekends).

Austin Knight Selection

Figure 4.1 Comparative qualification requirements in job advertisements: (a) *Le Monde*, 8 March 1988; (b) *The Sunday Times*, 17 April 1988.

candidates tend to refrain from using action oriented verbs, e.g. 'organizing', 'leading', 'deciding' and so forth. Instead they opt for verbs which are passive in their form or meaning: '*être embauché*

Responsable production

Intégrée à un groupe important et performant, cette société (130 personnes - 80 millions de francs de chiffre d'affaires) est spécialisée dans la fabrication en très grande série de petits composants mécaniques. Sa compétence technique, ses innovations permanentes et ses nombreux brevets lui permettent de répondre d'une manière très adaptée aux exigences de ses marchés et de jouir d'une excellente image de marque. Elle recherche le responsable de son unité de production. Sous l'autorité de la direction générale, il encadrera plusieurs ateliers regroupant une centaine de personnes et sera chargé de toute la gestion et l'organisation de la production, des services connexes et de l'animation des hommes. Ce poste s'adresse à un candidat âgé d'au moins 30 ans, ingénieur mécanicien diplômé d'une grande école (Arts & Métiers ou équivalence). Homme de terrain, il aura déjà réussi une première expérience d'encadrement d'une unité de production et maîtrisera bien les problèmes liés aux grandes séries. La rémunération proposée, fonction de l'expérience ainsi que l'évolution à l'intérieur du groupe, sont motivantes pour un candidat de valeur. Poste basé en banlieue Ouest de Paris. Ecrire à B. COULANGE en précisant la référence A/2643UN.

MEMBRE DE SYNTEC

PA

3, rue des Graviers - 92521 NEUILLY Cedex - Tél. 747.11.04

Lille - Lyon - Nantes - Paris - Strasbourg - Toulouse

Figure 4.2 Comparative emphasis on remuneration in job advertisements: (a) *L'Usine Nouvelle*, 28 February 1988.

comme ...' ('to be placed as'), '*chercher un emploi de ...*' ('to seek employment as'), '*collaborer, aider*' ('to be involved, to assist'). This linguistic bias is also noted by Laurence Wylie, who maintains that it is instilled very early on in childhood. He suggests that, if we look at the table of contents of a French geography textbook, we will find that all the chapters have nouns as titles (the soil, the vegetation, the climate and so on). In contrast to this, an American social studies book uses participles, indicating some kind of action, for its headings: growing rice, mining coal, etc. (in Santoni, 1981, 30).

Requiring a photo betrays the fact that the French have no equivalent of the label 'equal opportunity employer'. This is in contrast to typical job advertisements in Britain or the US which generally refrain from asking for photos for fear of accusations of discrimination.

As for the *curriculum vitae* itself, its content and format provide further clues. To start with, facts are stated in chronological order, unlike the American-style CV which starts with the career objective, then states current situation and works backwards. This difference is important in that one presentation emphasizes current achievement and motivation, irrespective of origins, whereas the other is concerned

Production Executive

North Midlands

To £22,000

LINK

An autonomous member of a major multinational Group, this very successful company manufactures high quality products for industry on a continuous basis in a modern plant at a pleasant North Midlands location.

A major expansion programme aimed at maintaining the company's position at the forefront of manufacturing technology is taking place and a talented Production Executive is required to lead and motivate a team of production supervisors.

You will play a leading role in improving productivity and further enhancing the company's automated manufacturing processes.

Aged 28/48, you will be a graduate in a Mechanical/Production/Materials Science discipline with comprehensive knowledge and experience of the latest Industrial Engineering and Manufacturing techniques—gained in a modern continuous process environment. Above all, you must possess drive, determination and total commitment to achieving targets and goals. If you can make an early impact, the job will provide a springboard to higher management.

Please send a comprehensive C.V. to J.N.B., Link Management Selection, P.O. Box 7, Neston, South Wirral, L64 7UG.

(b) *The Sunday Times*, 17 April 1988.

with the individual's background and verification of passage through 'obligatory' checkpoints. In other words, the French approach is less concerned with where you are now, than where you have been.

Another feature of the French CV is the relative absence of personal information. The contents are fairly dry and impersonal, stating qualifications, training and work experience but dispensing with the paragraphs of personal notes or details on sporting and social activities which are deemed so essential in Britain. Nor are referees included, presumably because the school attended is reference enough. As a result, the whole document need not exceed a single side of A4 paper (see Figure 4.3).

Education

The most striking feature of French management is the way in which one's education impinges, either directly or indirectly, upon one's entire career. As Alain Peyrefitte put it:

> *Il n'y a sans doute pas de pays au monde où les diplômes soient mieux respectés, leur validité aussi*

CURRICULUM VITAE

BOULNOIS Karine   Née le 21 mars 1965 à Soulac (33)

12 rue Edouard Lefebvre 24 ans
78000 Versailles   Célibataire
tel : 953.96.96   Etudiante

FORMATION

    1983 : Baccalauréat C – Versailles
    1985 : Admise à l'Ecole supérieure de commerce de Paris

LANGUES

    — Anglais   : courant
    — Allemand : bonnes notions

STAGES – EMPLOIS TEMPORAIRES

    – Juillet 1985 – Monitrice d'enfants
    – Août 1986 – Traductrice à Thomson-CSF Coopération.
    – Mai à septembre 1987 – Assistante Export chez l'Oréal.

DIVERS

    — Fréquents séjours en Angleterre
      2 séjours d'un mois en Allemagne
    — Présidente du Bureau des élèves (1986/87)
    — Permis de conduire B

OBJECTIFS

    — Dans l'immédiat, assistante au service du personnel,
    pour évoluer, à moyen terme, vers les responsabilités
    dans cette fonction.

Figure 4.3 Example of a French curriculum vitae.

persistante. (I cannot think of any country in the
world where qualifications have greater power or
longevity.)

(1976, 320.)

The royal road

As mentioned in the previous chapter, getting on the right track *(la voie royale)* is something which starts with *baccalauréat* options at secondary school. The *bac C* (maths option) is the first vital step in one's bid to reach a *grande école*. However, having reached the sanctum of one of these venerated establishments, lifelong career success is virtually guaranteed.

In most countries, educational pedigree is simply an entry ticket into a company. But in France it is an employment passport which often constitutes an assurance for life (a so-called *rente éducative*). *Grande école* graduates can look forward, not only to a 'golden hello', but to rapid promotion, not always based on results. As Peyrefitte explained:

> *En France, le diplôme est une fusée longue portée*
> *qui, sauf accident, vous propulse jusqu'à la retraite.*
> (In France, the diploma is an open-sesame which,
> barring mishaps, will see an individual through to
> retirement.)
>
> (1976, 320.)

France's top executives are reputedly the best educated in Europe. Students with high-level managerial aspirations as executives or administrators know they are best advised to attend the most prestigious *grandes écoles* for, even if they intend to set up business alone, it will enhance their credibility.

The generalist education provided by these schools is deemed to equip the graduates with the overall view to make it to the top, and that is reinforced by the companies themselves. Far from attenuating educational differences, companies accentuate them with élitist practices, notably high-flyer schemes and promotional ceilings related to qualifications, which help perpetuate the established order. Many of the *cadres* interviewed revealed that, with hindsight, they could quite easily have predicted their current situation simply on the basis of their educational luggage. By the same reckoning, they felt they could forecast the way their careers would unfold from now until their retirement. This suggests an unusually stable relationship between academic credentials and promotional ceiling – or as one *cadre* rather poetically explained to us, 'stellar trajectories are rare'.

This extensive (not to say exclusive) reliance on pre-experience education as an indicator of management potential allows the brightest prospects to be creamed off early and no doubt facilitates the apprenticeship to general management. 'Fast trackers' can be cosseted and given a secure setting in which to acquire the necessary skills as personal assistant (*attaché de direction*) to a senior manager. They are given training missions, encouraged to visit plants in the provinces or abroad – all this under the tutelage of a mentor who will help them make contacts and oversee their leap from specialist to general management. So, whilst educational capital may yield its best return early on in the career, it is used to beget other forms of capital, such as rapid experience. This skilful conversion strategy enables the holder to cast aside the crutch of education and point to an 'authentic' track record.

Graduation from the 'right' school also has repercussions on behaviour. Pre-conditioned into believing that they are bound for the boardroom, the would-be leaders start to act accordingly. Anticipatory socialization ensures that they acquire the demeanour and outlook of leadership. This self-belief is merely reinforced by firms which are eager to give them preferential career advancements, thereby establishing a well-padded CV and legitimizing their leadership positions. The implication is that bright young executives are perhaps encouraged to look good and keep their noses clean rather than fulfil their creative and intellectual potential. Critics might develop the view that those who reach the top are perhaps better at getting promoted than they are at running organizations.

From a positive viewpoint, the policy of using the grandes écoles to form pools of versatile talent obviously promotes healthy mobility and facilitates dialogue between educational, business, financial and public sectors. Indeed, the pervasive influence of the grandes écoles can be gauged by the comment of the Vice-President of Centrale's alumni association:

> Si l'on regroupait tous les anciens élèves des grandes
> écoles, on aurait devant soi la classe dirigeante de
> ce pays. (A list of all grandes écoles alumni would
> read like a roll call of France's ruling class.)
> (*Le Monde de l'Education*, April 1986, 10).

The institutionalization of *grande école* links

Another way in which education affects career progress is through old-boy networks. In many schools the durability of school links is institutionalized. At l'Ecole Polytechnique, for instance, all graduates high and low call each other *camarade* whether they have met before or not, and the lowliest X can write out of the blue to a famous colleague and be sure of help and sympathy. Having such an extensive network of contacts from the very start of one's active life is an immeasurable advantage.

A similar situation exists at l'Ecole des Arts et Métiers, which reputedly has the most efficient old-boy association to which graduates are automatically affiliated. Members receive regular journals and newsletters on salaries or career paths to supplement the annual directory listing alumni by name, region and company. One consultant in the interview sample admitted that before visiting any company he would check the association directory for a fellow 'Gadz'arts'[1] in that firm to fill him in on the prevailing situation. One production manager from the observation sample even confessed to having illicitly invited a colleague from a rival firm into the plant to show him how to solve a recurrent production problem. The graduates' freemasonry can clearly transcend corporate allegiances.

The purpose of alumni associations is basically three-fold: to promote the school's reputation, to help out in the search for a first job, and to facilitate mobility. Each association therefore runs a careers service which offers jobs to new graduates and restless old-boys alike. The HEC association allegedly offers 2,500 posts to the 300 or so students who graduate each year. More impressive still are the efforts made when alumni fall upon hard times. The association will pull out all the stops to find a job for (recaser) an unemployed member.

Likewise when it comes to promoting the school's name the associations can prove very helpful. For instance, the INSA (Institut National des Sciences Appliquées) association put pressure on the French electricity corporation (EDF) so that the company would recognize in its recruitment salaries the fact that the school had lengthened its curriculum to five years. Similarly, the Arts et Métiers association managed to persuade the French railways (SNCF) to open up certain posts previously reserved to the highest rated schools. On a less savoury note, the old-boys' association may also have some impact on the schools' own admissions policy. The head of a small business school actually confessed to setting a 30 per cent ceiling on the number of girls admitted to the school (Challenges, May 1987, 32). The reasoning behind this policy was that girls were a poor investment for the association since they were more likely to stop working, which would dilute the school's active network.

Bereft of these close-knit ties, mere university graduates in particular find it difficult to infiltrate the higher reaches of business. As the head of one university put it:

> Souvent, dans les grandes entreprises, les mafias
> d'anciens des écoles sont pour nous un mur
> infranchissable. (The old-boy networks in the large

---

1 'Gadz'arts' is a contraction of 'gars des arts et métiers' ('alumni of l'Ecole des Arts et Métiers').

companies often represent an insurmountable
obstacle for us.)

(L'Expansion, 7 March 1985, 83.)

Their lack of contacts in high places works against the university
students when they seek industrial placements which means they fail
to gain an initial foothold. Thereafter, their absence from positions of
authority in the more traditional companies becomes pathological. In
contrast to this, the *'gadz'arts'*, say, are renowned for their stranglehold over the automobile industry: Peugeot harbours 461 *'gadz'arts'*
out of 5,000 cadres according to figures published in *Challenges*
(March 87, 34) – something which cannot be explained away by distinctive competence. These collegiate ghettos are regularly condemned
in the press, but the criticism has the unwitting effect of boosting the
popularity of schools which guarantee employment.

What is more, the situation seems destined to deteriorate since
emulation is perceived as the only way forward. As a university head
explained:

> *Nos formations étant récentes, nous n'avons pas
> encore nos propres mafias.* (Our courses are recent so
> we don't yet possess our own mafias.)
> (*L'Expansion;* 7 March 1985.)

One can understand the desire to fight fire with fire, but the situation
seems rather hypocritical: on the one hand, the universities condemn
neighbouring networks, and on the other they try to constitute their own.

Adult education

As an adjunct to the present section, it is worth mentioning the area of
adult education. Since 1971, companies have been compelled by law
to devote just over one per cent of total wage bills to training. The
motivation behind this legislation seems to have been a desire to introduce some leeway into the rigid relationship between pre-experience
educational credentials and jobs. However, the anticipated impact on
careers has not really materialized. More often than not, it is the senior
management which decides who to send on management development
courses, which means that lack of training provides ready justification
for lack of promotion. So, post-experience education has done as much
to reinforce the educational pecking order as it has to break it down.

Of course, many *cadres* do upgrade their skills by attending management training courses, but these have little impact on career progress.
In France, no label earned at post-entry level will really make up for
inadequacies in pre-entry education. Even the most prestigious
establishments for senior executives such as the CPA, INSEAD, ISA,
ISSEC, CRC or CEDEP will only partly compensate a 'second-rate'

education. A post-entry diploma has a remedial aspect to it. It may give an engineer a managerial veneer but it will do nothing to augment the marketability of a graduate from the top *grandes écoles*. This is not an indictment of the pedagogy of these executive development centres but is a sign of the deference accorded to the top schools. It is also indicative of the attitude towards perfectability in France.

In contrast with the US, the acceptance of perfectability in France is low. French education is directed towards the acquisition of a well-established body of knowledge and attitudes. This finite view of knowledge carries over into management education where, to burlesque the situation, the best *grandes écoles* impart comprehensive knowledge which need never be updated. Those who attend these schools are deemed *formés à vie* (trained for life), further training being rendered superfluous. This attitude perhaps explains the pre-eminence of pre-experience education in relation to post-experience education.

Performance

In terms of career influences, the constant counterpoint to education is, of course, job performance. Any managerial selection system involves an implicit trade-off between performance in professional life and performance prior to entry (as measured by qualifications). The aim here is to try to assess the weight accorded to each element in the French context.

Track record

Most corporate recruiters genuinely believe that the value of a qualification is quickly eclipsed after initial admission to the company. One personnel manager from the interview sample explicitly stated:

> '*Franchi le cap du démarrage, le rôle du diplôme
> tombe vite à zéro.*' ('Having cleared the first hurdle,
> the power of the diploma soon disappears.')

Many of the *cadres* interviewed corroborated that idea, the general consensus being that a qualification could not be relied upon for support for more than five years. That is probably true in so far as the formal knowledge enshrined by the diploma becomes obsolete. However, what remains is a high-level start and the acquisition of a rapid and varied experience which the diploma has helped procure. This supersedes educational credentials as a promotion criterion but serves to promote the same population. What is more, *grande école* graduates who find themselves unemployed can count on an old-boy network to minimize the period of 'cold turkey' between jobs. So the claim that diplomas count for nothing, after initial recruitment, appears tenuous to say the least.

That is not to say that qualifications allow their holders simply to freewheel to power. Educational credentials must be allied to effort to produce their full effect. But assuming that *grande école* graduates can successfully negotiate the early stages, they will have the edge over less qualified colleagues, in making the transition to general management. The reason for this is that the responsibility for high level appointments falls in the hands of those already in power, rather than the personnel department. So, *ceteris paribus*, a chief will elect to surround himself with like-minded individuals who have emerged from the same mould, who speak the same language and have the same work methods. That way, the adaptation period is curtailed and the working relationship is more efficient. Co-optation in such cases probably has less to do with conscious discrimination than a feeling of intellectual empathy.

Social or technical competence?

As mentioned above, it is argued that after five or so years of professional experience, the diploma becomes irrelevant. This points to a shift in performance criteria whereby social competence gradually takes over from technical competence.

The relative importance of technical and social competence varies between firms – and, more importantly, between strata within a firm. Consequently, the type of competence expected of individuals will depend upon the particular stage they have reached in their managerial career. The value of technical knowledge, know-how and energy tend to diminish with age. Conversely, the socially acquired skills needed not to produce *per se* but to administer the production processes (such as the ability to delegate, resolve conflicts and motivate) increase as the *cadre* climbs up the organization.

It is in the latter half of one's career that the effects of attending the 'right' school come to fruition, as some individuals move from line jobs into positions of power that put a premium on such qualities as distinguished appearance, good manners, tact and good taste. Emphasis on social competence tends to favour the products of the *grandes écoles* who possess the necessary self-confidence and social wherewithal. So while companies ostensibly drop educational credentials as a means of selection, they replace them with credentials which elevate members of the same population.

In truth, the criteria for recruitment and promotion are easy to fudge. Companies can easily shroud qualification-based promotion in terms of 'behavioural' traits. The relative emphasis on technical or social competence is in the hands of the company and, in France, companies generally put a premium on social skills. This is most visible in the treatment of certain high flyers who are nursed through the obligatory period of operational effectiveness, skating over the surface until they are sucked up to the boardroom.

The acid test: 'self-made' men

Having ascertained that educational credentials will help establish an accelerated track record, how do those without qualifications fare? Or, to put the null hypothesis, is it possible to succeed without educational credentials?

The new, action-oriented mood in French business makes much of the fact that it is possible to do well without educational credentials. The more progressive journals have featured articles publicizing the successes of so-called *autodidactes* ('self-made' individuals). Recent issues of *Le Point* and *Challenges* have each devoted substantial pieces to those who have 'made it' without qualifications. But since both articles trot out the same set of success stories, one is left with the impression that these are merely exceptions which confirm the rule – and serve as excuses for a premature and hyperselective system.

In truth, a person's schooling (or lack of it) will always overshadow subsequent achievements. The primacy of the diploma is easily corroborated by taking a look at the appointments sections in newspapers or magazines. Newly appointed chiefs will place a diploma gained several decades past ahead of their penultimate posting in a prestigious company. The cryptic triumvirate of details, 'Jean Dupont, X, 53', tells initiated observers all they need to know about the individual, namely sex, school (X represents the crossed cannons of l'Ecole Polytechnique) and class (i.e. year of graduation).

It would seem that *'la diplomite'* ('qualification-itis'), as it is popularly known, is more acute than ever. Perhaps the greatest testimony to the pre-eminence of education comes from *autodidactes* themselves who, having 'made good', are still reluctant to admit to the appellation. Even in the wake of a new pro-business climate (see Chapter 7 on top management), the tag 'self-made' is a skeleton to be concealed rather than a source of pride.

An example from the group of managers whose work we observed in the course of the research makes the point exquisitely. The head of public relations had prepared a short résumé describing the *Président-Directeur-Général* (PDG, or French equivalent of managing director/chief executive officer). On reading it, the PDG (CEO) in question remonstrated quite violently with its composer for mentioning his lack of higher education. The PR man explained in all sincerity that nowadays 'self-made men' elicit nothing but respect and admiration. To which the worldly PDG replied:

> *'N'en croyez rien. On ne leur pardonne jamais de n'avoir été que des primaires!'* ('Don't you believe it.

*You're never forgiven for failing to go beyond
primary education!')*

The experience of René Monory, the former education minister who tried (unsuccessfully) to introduce selection prior to entry into the universities, is also revealing. He used to show off about not having passed his *baccalauréat...* until the day, in December 1987, when disrespectful students started chanting a set phrase borrowed from anxious parents, 'Monory, passe ton bac d'abord!' ('First pass the exam – then we'll see').

The stigma associated with a lack of education clearly persists irrespective of fashions – and there are perhaps good reasons (other than snobbery) for wishing to hide the fact in France. A 26-year-old, self-taught company head outlined two particular handicaps:

> *Quand on va voir pour la première fois des banquiers,
> ils trouvent qu'on est pas credible. De même, on ne
> peut pas embaucher immédiatement des diplômés,
> car, souvent, ils se méfient d'une entreprise dirigée
> par un autodidacte.* (The first time you go to see
> bankers, they feel you lack credibility. The same
> goes for taking on graduates, who are wary of
> companies headed by a non-graduate.)

On the other hand, *autodidactes* perhaps have the drive and courage which, according to one headhunter, their graduate counterparts tend to lack:

> *Ne réussissent que les élèves un peu placides,
> tenaces, attachés à un seul objectif: obtenir le
> diplôme. Les grandes écoles forment des gens doués
> d'une formidable force de travail et de concentration,
> mais peu préparés à prendre des risques.* (Those
> who succeed are generally calm, tenacious and hell
> bent on obtaining a degree. The *grandes écoles*
> produce individuals with a tremendous work rate
> and concentration, but ill-prepared to take risks.)
> (L'Express, 24 January 1986, 27.)

This view of *grandes écoles* graduates as rather timorous individuals was supported by a *cadre* interviewed who believed that, in France, competition was not seen as an end in itself in the American tradition – but rather a means to an end. Competition, as he saw it, was essentially aimed at achieving security. He explained that the French are prepared to expose themselves to great risks provided that the reward is guaranteed security, and cited admission to the *grandes écoles* as a prime example.

While *autodidactes* have certain advantages over graduates, primarily as a result of having nothing to lose, it was generally acknowledged that success would increasingly require a formal framework of theoretical knowledge. As one self-taught PDG explained to the researcher:

> 'A l'avenir, il ne suffira plus d'avoir du bon sens
> dans l'analyse et de l'audace dans l'action.' ('In
> future, neither commonsense analysis nor audacious
> action will be enough.')

This view of *autodidactes* as a dying breed was corroborated by a recent survey of company directors in *Le Point*. The article heralded, *'la fin du règne des autodidactes'* ('the era of the self-made man is past' – 5 October 1987, 54), which implies, perhaps misleadingly, that the *autodidacte* was previously in favour. The piece revealed that higher education, especially in a *grande école*, is virtually a *sine qua non* for rising to the top of large firms. Of the 200 top managers sampled 90 per cent were the products of higher education and of the remaining 10 per cent all had acquired some sort of legitimizing qualification in their professional life.

As regards the initial question about the possibility of success without qualifications, the answer has to be a qualified 'no'. It is unusual for individuals to make headway in traditional French companies without the official seal of higher education. On the other hand, in the less viscous environment of small or provincial companies, it is possible to climb by proving one's worth (company types in this sense are discussed below).

Career strategy

The notion of career strategy seems fairly weak in France. The managers interviewed tended to be vague about what they hoped to achieve by what age. No doubt this has something to do with a certain reticence to 'count one's chickens' or to appear overtly ambitious. To give some idea of the attitude, professional aspirations would generally be couched in terms of intellectual satisfaction or increased independence rather than more money, power or prestige. The few who did reveal specific goals and timescales had to be prompted to do so. It could be posited that this toned-down view of careerism is related to the rather predictable nature of career progression – and the fact that one's education holds sway over all other possible variables. This said, there are still a number of choices which will determine how quickly individuals reach their allotted station.

Company type

One of the prime decisions facing a new graduate concerns the sort of company to join – and depending on the school attended the choice can be quite vast. The lowliest of *grande école* engineers is likely to receive an average of two offers of employment on graduating, whilst a product of Centrale can expect up to fourteen (*L'Express*, 24 January 1986, 26).

Different companies offer different salaries, different career tracks and different responsibilities. Some promote on seniority, others on profits recorded. Ambitious young graduates therefore have to pick their way through a complex field of preferred opportunities. They have to judge which are the real opportunities and which are *voies de garage* (sidings). The fundamental question for new graduates is whether to opt for the safety of a large corporation or chance their hand in a smaller company where they may be given wider responsibilities.

There is a distinct sense of separate circuits in the managerial job market. On the one hand, there are the small companies, based in the provinces, with a higher incidence of *autodidactes* and an older age range. On the other hand, there are the larger companies, with their Parisian headquarters and a high concentration of young graduate personnel. This idea of a dual job market for *cadres* was confirmed by a production manager we interviewed who suggested that joining a small company was virtually an irreversible move. He claimed that opting out of the race for top positions in major corporations was tantamount to admitting that one was not cut out to work in an overtly structured and competitive environment. Consequently, large companies may have a few qualms about taking on someone with a small company background. Needless to say, the reverse is not true since small companies will be only too glad to hire people with experience of the way things are done in the major corporations.

One possible career sequence was summed up by the testimony of a student at INSEAD interviewed in Jane Marceau's study:

> 'One must make one's mistakes in a big company,
> prove one's efficiency in a medium-sized one and
> finish by earning a lot of money in one's own
> business.'
>
> (Marceau, 1980, 126.)

There is a general consensus regarding the companies which provide the best springboard into the business world as well as a blacklist of companies to avoid. At the top of the heap according to a survey in *Le Nouvel Economiste* (29 May 1987, 87) is IBM; though a number of other companies are rated higher in particular fields. For instance, Arthur Andersen or other consultancy firms are considered ideal for acquiring the coveted 'generalist' label without having to manoeuvre between functions for computing or management specialists, l'Oréal for research and marketing, Procter and Gamble for marketing, Rank Xerox for sales, Rhône Poulenc for production and research.

The high ratings of these blue chip companies is largely related either to security of employment within the company itself or the security of employment they confer upon those who pass through them. Colgate-Palmolive for instance, is renowned for its high turn-over of *cadres*, 50 per cent of which leave the company within five years (*L'Expansion*; 18 June 1987, 127). However, those who acquire its *étiquette* (label) emerge with a valuable *carte de visite* (calling card) which they can use anywhere. Accor is another such firm. A commercial director interviewed at the company was quite candid with us about the reasons that young graduates choose Accor:

> 'Ce ne sont pas les salaires qui les attirent – ils
> viennent ici pour faire leurs armes.' ('They don't
> come here for the money, but to gain their wings.')

Either way, the real appeal of these firms lies directly or indirectly in the security of employment. The primordial importance of security was corroborated by the findings of a recent survey in *l'Usine Nouvelle* (19 March 1987) which revealed an overwhelming desire by young engineers to join a large group which would provide well mapped out career possibilities. In many respects these preferences are latter-day manifestations of the French obsession with the security of civil service employment. The dream of many French parents, until quite recently, was to see their offspring enter state service – and even in 1982, a sur-vey revealed that 40 per cent of the youths themselves hoped to be-come civil servants (de Closets, 1982, 328).

In two of the small companies visited the heads were highly critical of this security-consciousness. The attitude of the *grande école* graduates was condemned on two scores: first for its sheer snobbishness, and secondly for the lack of adventure. They saw the graduates as con-formists, unwilling to try their luck in a post which would grow with them – opting instead for a future which was clearly mapped out from the outset.

What the small companies offer is a chance of wider responsibility. They are of course less concerned with qualifications, though that is probably through force rather than choice. One of the company heads visited was particularly pleased to have attracted a graduate engineer (albeit from one of the less prestigious schools) on to his staff. And this snob factor was noted by *l'Expansion*:

> Dans les PME, plus d'un patron est tout fier de se
> payer 'son' HEC ou 'son' polytechnicien, comme il
> se paierait une Rolls. (In many small companies, the

boss will take on a Polytechnique or HEC graduate,
in the same way as he would treat himself to a
Rolls.)

(L'Expansion, August 1977, 69.)

Mobility

The importance of manager mobility in France is largely dependent upon the prevailing norms within the sector or company. Personal mobility will be interpreted unfavourably in sectors such as heavy industry, banking or nationalized companies. On the other hand, it is generally viewed positively by PR firms, consultancy, computing, 'Americanized' companies and, generally speaking, in the sales function. Whilst this pattern of behaviour is similar to that in Britain, there is perhaps an underlying difference between the countries. The UK attitude, coloured by American views, is favourable in principle to mobility – whilst in France it is generally frowned upon.

In France mobility is not a universal sign of professional success and ambition. Indeed it is just as likely to be construed as the result of successive failures, or even instability, as suggested by the rather disparaging reference of one headhunter interviewed to *'les papillons aux CV tourbillonnants'* ('butterflies with whirlwind CVs'). Indeed, bright young graduates are warned not to be too anxious to respond to the offers of headhunters since they may get a reputation for instability. In the words of one headhunter:

> *Je me méfie beaucoup des gens qui collectionnent*
> *les employeurs. Celui qui change trop souvent*
> *d'employeur fait naître d'horribles soupçons, ou*
> *tout au moins soulève des questions bien légitimes.*
> (I am extremely wary of people who 'collect'
> employers. Changing jobs too often is bound to
> arouse suspicion, or at the very least legitimate
> queries.)

(Challenge, January 87, 50.)

Even where mobility is known to be motivated by ambition rather than 'flightiness', it may be regarded negatively. For instance, the career-minded financial director at one large company visited was described to the researcher as 'un escargot' ('a snail'). The implication was that he had 'no fixed abode' which made him slightly suspect and placed a question mark over his corporate loyalty.

Of course, the light in which mobility is interpreted depends to some extent on the age of the manager. Early on in a career, playing the field will probably be viewed positively, particularly since a young *cadre* may be anxious to shed the new graduate image by changing companies. However, later on (after 35), mobility is likely to be frowned upon.

Few of the *cadres* spoken to envisaged a change of company as part of their career strategy. Mobility was regarded as a last resort, when there is no other way out, rather than a positive means of gaining promotion or greater responsibility. They seemed unwilling to take a risk and relinquish the protection afforded by length of service in a company. Many *cadres* pass up salary or promotion opportunities for the security of immobility.

There is a paradox here to which we should draw attention. Countries which favour generalism in management usually favour manager mobility as well: the USA is the obvious example, and these American norms are reflected in Britain. France, on the other hand, is unusual in favouring generalism, but not on the whole favouring mobility. Other countries which, like France, are negatively oriented to mobility – East and West Germany, for example, and to a lesser extent the Netherlands and Scandinavia – tend to have a more specialist view of management, expecting individual entrants to be qualified to work in a particular function or department, and either to make their whole career in this function, or to rise to general management on the basis of experience in a single function.

This generalized desire to stay put was even more acute among *autodidactes*, for whom changing company was synonymous with loss of responsibility, salary and status. The reason for this is that they lack an officially sanctioned degree to certify their value to prospective employers. The fate of the *autodidacte* is basically tied in with his employer's and promotion relies on the firm's growth. This is in contrast with, say, Britain where the self-taught individual would, first get credit for having done the job, and second, be less disadvantaged in a culture that is not so self-consciously intellectual.

By the same token, *grande école* graduates possess the official seal of approval which allows them to roam freely in the job market. Again we see the ubiquitous effect of qualifications which enable their holders to accumulate experience in different companies. This, in turn, provides justifiable grounds for discrimination when they apply for senior positions – something which is confirmed by a report in *Le Point* (5 October 1987, 54) citing a diversified career as a common trait among those who reach the top. Ironically, the widespread immobility at middle management level serves to legitimize the right to power of the few who are mobile. So, whilst French managers cannot make a career out of mobility alone, mobility can assume the role of distinctive competence which justifies a senior position.

If French companies do not place a very high premium on mobility in general, there is one form of mobility which can prove particularly 'rewarding', namely mid-career transfers from the public to the private sector. Of course, this form of mobility is not exclusive to France. Similar migration patterns occur in Japan from government to government-related industry and in Israel where transfers from military to business circles prevail. However, there is a sharp contrast between France and her two biggest neighbours, Britain and West Germany, neither of which really indulges in this practice – with the possible exception of the British penchant for appointing status lenders to non-executive positions on boards of directors.

In France, then, added value may be obtained from entering public service[1] and using one's privileged knowledge of its workings as a springboard for a second career in industry, and the donning of 'golden slippers', *pantouflage*. It is a sign of their relatively smooth transition that the extent of the phenomenon is so little known. The one-way irrigation of the business élite by civil servants is eased by the social and educational proximity of the two groups. The French tend to regard it as professional mobility rather than sectoral transition.

The headline-grabbing instances of *pantouflage* associated with nationalized companies and changes of government are simply the tip of the iceberg. Beneath the surface there is a steady, osmotic flow from the public sector (including the armed forces) to the private sector. The pattern is a classic one: transfer usually takes place in the mid-thirties, by which time the *cadre* has ample public sector experience to offer, as well as an appreciation of career limitations (in public service), yet sufficient drive left to make an impact in the private sector.

The circumstances for leaving vary. Some respond to an offer, others take the initiative, having carefully cultivated contacts when in office (see Figure 4.4). Customer firms often save posts for those who have placed state orders with them.[2] Either way, ex-civil servants have numerous trumps to play with a prospective employer. They possess intimate knowledge of the rules and regulations. They have friends in high places and can facilitate dialogue with those who administer – and even if they cannot play on personal contacts, they are *au fait* with the way political and governmental networks operate; they know how to lobby and, having themselves been on the receiving end, know when and where to apply pressure. What is more, their high-level training permits a rapid grasp of complex problems. In the French context, then, perhaps as a result of state involvement in company affairs, ex-civil servants clearly have something to offer most employers.

The most sought after specialists are the *inspecteurs des finances* who, by means of *pantouflage*, virtually monopolize the higher reaches of the banking sector (Société Générale, Crédit Lyonnais) and the nationalized insurance groups (UAP, GAN), not to mention the political spheres. The reason for their popularity has less to do with

---

1 A civil service career is still prestigious but increasingly it is regarded as a short-cut to senior positions in the private or nationalized sectors, rather than an end in itself.
2 This in spite of legislation (art. 175 of the Penal Code) prohibiting entry into client companies within five years of resignation (*L'Expansion*, 8 October 1987, 153).

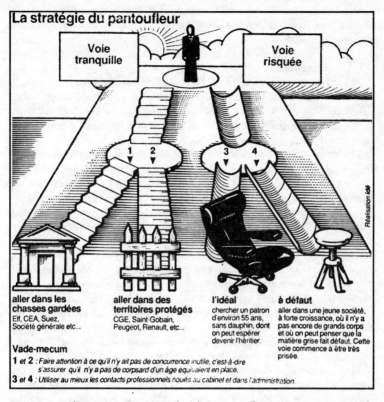

La stratégie du pantoufleur

Voie tranquille

Voie risquée

1 2 3 4

aller dans les chasses gardées
Elf, CEA, Suez, Société générale etc...

aller dans des territoires protégés
CGE, Saint-Gobain, Peugeot, Renault, etc...

l'idéal
chercher un patron d'environ 55 ans, sans dauphin, dont on peut espérer devenir l'héritier.

à défaut
aller dans une jeune société, à forte croissance, où il n'y a pas encore de grands corps et où on peut penser que la matière grise fait défaut. Cette voie commence à être très prisée.

Vade-mecum

1 et 2 : Faire attention à ce qu'il n'y ait pas de concurrence inutile, c'est-à-dire s'assurer qu'il n'y a pas de corps d'un âge équivalent en place.

3 et 4 : Utiliser au mieux les contacts professionnels noués au cabinet et dans l'administration.

Réalisation idé

Figure 4.4 Alternative strategies for the *pantoufleur*. (Source: *Le Monde Affaires*, 19 March 1988.)

the skills they have acquired from verifying public accounts (to ensure that state funds are not misspent), than with their intellectual and social attributes. Each year the top five graduates of l'ENA invariably opt for the *Inspection des Finances* which is considered the best of the élite *Grands Corps de l'Etat* (senior branches of the civil service). It therefore has a prestige without parallel in the UK – even entering the Foreign Office cannot hold a candle to it. So, to bag an *inspecteur* is considered a real coup for any company which manages to do so.

At a somewhat lower level, the foremost '*pantoufleurs*' in terms of number are ex-service personnel, who can foresee their likely *bâton de maréchal* (promotional ceiling) and find an escape hatch in the armaments or electronics sectors. A few large companies can even boast their own clan of 'St Cyriens'[1] to go alongside groups from Polytechnique,

---

1 St Cyr – French equivalent of West Point or Sandhurst.

Centrale or Arts et Métiers. Occasionally, civil servants will equip themselves with a legitimizing managerial qualification prior to making the transition.

Functions

Social prestige (noblesse) is an important notion in French industry. On a sectoral scale, the noble domains are those with a high capital intensity in which the problems of manufacture are secondary to those of conception, such as aviation, space, nuclear energy, telecommunications.

The same attitude manifests itself at functional level where the perceived nobility of an activity, its interest and its variety often outweigh remuneration factors. Conception functions, which are cerebral rather than operational, have higher status than execution functions. But the level of differentiation goes further than that. Perhaps the most striking example is the technical domain with its ambivalent antecedents. On the one hand, there is the scientific tradition and the pure and disinterested quest for knowledge where mastery of the world is based on the power of the mind. And on the other hand, it is rooted in the world of labour, of work which makes man subservient to machines, which dirties the hands and wears out the body. The distinction between these two traditions even takes material form, with mechanical engineers developing hard, calloused hands while electrical engineers develop fine fingers for dextrous work – a real throw back to peasants and aristocrats (*La Revue Française de Gestion*, October 87, 45).

The essential criterion in determining prestige seems to be the degree of immateriality of the task. In engineering, electronics has a higher element of abstraction and therefore of purity and nobility, which places it above electrical engineering with its high currents, and way ahead of mechanical engineering, which requires brute force! The same goes for other functions. In the commercial function, for instance, dealing with immaterial flows of funds is more prestigious than dealing with tangibles. As one student from the renowned business school INSEAD put it to Jane Marceau:

'It is nobler to sell money than socks.' (1980, 113.)

The degree of immateriality also appears to be the foundation for the functional hierarchy. The more ethereal specialities like finance, marketing or the current vogue function, communications[1], are deemed more uplifting than the utilitarian functions like purchasing or production. In fact the greater the physical, as well as intellectual,

---

1 The communications function in France is responsible for internal and external corporate communications – functions discharged in Britain by both PR and personnel departments.

distance from the shop floor, the higher the prestige of the function. The point is reinforced by Boltanski:

> The highest positions are those in which one need
> not be aware of labour, labourers, or production but
> only of such abstractions as commodity and cash
> flows, high technology processes, and investments.
> (1987, 249, Eng trans.)

British readers might justifiably question whether France is any different from the UK in this respect. After all, the view of production as low status and finance as high status is not exclusive to France. This is true, but we may posit that different causes lie behind the same reality. What is valued in France is abstractness as a concomitant of intellectuality. Thus, finance has high standing because it is associated with maths and cleverness while production is a victim of its perceived lack of intellectual challenge. In Britain, on the other hand, a similar pecking order has a very different basis. The pecking order is determined by traditional anti-industrialism. It follows that the most prototypical industrial functions such as production, evoking the 'dark satanic mills' of the industrial North, are devalued. And at the other end of the spectrum, functions like finance, with their professional affiliations, are high prestige.

Unfortunately, in the French context, this rather neat intellectual stratification of functions has been upset by two recent trends. One is the ambiguous position of computing. Computing is not considered a particularly noble area, not least because experts in the field tend to be products of the university system (data processing is one of the very few areas along with, say, law and taxation in which recruiters might specifically seek out a university graduate as opposed to one from a grande école). On the other hand, the introduction of computing into departments like engineering design and operations management has rendered these more abstract and has helped to raise their status.

The other influence is the action-oriented mood which has emerged in the last decade (see section on the new breed of managers in Chapter 7) and seeks to promote results, performance and ability in the field. This has raised the profile of functions like sales and production in which young graduates square up to practical problems and show concrete results. It has become fashionable among 'young pretenders' to show that their grande école background has not impaired their pragmatism. So, although a function like production is not the way to the top, a spell in production can be a useful career move. The only problem is when to break out of the production function in order to pursue one's ambitions. As one engineer explained in l'Express:

> Si vous restez à la fabrication trop longtemps, on
> vous enferme dans un ghetto. Aucune chance de

>faire partie un jour de l'état-major de l'entreprise. (If
>you stay too long in production, you get locked in to
>a ghetto and you can kiss goodbye to your chances of
>ever reaching the higher echelons of the company.)
>
>(24 January 1986, 26.)

Or as one production manager from the group we interviewed explained:

>'Quand on a les mains sales on a les poches vides'.
>('Dirty hands go with empty pockets.')

This view of production as fairly low status is of course not exclusive to France – a similar case has been made in Britain. However, we may again posit that different influences lie behind the same reality. In the UK, production is tarnished by the low status of industry. In France, production suffers from its lack of intellectual standing. This pattern seems to prevail throughout French organizations with a devaluation of functions not associated with cleverness or intellectualism.

There are other functions which are best avoided if one hopes to make rapid progress. Until recently, these included the management of human resources (or personnel) as it was known, which came low on the list of priorities in a firm. This could be seen in the quality of recruits to the function (often ex-NCOs). The subsequent rise of this function is mirrored in the titular evolution of those in charge, starting with 'chef du personnel', moving on to 'responsable des relations sociales' and latterly 'directeur des ressources humaines'.

Purchasing, on the other hand, still appears to be the Cinderella function in French organizations. It is often left to non-qualified technicians and occasionally serves as a final resting place for 'old retainers' for loyal and faithful service. The same used to be true of the training function, which as mentioned earlier now benefits in France from obligatory expenditure (just over 1 per cent of the payroll). As with personnel, there are signs of a realization of the strategic value of these functions (particularly in the large companies) but their heads remain relatively underqualified.

The best-paid functions, according to Le Nouvel Economiste survey (29 May 1987, 83) are still finance and marketing. In the late 1960s marketing was considered the up-and-coming function. Today, communications has taken up that mantle and is regarded as a useful professional springboard since it offers a global perspective of the company and privileged relations with the PDG.

Sales too is well-paid but lacks prestige because it is the domain par excellence of the autodidactes. Sales, in France, is one of the more 'open' functions in which personal qualities and performance outweigh educational references. The problem for those who choose this function is to switch to another function before they reach forty and lose the energy and ambition which sales demands.

The main priority for anyone who goes into manufacturing (or, for grande école graduates, research[1]) is to look for complementary functions to try to gain a 'global' view of the company and help them make the transition to top management. This brings us on to the question of whether it is best to stick to one function or to zig-zag – in other words, whether to be a specialist or a generalist.

The foremost engineering schools like Polytechnique and Centrale have always prided themselves on their breadth of teaching. Indeed, the training received at Polytechnique is so broad that its graduates generally go on to more specialized post-graduate écoles d'application of which the most superior are the Ecole des Mines and the Ecole des Ponts et Chaussées. Even in the face of increasing knowledge, the engineering schools have resolutely avoided focusing on particular specialities. As one head of personnel from our interview sample put it, 'moins un diplôme sert, plus il est recherché' ('the less use the qualification, the greater its market value').

And Weiss confirmed that notion in his description of l'Ecole Centrale:

> In the generality and comprehensiveness of his
> curriculum lay the basis of the Centrale engineers'
> claim to industrial aristocracy, the right to direct
> large enterprises, the possession of qualities
> radically different from the 'skills in certain
> specialities' taught in the less exclusive schools.
>
> (Weiss, 1982, 255.)

To this day, the intricate grande école hierarchy (as witnessed by starting salaries or job offers), still ranks the most general scientific schools ahead of their more specialized counterparts. The distinction even extends to the top commercial schools which pride themselves on their generalist ethos. Their curricula are geared to giving the students an overall appreciation of company matters, and the bias towards general management features prominently in their literature. They aim to produce polyvalent products capable of filling posts in any sector – leaders for every occasion.

Clearly, the tradition of generalist engineers who oversaw France's early industrial expansion in the latter half of the nineteenth century still taints French corporate perceptions. The cadres we interviewed were fairly unanimous in their belief that it is the generalists who make it to the top. This means that at some point in their career, ambitious

---

1 The 'super typical' career path, according to Benguigui and Monjarder (1970) is: grande école – R & D – general management.

young *cadres* must make a break from the specialist niche which they may occupy and demonstrate their skills in other areas. Of course, not just anyone is deemed capable of switching functions at the drop of a hat. It requires the sort of adaptability instilled by the top schools.

This raises an interesting point concerning the French perception of the universality of management. On the face of it, the French notion that its *grandes écoles* produce a universal élite shares something with the American notion of managerial man, who can manage any industrial or commercial undertaking. Both approaches claim universality – however, on closer examination the foundations for managerial polyvalence differ radically.

For the Americans, universality resides in the training. Conventional wisdom in the United States is that management is a discipline that can be taught and learned and has principles which are generally applicable. For the French, on the other hand, it is the man who, by virtue of his intellectual quality, can adapt to any situation. Polyvalence stems from the person as an 'intellectually finished product', not the imparting of particular skills and techniques. In some ways, the French manager is closer to a professional version of the British tradition of the 'gifted all-rounder' who can turn his hand to anything – but in France the *raison d'être* is measured intellectual performance, and in Britain a diffuse notion of leadership.

Overview

From the preceding description of career influences, it is apparent that education is the linchpin. Without qualifications, horizons will be limited; but with them, other trump cards such as wider experience and 'healthy' mobility may be played. So, while companies maintain that a qualification counts for little after initial admission, it in fact provides an unassailable head-start which becomes self-perpetuating. The intention of this section is to look at some of the consequences of such a system.

Grande école graduates are expected to be competent when joining a company and are often appointed directly to a position of *cadre*. Ironically, this rather premature allocation of responsibilities can be just as demotivating for the lucky few as for those excluded. The former see little need to prove themselves since they are already guaranteed preferential career advancements, whilst the latter must resign themselves to an atrophied career. As Pierre Mannoni, himself an *autodidacte*, put it:

> Pendant encore des décennies, ce Moyen-Age
> scolaire dans lequel nous vivons va étouffer des
> personnalités, des potentialités de façon

irreversible. (We are still living in the educational
Dark Ages. For how many more decades are we
going to sit idly by while great talents and potential
are permanently stifled?)

(*Challenges*, April 1987, 36.)

A multitude of candidates are discouraged from applying for posts simply because they come from 'inappropriate' backgrounds. The discrimination becomes self-fulfilling, with *autodidactes* not applying for jobs formally open to them but, *de facto*, reserved for *grande école* graduates. They learn to tailor their expectations to organizational realities. As Boltanski explained:

Self-taught *cadres*, especially those of middle- or
lower-class background, have almost no hope of
obtaining positions of power, which are monopolized
by graduates of the *grandes écoles* and/or *cadres* of
upper class background with inside contacts.

(Boltanski, 1987, 261 (Eng. trans.).)

This lack of career opportunities may also help to account for the long-standing malaise, often referred to in the press and discussed in Chapter 2, among middle managers. It seems natural that prematurely curtailed career aspirations contribute to poor motivation and morale.

What is more, not much has come from management 'catch-up' programmes which have been used to justify promotions rather than encourage managers to improve their skills with the incentive of promotion. Irrespective of the way companies try to sell management training, the general feeling is that access to the corridors of power is on a one-shot basis. If one misses the boat as an adolescent, the chances of recovery later are remote. Whilst it appears unfair, this practice is more or less accepted because the criteria used are unequivocal and known to all. The road to the top is well signposted which means that dispersal of talent through misinformation is minimized.

On the upside, of course, the notion of predetermined career paths probably limits unproductive political rivalry since only a few can have pretensions of power. What is the point of jockeying for position when the race is a foregone conclusion? It also renders promotion of *autodidactes* a particularly powerful signal.

There are obvious social and political advantages to promoting *autodidactes* in a country where they are generally kept down. For a start it advertises effort as the way up. Secondly, the risk involved is minimal since loyalty and conformity to company norms have been ensured by a lengthy process of socialization and selection.

The few *autodidactes* who rise through the ranks are unlikely to condemn the workings of a system from which they have emerged

73

with more than they could have expected. Furthermore, they may have gained access to their position at a high cost to their private lives – those who have more obstacles to overcome tend to over-invest in their new roles and positions. They are likely to be hypersensitive to withdrawal of the trappings of *cadre* status which they have worked hard to acquire – so dissent will not come from this quarter.

This brings us to another point. Possibly, it is the very paucity of career opportunities for the vast majority of middle managers that causes the excessive attachment to status symbols and acquired rights. Bereft of real career aspirations, the *cadre* finds surrogate 'achievements' to motivate him.

The attachment to status symbols is revealed by Boltanski in his description of the way companies coerce an individual into resigning. He suggests that this can be achieved simply by withdrawing some of the previously granted privileges but without touching the salary. For instance, not being invited to meetings or informed about events are exclusionary processes which soon become unbearable. Ostracism will render the *cadre* paranoid and his belief in his worth will be undermined to such an extent that he will either resign or end up making mistakes which justify the attempt to get rid of him. Boltanski (1987) quotes a *cadre* who outlines the procedure:

> They'll transfer you from one department to another.
> Or they'll assign you work below your level. You're
> supposed to be an executive and they'll treat you
> like an errand boy. If the man's got a weak character,
> he'll resign. To hold on you've got to be tough. They
> don't invite you to meetings and conferences, they
> don't tell you what's going on, so you look like a jerk.
>
> (264 (Eng. trans.).)

Instances of this kind would seem to point to an underlying flaw in the French management selection process which condemns the majority of the population to the 'scrap heap' before entering active life, whilst guaranteeing the 'lucky few' uninterrupted career progress. In fact, there is growing concern voiced about the psychological effects on French society of such a system. It leaves a disillusioned and frustrated majority with the demotivating prospect of limited advancement, since the upward limits on promotion are basically determined by the diplomas held at the start of a career.

As one personnel director explained to us, a more diversified management recruitment base seems desirable on two grounds: first to recapture those talents which have somehow strayed from the *porte principale*, and secondly to introduce a little more rivalry into competition for the top posts.

The degree of existing system which sets excessive store by

qualifications were perhaps best exemplified by another personnel director from the sample of companies visited. He explained that the number of *cadres* recruited last year fell almost evenly into three categories: those taken on by the personnel department, those poached from other companies by headhunters and those recruited '*par relations*' ('on personal recommendation'). Of the three categories, the highest turnover was among executives recruited by headhunters (75 per cent of whom had already left); next came those recruited through recommendations (30 per cent had left); finally came the managers recruited by the personnel department itself, of which none had left.

Although there was undoubtedly an element of bragging about these revelations, the varying success rates underlined a very important fact: the best qualified people, who corresponded ideally to the head-hunter's spec (based on academic qualifications), were not the best suited to the company's needs. In other words, educational credentials may not be the best means of testing managerial potential, or as the same personnel manager put it:

> '*On ne doit pas chercher les meilleurs, mais les mieux adaptés*'. ('Our aim is not to find the very best, but the best suited.')

Chapter Five

The nature of
work relations

'C'est sûr qu'à l'égard des rapports de travail les
Français sont plutôt constipés.' ('There's no doubt
that in terms of work relations, the French are not
particularly at ease.')
(Conversation with Pierre Salbaing, Vice-President,
                    Conseil d'Administration, L'Air Liquide.)

This chapter takes its cue from the seminal work of Michel Crozier on
work relations in a bureaucratic context in France. Crozier identified a
number of themes which he believed characterized French organizational interaction, notably the isolation of the individual, the avoidance
of face-to-face relationships, the compartmentalization of the organization, the struggle for privileges and the lack of constructive solidarity.
The aim here is to put our view side by side with that documented so
well by Crozier in the 1960s.

Impersonal

Our immediate impression of the ambience of the traditional French
office is that it is less chummy and relaxed than the equivalent in
Britain or the USA. An obvious manifestation is the relative absence of
joking around (ribbing, running jokes, self-deprecation), probably
because humour exposes one's personality. Or again, 'slouching'
(sitting on or putting one's feet up on desks) is uncommon. Interestingly,
the only French manager we saw who actually provided evidence to
the contrary was a trainee store manager at Carrefour, who happened
to be an English expatriate and readily rested his feet on the nearest
available surface. This theme of non-verbal expression is explored
in much detail by the American sociologist Lawrence Wylie, who
maintains that the French are far more upright in their posture and
controlled in their movements than the Americans:

> The French have a sense of vulnerability about their
> bodies that is greater than that of Americans who are

less worried about their body boundaries.

(in Santoni, 1981, 38.)

Social interaction in France makes a clear distinction between personal and professional relations. The role played in the office can easily be kept distinct from the person occupying the role through the use of a battery of props (explored in Chapter 6). This is indeed one of the paradoxes highlighted in our first chapter. At its extreme French *cadres* can exhibit astonishing awareness of their own 'split personality'. For instance, one production manager explained his actions to us by saying, '*qu'est-ce que vous voulez, je suis bête et discipliné – je fais ce qu'on me dit*' ('What do you expect? I'm well disciplined but unthinking – I do as I'm told'). In this assertion the *cadre* was demonstrating an ability to pull away from, and judge, his professional actions. An even more striking example of this distinction between the individual and his function was provided by Lawrence Wylie who quotes Montaigne's approach: '*Montaigne et le maire de Bordeaux sont deux*' ('Montaigne and the mayor of Bordeaux are separate') – which provided convenient justification for his leaving Bordeaux at the time of the plague (in Santoni, 1981, 61).

The notion of impersonality is developed by Desmond Graves, who suggests that the French tend to regard authority as residing in the role not the person. According to Graves, it is by the power of his position that a French manager gets things done (what Chester Barnard termed structural authority). This is in contrast to the Anglo-Saxon view that authority is vested in the person (personal, charismatic or moral authority). The distinction between the two cultures implies that a Frenchman will accept responsibility so long as it is attached to his role but will not actively seek responsibility, as a British manager might, for it adds nothing to his stature. As Graves puts it:

He is '*le responsable*' – but not, as in our culture,
'the person responsible'.

(1973, 293.)

This counterposing again helps to explain the paradox to which we drew attention in the first chapter, where the French are critical of orders but willing to accept big power differences.

The desire to keep function and personality separate has repercussions upon the nature of social contact. It is not possible to reconcile cordial relations and formal (as opposed to personal) authority. Consequently, office colleagues do not often try to meet each other socially, and there are few signs of fraternization between staff of differing grades. This is corroborated by Renaud Sainsaulieu who states:

> *En ce qui concerne les relations interpersonnelles*
> *d'amitié, elles sont assez faibles et fragiles,*
> *en ce sens qu'elles ne débordent pas les limites des*
> *catégories formelles des rangs et des statuts officiels.*
> (Interpersonal friendship ties are fairly weak in so
> far as they rarely transcend the formal boundaries of
> rank and status.)
>
> (1977, 245.)

It is noteworthy that even in the more homely environment of a firm *à dimension humaine* (of human proportions) that we visited, the boss still insisted his staff call him *Monsieur*.

This low-level social openness finds spatial expression in the office layout where personal space seems to be a matter of some importance. Open-plan offices are scarce at *cadre* level and can cause quite a stir if they are imposed. Again the only exception encountered was an American subsidiary whose corporate culture is based on egalitarianism, an integral part of this being the total absence of personal offices. The French like to have a 'territory' to call their own – and the impregnability of the sanctuary tends to increase with organizational status. Three of the PDGs (CEOs) observed had soundproofed doors, great unwieldy things which were almost permanently closed and which simply encouraged people to seek access via the secretary's office. At lower levels glass partitions tended to be blocked out with posters and doors were generally closed – and one maintenance manager even had a spring-loaded door which shut automatically. Such clues tend to indicate low emphasis on dialogue, teamwork, confrontation of opinions as well as a negative view of conflict.

Formal

The pattern of interpersonal relations is formal. The French seem to adhere to a classical conception of management which favours work in isolation, punctuated by formal meetings. Such an approach restricts exchanges to a highly codified framework which precludes the need for personal involvement. This is in contrast, say, to the American approach, highlighted by Kotter (1982, 88) which is more interactive and unstructured.

A number of *cadres* in the sample commented on their preference for getting things done through formal meetings. One PDG (CEO) went as far as to say, *'c'est la seule façon de faire avancer les choses'* ('it's the only way to accomplish anything'). Meetings were seen as an opportunity to bring conflicts to a head ('déclencher l'orage' – to start the storm') or to obtain firm commitments from individuals thanks to peer group pressure. Meetings also constitute an economy of effort in that they allow information to be given quickly and clearly – particularly messages which are not transmissible in an office or casually.

There is therefore a case for suggesting that the French *cadre* is a meeting specialist, in much the same way as his Anglo-Saxon counterpart might be considered an adept troubleshooter. Certainly, meetings provide the *cadre* with a stage on which to display his oratory skill. The whole event is a sort of microcosm of organizational life where status can be enhanced by skilful advocacy and stylish expression or lost by poor eloquence. The agenda is known in advance as are the people attending and the proceedings are formalized – this reduces uncertainty and provides a perfect occasion for furthering personal aims or doing down opponents.

In some companies, there were complaints that the number of meetings was in fact becoming excessive – these companies were deemed to be suffering from *la réunionite* (meeting-itis). One PDG (CEO), whose American MBA gave him different terms of reference, posited that meetings were in fact status-lenders since they reduced access to the person in question. There were also hints that meetings were a means of self-justification – as one *cadre* explained, '*ça meuble une journée*' ('it fills up the day'). In this respect, meetings are comfortingly tangible and make what one has done at the end of the day easy to recall. This view of meetings as showy rather than functional was put more forcefully by a cynical production manager who revealed, '*parfois on parle pour le compte rendu*' ('sometimes we talk in order to have something to record in the minutes'). In such cases the importance of the meeting may lie elsewhere, for instance in terms of who has not been invited.

Another sign of the attachment to classical principles can be seen in the continued distinction between thinkers and executors. Corroboration of the lingering influence of Taylorism is perhaps seen in the way the French have embraced quality circles and discussion groups – working groups outside the normal hierarchical channels. The alleged intention of these new means of participation was to tap the resources of the entire personnel. Unfortunately, these groups have not provided the anticipated antidote – they have reinforced existing hierarchical relationships rather than opened up the way for wider involvement. Instead of using these informal work groups to designate their own spokesmen, many companies have imposed hierarchical heads – thus, underlining from the start a lack of faith in the personnel to elect sensible leaders and the fear that it would give rise to *une hiérarchie parallèle* which might undermine the so-called *hiérarchie naturelle* (chosen by the laws of nature?).

Furthermore, management still appears unconvinced by the capacity of those at the base to think for themselves. The entire management group at one company we visited attended an exposé on quality circles. The organizer started by detailing a handful of 'irrefutable' principles, along the lines 'we can improve productivity if we increase worker commitment'. When he reached the principle about each worker being an expert in his own work, the meeting hit a sticking point. A protracted discussion ensued about the validity of the statement, and the outcome was a redefinition which did away with the word 'expert'. What is more, this could not be dismissed as a one-off case of linguistic 'nit-picking'. It represented a serious lack of faith in worker aptitudes – something which was reiterated by the reaction to a subsequent statement: *'Il existe des reserves d'intelligence inemployées'* ('there are untapped intellectual seams'). Once again, the *cadres* felt they could not let the proposition pass unchallenged and suggested that *'intelligence'* be replaced by *'ressources'*.

Hierarchical

Thanks in part to the American scientific management practitioner, Frederick Taylor, the popular conception of an organization is that of a human pyramid, rather than, say, a well-oiled machine, a market or a beehive. This layered view of the organization can be seen in the nature of work contacts which are faithful reflectors of rank. For instance, one *cadre* explained that, as a rule, he would telephone a subordinate, but go and see a superior. Another manifestation of this desire to avoid contact with lesser mortals can be seen in the widespread use of secretaries to set up calls in other companies. In this way embarrassing rejections and lengthy explanations can be avoided. This practice is generally justified by the preciousness of the boss's time, though as one PDG (CEO) rightly pointed out, no sooner has he resumed work than his secretary will interrupt him. What is more, the use of an intervening filter to save time begins to look dubious when one considers the following exchange witnessed between a *cadre* and secretary:

> 'It's M. Dupont on the line.' – 'Not now, I'm
> busy.' – 'He says its urgent – something to do with
> tomorrow's trip.' – 'What does he want to know?' –
> 'If M. Leroi will be coming along too.' – 'Tell
> him no!'

The duplication of effort together with the possible misinterpretation given the intervention of a third party makes the use of a secretarial barrier look less than necessary. But as one PDG (CEO) explained:

> *'C'est pour les gens un peu péteux qui veulent se
> faire annoncer.'* ('It's for people who are a bit full of
> themselves').

This keen sense of hierarchy militates against the mixing of various strata. For instance, the decision by a senior *cadre* we observed to take his son skiing on a works council holiday was greeted with much surprise by colleagues and subordinates alike. Such trips are theoretically for the benefit of all personnel but hitherto no senior managers had ever 'deigned' to mix with subordinates on such an intimate exercise.

Status consciousness was also visible at a company visited which refused to send senior and intermediary *cadres* on the same training courses. The logic behind that decision was that the benefits of training might be lost if the participants felt inhibited by the presence of superiors or subordinates – particularly in view of the potential loss of face which accompanies the learning situation.

In-house training can prove particularly disruptive with the trainers moving about between hierarchical levels and upsetting the established order. Computing is a notable example of an area which has thoroughly confused the neat 'intellectual/manual' boundary. Indeed, it has caused so much trouble that, as the head of a computing department explained to us, it was the subject of rare consensus among the departments:

> '*Ils peuvent tous se mettre d'accord pour dire du mal de l'informatique.*' ('Slagging off computing is about the one thing they can all agree on.')

At a group level, status consciousness is made explicit by the collective designation of the management ensemble as *la hiérarchie*. It is a term which is borrowed from the bureaucratically organized hierarchy of the church. An example of its usage in business is:

> '*En France c'est l'appartenance à la hiérarchie qui légitime l'autorité de l'agent de maîtrise. Il commande parce qu'il a été choisi par la direction à cette fin, choix qui le distingue et l'éloigne des ouvriers.*' (In France a first-line supervisor derives his authority by virtue of belonging to the management group. He gives the orders because he has been chosen to do so, a choice which sets him apart from the workers.)
> (*Revue Internationale du Travail*, January/February 1985, 1–16.)

Segregation could also be seen in the existence at most companies of separate canteens for workers and management, common enough in Britain, of course, but unusual in Germany, Switzerland and Scandinavia. And even where there was a single dining-hall, it was not uncommon to see unofficial 'territories'. This 'intellectual apartheid' was sometimes cloaked in practical considerations – for instance, one company had a notice which designated one canteen for 'people in civilian clothes', the aim being to avoid mixing overalls and suits. Yet it transpired that production managers would change out of their overalls while secretaries would eat with the workers. Perhaps more striking was the fact that in the canteens people would generally eat in small groups rather than fill up tables with spare seats – again with very obvious layering by rank.

This awareness of hierarchy is reinforced by constant references to *la voie hiérarchique* (the formal chain of command). Individuals were discouraged from bypassing intermediary levels when communicating since it undermined the authority of intermediary levels and in some cases robbed them of their *raison d'être* (i.e. as information passers). Confirmation that French managers actually adhere to formal channels of communication is provided by Desmond Graves. He noted that the actual contacts of the French manager were very much in line with what one would expect after examining the organization chart. This, incidentally, was in stark contrast to British managers, who showed few qualms about breaching organizational protocol and whose 'patterns of communication bore no relation to the "official" organization chart' (1973, 296).

In France, circumventing is only permissible if the person who should have been informed does not hear – or else it constitutes a loss of face. This notion is confirmed by Boltanski (1987, 263 (Eng. trans.)), who maintains that one of the prime means of 'encouraging' a *cadre* to resign is to deprive him of information.

In effect, the hierarchy is as much supported from the base as it is maintained from the summit. Those on the bottom see emulation of those above as the only way up – so they mimic the attitudes of those at the top and unwittingly bolster the existing system. The notion of a professional pecking order permeates every stratum right down to the base. Even workers think in terms of more or less honourable professions. Skilled workers are referred to as *l'aristocratie ouvrière* (the manual aristocracy) in relation to unskilled workers. Thus, the workers are merely echoing the distinction higher up in the hierarchy between, say, graduate engineers in the noble speciality of electronics and graduate engineers in the 'common' field of mechanics.

Of course this stratification rests upon more than the historical distinction between what is 'noble' and what is not. The French researcher Marc Maurice drew particular attention to the qualification hierarchies and wage structure with the evocative '*grilles de classification*' ('classification matrices') which pit manual versus non-manual, skilled versus unskilled, supervisory versus non-supervisory and line versus staff *cadres* (Maurice et al. 1986, 252).

Partitioned

Segregation within French firms is not merely horizontal but also vertical. This is perhaps a collective manifestation of the way individuals seek a personal 'territory'. There were numerous allusions to *le cloisonnement* (partitioning) at the firms visited. The clannish nature of interpersonal relations is partly due to the alumni of prestigious *grandes ècoles* who tend to congregate in particular companies. But the practice is not restricted to the élite. Indeed, François de Closets names taxi drivers, bakers and pharmacists as three of the prime offenders in the perpetuation of *numerus clausus* (closed shops – 1982, 280). And Crozier supports this view when he says:

> At all levels of society the French, once they gain
> entry into an influential group, instinctively try to
> keep others out.
>
> (1982, 26.)

The French propensity for forming cliques was mentioned spontaneously by a number of interviewees. They alluded to *l'esprit de clan* (clannish mentality), *les chasses guardées* (preserves), *les petites bastilles* (small fortresses), *les querelles de chapelles* (warring factions), *les castes* (casts), *les fiefs* (feudal estates). The head of one small company in the survey explained how he was forced continually to reshuffle the personnel around the offices in order to break down cliques.

The essential function of the above-mentioned cliques is to protect and empower their members. It was noticeable, for instance, that once a right had been gained by a group, there was no way it could be abolished – it became un *droit acquis* (an acquired right). Two examples from our study involving bonus payments may serve to illustrate the point: one PDG (CEO) was trying to find a new appellation for a *prime de période de pointe* (a bonus for rush jobs) since the title no longer corresponded to reality. Another head was tackling a similar misnomer – une *prime qualitative* (a quality bonus) which had become institutionalized and had lost its exceptional nature. In both cases, suppressing the bonus was out of the question since it would be equated to a drop in salary. They had become acquired rights, and the only option was to rename them in order to show awareness of the situation.

So in spite of the much-vaunted egalitarianism associated with the French Revolution and the First French Republic, the French are deeply attached to the accumulation of privileges and distinctions which divide them – an idea that was introduced at the end of Chapter 1 with our provocative hexagon. As René Remond put it:

> *L'attachement à l'égalité et la course aux privilèges.*
> (A passion for equality and a race for distinction.)
>
> (Reynaud, 1982, 37.)

Functional differentiation too is strong, as reflected by interdepartmental relations. The following complaints are culled from observation and interviews:

> *'Le siège ne connaît pas nos problèmes.'* ('They don't understand our situation at head office.')

> *'La filiale cache tout et fait n'importe quoi.'* ('They put up a smokescreen and do what they like at our subsidiary.')

> *'La production s'en fout.'* ('Production doesn't give a damn.')

> *'Le personnel fait du social sans mesure.'* ('The personnel department is obsessed with social considerations.')

> *'Les ventes ne pensent qu'à faire du volume.'* ('The sales department only think about their sales figures.')

> *'Le marketing crée ses produits sans écouter l'avis du terrain.'* ('Marketing doesn't pay a blind bit of notice to those in the field when it dreams up its products.')

These informal complaints are not all that different from what Keith Lockyer, for instance, identified in British industry (Lockyer and Jones, 1980). He established a sort of functional 'who hates whom' table which mapped out interdepartmental friction in British companies. What is surprising, then, is the apparent absence of corresponding French research into interfunctional conflict. The only real exception to this is probably the well-documented division between production and maintenance which Crozier first depicted in his classic study of a cigarette company (Crozier, 1964). More recently, Maurice *et al.* produced similar findings when comparing France and Germany. They quote a *cadre* who explains:

> At informational meetings for all personnel you have to be very careful when you mention either maintenance or production, because you get the

feeling that one false step can arouse two hostile armies.

(1982, 264.)

From the present research too, there were signs that the conflicting interests of the two departments have not yet been resolved – and with the gradual takeover by production of routine maintenance the situation was sometimes aggravated - *'chacun tire la couverture de son côté'* ('everyone's pulling the covers their side').

At one particular production plant in our sample efforts were being made to integrate the two functions in order to ease authority problems. These problems stemmed from the fact that maintenance men were geographically isolated from their boss, and unaccountable to the production supervisors – which meant they did very much as they pleased. As one neutral, *cadre* explained, *'le médecin se fait attendre'* ('everyone awaits the doctor'). The production manager in that plant reiterated the point by referring to the maintenance department as 'l'état dans l'état' ('a state within a state') - suggesting that little had changed since Crozier's classic study from the 1960s.

Political

Manifestations of political behaviour were less overt than in Britain or the USA, and French managers did not seem to derive the same sort of pride in divulging their political manoeuvrings as do their Anglo-Saxon counterparts. However, there were signs that political games were being played.

If we take written communications as an example, we can see that the coded nature of the interaction need not impair political thrust. To start with, opting for the written form, particularly in companies with a mainly oral culture, is in itself a powerful signal – it can be seen as *une agression* (an attack).

One administrative director in our study sent the purchasing manager a memo expressing his annoyance over some misdemeanour – this in spite of the close proximity of their offices and the fact that they saw each other regularly. The note was obviously motivated by the desire to register displeasure without overt confrontation. The administrative director knew he had made his point (*'marqué le coup'*), but by restricting the communication to the two parties (no other copies), the receiver knew there was no real malice.

In terms of contents, it would seem that almost anything is a good enough pretext for a memo, even if it is not adapted to the nature or the value of the information. We came across an interesting example at one of the large companies visited. The memo, which every single *cadre* had received, urged all personnel to cut down on the number of unnecessary photocopies (there's nothing like leading by example) –

this in spite of the fact that the boss in question saw the entire management staff each morning for a meeting. Here the aim had been '*de laisser une trace*' ('to leave a trace') so that no one could claim they had not been informed. In view of such excesses, it is hardly surprising that one *cadre* complained of '*incontinence en matière scripturale*'. The resulting inflation of archives is tremendous because no one dares throw anything away – to wit, a manager who, on cleaning out his new office, found four drawers, each one packed with the archives of one of his four predecessors, like prehistoric strata.

Besides the contents, hidden messages can be transmitted in anodyne form in the list of recipients or date – details which the French manipulate with subtlety. One *cadre* explained that in certain cases, the importance of a memo lies in its timing rather than its content. The author may be trying to prove speedy reactions to events or a recent development.

As regards who the memo is dispatched to, there are a number of categories. First, there are the immediate recipients (*destinataires*) who are meant to act upon the information. Secondly, there are those who are not intended to take action but simply need to be informed, covered (*une note-parapluie*) or flattered. Finally, there are the unofficial recipients who receive an extra copy, sometimes termed a 'blind copy'. While these categories appear fairly clear-cut, one *cadre* explained that it may well be that the key recipient is in fact camouflaged in the category headed 'copies'. Another important point about the list of recipients is that it should reflect organizational status. Woe betide a *cadre* who places the PDG below a head of department, even his own, in the list of *copies*.

Further evidence of political behaviour in communications were the rumours which seemed to preoccupy several bosses. There were several references to *les bruits de couloirs* (rumours) or *le téléphone arabe* (the grapevine). Indeed a survey in *Le Nouvel Economiste* (12 May 1980) placed rumours ahead of one's immediate superior as a means of gaining information.

The importance of this form of information in the French context may be a reflection of the relative inefficiency or rigidity of normal channels of communication. It is only natural for rumours to flourish when there is an imbalance between the supply and demand of information. The rumour in France perhaps has a democratizing influence in an otherwise élitist system of communications – as one *cadre* put it, '*c'est le marché noir de l'information*' ('it's the information black market'). The speed of propagation easily outstrips official channels and responds to dual needs of the personnel: to be informed early and to make out one is privy to 'inside' information. It is from these needs that rumours derive their efficiency – they are sucked up by avid receivers and immediately re-emitted, though not always intact.

The managers we interviewed were aware of the possibilities of deliberately starting rumours but they showed wariness about indulging in a practice over which they had no control and which could easily backfire. The head of one production plant was particularly annoyed that every piece of unofficial information released, however positive, was somehow twisted to sound negative by the time it reached grass-roots level. He surmised that people heard what they wanted to hear, not what they were told – though he conceded that they (the *cadres*) did not always make things clear when they had something unpleasant to say. So any complaint that messages were not being received properly was partly '*une autocritique*'. What is more, the speed with which the message spreads depends on its content – as one *cadre* explained it is one thing intimating there may be a pay rise; it is quite another trying to get safety procedures respected.

The fact remains that beneath a formal exterior, French work relations make way for more supple practices – which probably serve to make the formal system workable and therefore contribute to its persistence.

Work versus social relations

One might be tempted to say that the above description shows a relatively low carry-over in France from the social to the business setting – with individuals maintaining a permanent façade at work. This assumes that the professional persona is something which is donned before going to work in the morning. That is not necessarily the case. The relative impersonality and formalism found in organizational relations is echoed in French social life. If one looks at the traditional pattern of interpersonal relations inculcated in the basic associative life of a village, one can see the roots of the work relations described above.

The principles that indiscriminate friendship exposes one to manipulation, that property should be enclosed, that outsiders are not to be trusted – these defensive solidarities are all legacies of the village mentality which still has a strong hold over French social relations. As Wylie points out, the basic social arrangement in France is the circle – a person is responsible only to people in his own *cercle* and indifferent to people outside it. French dislike for people outside their own *cercle* is epitomized by Sartre's phrase, '*l'enfer c'est les autres*' ('Hell is other people' – *Huis clos*, scene V).

Overview

Whilst it would be foolish to suggest that the above description is universal, it certainly prevails in French companies. French work relations are, on the whole, more highly structured and more detached.

From an Anglo-Saxon stance this may appear like a tremendous indictment of the French organizational model. However, in the French mind this lesser investment of the self is considered a means of preserving personal choice, independence and individual dignity.

It is noticeable in France that those companies which do try to impose a more informal style of work relations are often unpopular. There is a widespread belief that cordial relations merely serve as a means of motivating (and manipulating) cadres, of dismantling hierarchical and functional cleavages, and of encouraging a certain freedom of expression which facilitates decision-making – in other words, as an instrument which cleverly subordinates the interests of the individual to the interests of the firm.

This resentment towards informality as a manipulative device may explain the relative flop of Kenneth Blanchard's One Minute Manager in France. The transparency of his proposals was rather too much for French managers. Indeed, one cadre maintained: 'I would not take kindly to being patted on the shoulder – not in the professional context at least' – which reinforces the idea put forward earlier in the chapter that the French do not like their body space violated.

Clearly, in the French context, the desire to avoid conflict and to be protected from arbitrary decisions and manipulation are more important than the immediate gratification provided by social contact. The idea is supported by Wylie, who studied a French village in the Vaucluse. He describes a boy who wasn't bright, never got into trouble and worked very hard. Why? 'Pour qu'on me laisse tranquille' ('So I'll be left in peace' – in Santoni, 1981, 60). The desire for independence, even at the expense of not doing what you want, seems important in France.

This chapter basically concurs with Crozier's view of French work relations as impersonal, formal, compartmentalized... in short, predictable: consider here the much vaunted low tolerance for ambiguity in France, discussed in Chapter 1. There is certainly an undercurrent of informal circles which help to 'oil the wheels', but that influence is better concealed than it is in Britain or America. Finally, it is posited that the dual roles played by French managers do not reflect a split between social and professional circles – but rather a broader distinction between public and private life.

We have now set the scene for the following chapter on business rituals – the desire for ritualization being a manifestation of the desire to preserve distance and independence.

❙Chapter Six

Rituals in French business

> 'L'informalité est un aspect du management à
> l'américaine qui n'a pas achevé la traversée de
> l'Atlantique.' ('Informality is one aspect of the
> American managerial model which has not achieved
> the Atlantic crossing.')
>
> (Conversation with Philippe Loridan, PDG of
> Treifus-France S.A.)

Any attempt to characterize French management would be incomplete without an examination of the country's business rituals. They are reassuringly conspicuous, often physiological, manifestations of differences between cultures. They are concrete not abstract, and do not rely on value-laden interpretation but are accessible to simple observation. This adds to their intrigue; they go unquestioned by the initiated – only an outsider is likely to be struck by their existence or draw attention to them. Indeed, the inclination to dismiss business rituals as anodyne trivia (unworthy of serious study) is perhaps another motive for delving deeper.

Closer examination suggests that these ceremonial singularities of French management in fact represent the visible part of the proverbial iceberg – and, as such, are inextricably linked to the submerged part which supports them. They are more than benign symptoms. They actually serve to reinforce many of the deeply rooted traits of French management – and can only be interpreted in the light of wider issues such as hierarchy, networks and cliques, formality, respect of the individual and the role of women in organizations. In this respect, the investigation of rituals acts as a focus for some of the themes already discussed.

Greeting

Perhaps the most striking ritual for the business visitor to France is the shaking of hands on meeting and parting. This gesture, together with kissing as a form of greeting[1] are renowned as typically French customs.

---

1 Occasionally kissing is seen in organizations – primarily between women, but sometimes mixed sex and more rarely involving *cadres*.

In the formal business setting the procedures regulating handshaking are fairly rigid and institutionalized.

Etiquette demands that the superior stretch out his hand first[1], or if a woman is involved, that the initiative come from her (even if she is the junior party) since it might be construed as forward for the superior to offer his hand. If the individuals are of equal hierarchic status, the onus is on the entrant to approach the others and they are required to make some semblance of rising to greet or bid farewell. In practice, individuals only rise when confronted by a superior (or visitor) – colleagues are treated to a summary lean forward or nod of the head, and a token hand on the arm of the chair (as if to rise).

According to Sanche de Gramont:

> The hand should not be squeezed, brandished or slackly dropped; nor should the shake be too brief (discourteous) or prolonged (familiar). It must be straightforward and without brusqueness. (1969; 295.)

Ostensibly a plain dichotomous (i.e. it may be either performed or not) gesture, handshaking in fact offers managers considerable scope for passing on messages – whether reflecting moods or relationships. Consider the following examples all taken from our periods of observation in French companies:

1. A maintenance manager offered his hand to one of his foremen. The latter responded by holding out his wrist, indicating that he had a dirty hand. The maintenance manager symbolically insisted on shaking his hand irrespectively. In doing so he earned respect and enhanced his image as a robust manager who, in spite of his *grande école* education, was not too proud to dirty his hands alongside his subordinates. An interesting twist on the theme was witnessed at another factory where a disgruntled worker displayed a subtle lack of respect for his superior (and the visiting academic) by stretching out a dirty hand, which the manager (having instigated the salutation) was committed to take.
2. After losing face in front of his boss because of a peer's criticism, a head of department marked his anger the following day by delaying his handshake with the *provocateur*. The rules governing salutation

---

1 We observed one case where a *directeur* refused to acknowledge a subordinate who had the affrontery to extend his hand unsolicited – a cardinal sin.

are so compelling that a minor transgression is highly significant, and by momentarily withholding acknowledgement upon entering the office, the offended party had clearly registered his displeasure – ostracism in France is not to be shaken by the hand. Boltanski quotes a graduate engineer who engaged in political activity embarrassing to the firm. His colleagues made their feelings known to him through exclusion: 'After a while some guys refuse to shake your hand' (1987, 262, English trans.). All this seems to reflect a wider cultural need to acknowledge the existence of people around you – a mark of respect for their individuality.

3. A popular *cadre* returning to see old colleagues following a promotion to another sector was greeted with an 'augmented handshake', in other words, a double-handed clasp which went beyond the expected formality of a simple handshake, thereby expressing closeness after a lengthy separation.

4. A production manager carried out systematic tours of the works three times a day with the sole purpose of shaking hands with every foreman on each of the three shifts. He did not have to concoct some pretext for dropping in on them since *'pour faire un tour de mains'* ('to shake their hands in turn') was reason enough. Needless to say, it also helped him to manage proactively since it both allowed him to *'prendre la température'* ('test the water') and to pass on messages *'entre quatre yeux'* ('man to man').

In a similar vein, Theodore Zeldin cites a teacher who complains, 'In my *lycée* the headmaster shakes the hands of the *agrégés* (highest qualified teachers), holds out two fingers to the *certifiés* and merely nods distractedly to all the other teachers' (1980, 386). Less caricatural versions of this 'physiological segregation' were witnessed with people greeted more or less cordially depending on their rank. Favouritism based on intellectual accomplishments or long-standing association, was explicit in terms of the people a top manager would deign to acknowledge.

Clearly, the handshake acts as a channel for expressing moods or reinforcing authority relationships which go far beyond the basic signal of lack of hostility – though it has retained this essential aspect of partnership or conciliation at the end of a tempestuous day. It also signifies respect for colleagues and enables the superior to boost morale among workers who rarely get a chance to see him and set much store by *la poignée de main du chef* (the boss's handshake). It is a psychological stroke (literally) which has shades of Ken Blanchard's 'hand-on-the-shoulder' recommendation (1983, 41) – but even this gesture is not a viable substitute since it can seem patronizing or out of place. In fact, managers in cultures where handshaking is not the norm have to resort to other, less tactile means (such as tone of voice) to convey the same messages.

In this respect, French managers are blessed with what amounts to an uncontrived point of contact. Unlike their Anglo-Saxon counterparts, they do not have to engineer a convoluted excuse to see someone, or wait vigilantly to 'catch them doing something right' (Blanchard, 1983, 41). The French manager can legitimately go and see a colleague simply *pour lui donner le bonjour* (to bid him good day) – the handshake needs no ulterior justification. What is more, because it requires the participants to invade each other's personal space and look each other in the eyes, it provides an ideal opportunity to pass on confidential messages, and to pick up early-warning signals. One PDG (CEO) in our study looked upon it as a fairly accurate psychological barometer. He recalled an occasion when he had gone to introduce himself to the staff of a newly acquired company: on shaking hands with the personnel he had consciously noted two individuals who did not look him straight in the eye. He later learned that they had been the most vociferous opponents of the takeover.

Used wisely, the handshake can prove an invaluable tool for proactive management. The production manager is perhaps its foremost beneficiary in that he is able to glean information early, thereby allowing him to pre-empt future problems; and the benefits are not entirely one-way in that the manager is also making himself accessible to workers and can anticipate their needs before these lead to problems.

Yet the handshake is also a channel for less 'salutory' messages. For instance, it reflects and perpetuates that distinctive feature of French management, the hierarchy. Touch is traditionally related to dominance, whether between sexes, generations or classes. Paradoxically, while handshaking reduces the physical distance between individuals, it reinforces the organizational distance between them. The distinct set of rules which govern the salutation display leave those involved in no doubt as to who is boss. It is a power gesture in so far as it is instigated by the superior and, if carried to extremes, can be a faithful guide to the rank of the interlocutors.

This physiological manifestation of inequality is compounded linguistically by the *tu/vous* distinction. The combination of these power signals leaves the participants under no misapprehension as to which of them is the senior. Thus, French managers neatly side-step the problem of asserting their authority. They are provided with the means of doing so without having to invest their personality – simply by displaying the trappings of authority.

Form of address

For all its egalitarian claims, even the French Revolution had no lasting impact on formalism. The *vous* form of address was briefly abolished (along with *Monsieur* and *Madame* which were collectively replaced by the androgynous *Citoyen*) but soon reinstated. This was inevitable – *vous* and *tu* are power pronouns that situate class status and reflect a society which accepts social inequality as natural, a structured society by general Euro-American standards in which each individual has his appointed station and says *vous* to his superior.

Of the countries which retain the formal/informal distinction, France is perhaps the most 'miserly' with its *tu* – in contrast, say, with Sweden where the polite form is virtually obsolete. Certainly in France, the *vous* form of address is *de rigueur* in business circles. Like the handshake it is subject to a number of rules – the basic one being that it is up to the superior to determine which form of address to use, since this defines the relationship. As with the handshake, one of the present authors has actually witnessed an instance of an 'irreverent' subordinate (who foolishly tried to instigate a more familiar relationship) receive a firm put-down with an emphatic *vous* in the superior's response to accentuate the social and hierarchical distance between them.

A more subtle, but equally effective, snub is attributed to François Mitterrand (reported in *L'Express*, 1 March 1985, 33). On emerging from a particularly successful party congress, a fellow Socialist ventured, '*On se tutoie?*' ('Shall we drop the formalities?'), to which the President replied distantly, '*Si vous voulez*' ('If we must') – or, to put it another way, 'No!' Mitterrand is in fact renowned for his aloofness and one of the claims to fame of François Dalle (the PDG of the famous cosmetics and toiletries company, l'Oréal) is that he is one of the very few people to use the familiar form of address with the President.

Fortunately, most subordinates know their place and would no more dream *de tutoyer le chef* (of being familiar with the boss) than refuse to shake his extended hand. Many of the *cadres* spoken to, confessed '*J'ai du mal à tutoyer*' ('Familiarity does not come easily to me'), notably with regard to older or more senior colleagues. The resilience of this norm can be gauged from the reaction of one secretary to our hypothetical suggestion that she employ the familiar form with her boss. She was adamant that even with his blessing, she could not 'bring herself' to do so (as though mortified at the very thought). Her boss in fact corroborated this by admitting that he would not address her as *tu* for fear of undermining his power. He felt that a familiar relationship would leave him vulnerable because 'people' (impersonal) were prone to take advantage of it – and use it as a lever for favours. The French believe that friendship obliges, exposes the 'friend' to manipulation, and makes him dependent – a fundamentally intolerable situation, if we are to accept Crozier's theories on the subject (see Chapter 7).

Basically, there is a profound apprehension that a relationship will degenerate if one reveals too much of oneself, so distance is artificially maintained using the polite form. Many *cadres* made it a rule never to use the *tu* form. This was particularly so among the older *cadres*, for whom *tutoiment* was tantamount to 'sleeping together' – the allusion is not so far-fetched when one considers the revelation of one of the bosses interviewed, a 58-year-old, who admitted that he had never once addressed his parents as *tu*. He added that *vous* could, quite easily, be reconciled with friendship but that familiarity made reprimand difficult. The use of the *vous* form was primarily motivated by the future need to sanction or, worse still, make a subordinate redundant. Censure is regarded as far more *sanglant* (scathing) in the *vous* form.

Thus, to use the *tu* form one had to be fairly confident of not needing subsequent recourse to the *vous* form since back-peddling is out of the question. It is a one-way move, though there were rare exceptions: for instance, two *cadres* on familiar terms reverted back to the *vous* form when one of them was promoted to be the other's boss – though in private they remained on *tu* terms. This use of *vous* as a face-saving device was also witnessed with a *cadre* during one of the interviews. We were interrupted by another *cadre* who addressed his colleague as *vous*. It later transpired that the two were on familiar terms but that the 'intruder' had refrained from showing this out of respect for his colleague in front of an unknown party.

As a rule, people of the same generation or organizational/educational status are likely to use *tu* more readily with one another. One *cadre* listed those colleagues with whom he was on familiar terms and mentioned one '*que tout le monde tutoie*' ('that everyone calls by his first name'). This at once implied a certain lack of authority (you do not say *tu* to someone you respect) and a congenial disposition (or to someone you dislike). From his own experience, the *cadre* recalled that the turning point had often been an event (long car journey, shared hotel room...) whose relative intimacy rendered the *vous* form absurd – this would prompt an anxious (for fear of rejection) '*C'est bête quand même...*' ('it's a bit silly after all') and a transition to the familiar form. It is striking that the watershed for relaxing these formalities was frequently when those concerned were away from the traditionally rigid setting of the workplace.

The widespread use of *vous* means that any derogation of the practice is all the more significant. In other words, the *tu* form of address derives its political power precisely from the fact that *vous* is the norm in business.[1] Thus, the accelerated, or in some cases obligatory, use of *tu* is a powerful weapon in forming a clique and warding off unwelcome intruders. Mutual *tutoiment* effectively seals a clique in a highly

---

1 To invert the old adage 'It is the rule which reinforces the exception' – were it not for the widespread use of *vous*, the familiar form would not have so much impact.

'visible' way – and numerous old-boys' associations, as well as less formal networks, employ this device to their advantage.

France's top *grandes écoles* (l'ENA, Polytechnique, HEC, Arts & Métiers...) are particularly fond of the ruling that their alumni should address their cohorts as *tu*. This, according to one cynic, in spite of the fact that they did not know one another at school and would probably have despised one another heartily if they had.[1] *'Le fait d'avoir posé ses fesses sur les mêmes bancs'* ('the mere fact that they had shared the same benches') is regarded as reason enough for familiarity.

It is said that ex-Polytechnique students must *tutoie* anyone who was up to seven years above or below them – a ruling presumably designed to spare the sensibilities of senior members. In other schools the exigency is less restrictive but equally binding, even at official functions. For instance, at one international conference attended by one of us, the guest speaker, Yvon Gattaz, acknowledged the chairman's introduction with *'Je te remercie...'* ('thanks a lot'). Many of the foreign guests were visibly taken aback at this sudden injection of informality – little did they know that the two protagonists were both graduates of l'Ecole Centrale.

Directories lend weight to this peculiar form of exclusion rite by listing alumni according to occupation, company and position. Every self-respecting association publishes a directory, thereby reinforcing the popular image of old-boy networks as *les mafias*. The directory of the Ecole des Arts et Métiers actually includes a bookmarker-cum-advertisement which addresses members informally: *'As-tu payé ta cotisation?'* ('Have you paid-up your subscription fees?'). The clubbish-ness of this approach is replicated in a recruitment poster for the communist-based union, the Confédération Générale du Travail (CGT). The poster urges workers to renew their membership: *'Prends ta carte CGT'* (see Figure 6.1).

All this reflects the exploitation of the familiar form of address as a utilitarian device rather than to denote friendship – but its 'misuse' is not confined to institutionalized solidarity. There are informal examples in most organizations of politically motivated cliques. These coalitions constitute privileged arenas in which people already possessing social capital (i.e. connections) congregate in an attempt to make that capital fructify – by making useful contacts. On these occasions, the *tu/vous* distinction acts as a powerful barrier to entry.

A typical example of *tutoiement politique* (political familiarity) was experienced by one PDG (CEO) who was invited to a product launch by a company manufacturing a complementary product. He accepted

---

1 This comment has a ring of truth about it in so far as French education in general, and the élite *grandes écoles* in particular, are notorious for promoting individual effort (sym-bolized by the dreaded final year rankings) over joint effort – an approach not particularly conducive to developing friendship ties.

As-*Tu*
Payé
ta cotisation ?

Cotisation 1986

–	de soutien	580 F
–	membre actif	470 F
–	retraité suivant possibilité	à 290 F 580 F
–	promotion (82, 83, 84) au minimum.	120 F

———

Chèque Bancaire :
Association des ingénieurs ICAM.

Virement Postal :
Compte 90-11 P LILLE

———

Pense aussi
à la caisse de Secours.

Figure 6.1 Use of the familiar form of address to denote membership. The CGT urging workers to pay their dues and the bookmarker reminding alumni of l'Ecole des Arts et Métiers to pay their subscriptions make strange bedfellows.

the invitation as a useful opportunity to make a few new contacts but was disappointed to find that everyone knew (or pretended to know) everyone else. He was made to feel awkward, an outcast, simply because '*ça se tutoyait à tours de bras*' ('they were all "in" with each other'). The conspirators had rendered the clique 'impregnable' simply by using the *tu* form. Their familiarity with one another, whether genuine or (as he suspected) cosmetic, barred his entry. The familiar approach acts as an expression of group membership – and as such constitutes one of the pillars of French tribalism (this propensity for forming clans and *cloisonnement* is discussed in Chapter 5 on work relations).

Having seen what it is like to be on the outside looking in, it may be interesting to quote a boss who happened to be plugged in with the people that mattered. He took great pride in explaining:

> '*Je suis personnellement ami à tu et à toi avec tous les présidents de ligue. Aucun de nos concurrents n'a ça. Aucun. Ils viennent là en spectateur.*' ('I am on familiar terms with every single president in the confederation. There's not one of our competitors who can make that claim. Not one. They all attend as spectators.')

An interesting twist on the protective use of *tu* was provided by the senior management at a car plant. The personnel manager, who was part of a so-called *organigramme en rateau* (i.e. where all heads of department are on the same level), was *de facto* the plant manager's right-hand man. Now this was probably fully justified in so far as his detachment from operational problems made him a valuable advisor. However, it was reinforced by a psychological barrier which set him apart from his 'peers' – he shrewdly insisted on remaining on formal terms (like the boss) with his colleagues (who all addressed one another as *tu*), thereby asserting his 'authority' over them and keeping potential usurpers at bay.

Another amusing variation on the political use of *vous* was revealed by a young *cadre* who envisaged rapid promotion and took the precaution of addressing everyone as *vous*. This was a conscious decision based on the reasoning that subsequent promotion might prove embarrassing for people with whom he had previously been on familiar terms. The anticipated promotion materialized and the transition was smooth, thus confirming this useful tip for potential high-flyers. As already mentioned, a rather less elegant solution to the same problem resulted from the promotion of one *cadre* as boss of his previous colleague. In order to avoid embarrassment to the senior *cadre*, they conspired to revert to the formal *vous* – in public at least.

97

Further nuances in relationships are revealed by the way in which people are addressed – such as the title used. The French seem very keen on formality: the referee is *Monsieur l'Arbitre*, just as the policeman is *Monsieur l'Agent* and any ex-chairman expects to be addressed till his death as *Monsieur le Président*. Even graduate engineers will be referred to in jest as *Monsieur l'Ingénieur*. Older people especially like being called by their titles both in letters and speech. This may be a sign (as suggested by a *cadre* with twenty years' experience in America) that, '*on se prend trop au sérieux*' ('we take ourselves too seriously'). Others regard this deference, not so much as a sign of acceptance of the hierarchy, as a mark of respect for individual dignity. Whatever the motivation behind it, formality seems to result in a bolstering of the traditional hierarchy.

French managers certainly appear socially reserved by Anglo-Saxon standards – especially in comparison to their American counterparts, who value informality and at least the appearance of equality in human relations and are quick to seize upon Christian names. This difference in approach was quite striking when companies we visited received incoming telephone calls from abroad. The direct manner of Americans in particular often jars in France. On a number of occasions the caller provoked a stir at the reception by asking for 'Philippe' or 'Pascal'.[1] Some French *cadres* have taken this as a cue to modify their own communications with other countries – by making the awesome concession of including their first names when signing letters.

In France, close relations between *cadres* are indicated by use of the surname – without *Monsieur*. The secondary importance of the forename can be seen on envelopes where addresses bear the surname followed by the initial (or name), rather than vice versa – a habit which is ingrained at school and perpetuated by the administration. The relative redundancy of the first name was emphasized by the difficulties faced by secretaries when attempting to fill out forms requiring the forename. On more than one occasion colleagues of the *cadre* in question were unable to help the secretary. This French preference was made explicit by one *cadre* who was unable to respond to an American request for full names (to fill out hotel reservations) and could only offer a sheepish, 'In France people do not call themselves by their first name'.[2]

---

1 This may be a learning point for foreign callers who, in their myopic attempt to play down status distinctions such as titles by eliminating 'unnecessary' formalities, succeed only in making themselves comfortable, whilst their French colleagues become uneasy or even annoyed.

2 The fact that formality is the rule may be inferred from the surprised reaction of an experienced *cadre* on entering a new company: 'I was kind of surprised, because in business you don't see people slapping each other on the back very often and calling each other by their first names, at least not for long' (Boltanski, 1982, 301, English trans.).

As with the predominance of the *vous* mode, the almost exclusive use of surnames loads the use of forenames with significance – they can even become prized rewards if used sparingly. According to one *cadre*, his PDG called only five or six people by their first names[1] – they did not reciprocate, but it was nonetheless considered '*une marque d'estime extraordinaire*' ('a real honour'). One of the privileged few was Pierre who was more important in the company when the current PDG had started out 22 years ago; in this case it was a mark of affection for a senior employee.

A fascinating reversal of this trait is practised by workers who prefix the PDG's first name with *Monsieur*. This is particularly the case in traditional family firms which harbour several family members bearing the same surname, such as Michelin where the current patron is endearingly known as 'Monsieur François'. While this signifies a certain closeness, it also smacks of paternalism.

The qualifying prefix *Monsieur* is reserved for superiors or visitors and is generally abandoned with colleagues and subordinates. However, it will be used if the superior seeks to emphasize a point (usually negative). For instance, '*J'ai quelque chose à vous dire, Monsieur Dupont*' (which is reminiscent of the way a mother might signal disapproval by calling out her child's full name). It can also be used to indicate role reversal, as demonstrated by a PDG who had to reprimand a junior *cadre*. On their next encounter the PDG made a point of showing there were 'no hard feelings' by mimicking subservience, '*Très bien Monsieur, je m'en occupe*' ('Very good Sir, I'll take care of it'). The essence of this joke-cum-reconciliation lay in the inversion of the formality expected in hierarchical relations.

Another nuance in the art of interpersonal one-upmanship is provided by the use of the whole name and the omission of *Monsieur*. Strictly speaking, this is a breach of business protocol but it can provide a significant psychological edge. For instance, a request to speak to Jean Dupont has a touch of Anglo-Saxon irreverence about it – implying that the person asked for does not impress the inquirer.

The French organizational context provides its players with the means to assert their authority without having to reveal their personalities. They have at their disposal numerous physiological and linguistic signals which provide a ready-made delineation of authority. Their British counterparts are bereft of such messages and have to project authority in their tone of voice or attitude – both of which are more open to misinterpretation.

This finding also seems to fit in with Theodore Weinshall's theory (1977, 248) that French managers see authority vested in the role as

---

[1] This does not imply that he also used the *tu* form with them – *vous* and the first name are perfectly compatible – they denote affinity whilst preserving distance. The permutations are numerous.

opposed to British managers who see it vested in the person. In France then, authority requires a lesser investment of the 'self' – the handshake, the title and the form of address are stage props which help maintain authority whilst simultaneously protecting the real individual. In short, business etiquette equips the *cadre* with the weaponry to assert his authority, whether or not he has the personal attributes to back it up. This perhaps corroborates Crozier's belief that the French are uncomfortable in face-to-face relationships since they have organized rituals to cover the anxiety.

It would seem that the French have concocted a system of authority relations which minimizes the personality element – and makes it possible for those without experience to exercise authority. To distort the motto of Winchester school (coined nearly six centuries ago), in France, 'manners makyth the manager'.

Written rituals

On presenting an English secretary with a draft copy of a letter to be typed up in French, she gave it a cursory glance and immediately remarked on the apparent absence of a closing salutation. It had to be pointed out to her that the whole of the last paragraph, beseeching the receiver to accept the assurance of most distinguished sentiments, was the French equivalent of 'Yours faithfully'.

Furthermore, there are infinite possibilities for signing out depending on the impression one seeks to make on the receiver. For instance, a senior civil servant will send a lowly colleague *l'expression de ma considération distinguée*, an equal his *haute considération* and a high-ranking superior his *très haute considération*. In the business world, the formalities are not quite so strictly defined, but similar rules operate. The sender can bestow anything ranging from the basic *vive considération* to the more lavish *sentiments respectueux* or even *entier dévouement*, depending upon the perceived relationship with the receiver. The permutations are full of nuance and secretaries generally need an etiquette guide at hand to avoid a regrettable *faux pas* – in other words, to ensure that the signing out phrase conveys sufficient deference given the relative status of sender and recipient. What is more, the courtesy and status-consciousness bear up even under the utmost pressure of deteriorating relations. This can lead to a signing out phrase which is in striking contrast to the tone of the letter (see Figure 6.2).

Another feature of French business correspondence is its impersonal nature. Letters open rather stiffly with *Monsieur* (even if the recipient is known to be a woman) or *Monsieur le ...* (plus a title), and end with the stylized formality mentioned above – there is no presumption of acquaintanceship. By convention, even the content is disconcertingly

Paris, le 02 Septembre 1987

Monsieur,

J'accuse réception de votre courrier en date du 29 juillet, qui ne me surprend, ni ne m'attriste, mais m'irrite au plus haut point.

Je ne peux en effect pas accepter le ton que vous vous croyez autorisé d'utiliser. .

Il me semble que je suis celui qui est en droit de demander des explications, et que vous tentez bien maladroitement de renverser cette situation.

D'autre part, et que pour les choses soient claires, sachez que j'entends m'entretenir avec Monsieur   tant que lui et moi y trouverons convenance et que je n'envisage pas d'utiliser les services de quelconques intermédiaires pour ce faire.

Enfin, puisque Monsieur   a été informé de notre différend tant par vos soins que par les miens, je pense qu'il serait heureux qu'il accepte d'assister au prochain Conseil d'Administration du CILBO. Je compte en effet sur cette occasion pour aborder aussi précisément que vous le souffrirez la situation pesante que je vous soupçonne, ainsi que ce Monsieur   , de créer volontairement.

Je terminerai en vous précisant:

– Que c'est au titre de la SARL T.A.T. que j'ai été réélu, et non PAT-MULTIPREST.

– Que dirigeant une SARL, j'en suis le gérant et non le PDG.

– Que m'écrivant en qualité de Président au CILBO le Conseil peut et doit être informé de notre litige, la mention "Personnelle et Confidentielle" me paraissant déplacée.

Vous souhaitant bonne réception de la présente, et dans l'attente d'une convocation pour le courant septembre, je vous prie d'agréer, Monsieur, l'expression de mes salutations très distinguées.

                                Jean-Pierre COIMET
                                LE GERANT

Figure 6.2 Contrast between tone and content in a business letter.

cold from an Anglo-Saxon standpoint. The aim seems to be to preserve anonymity. There is no sign of the familiar approach which characterizes Anglo-Saxon correspondence. Even if the individuals parted on the warmest of personal terms, the follow-up correspondence is unlikely to make reference to that cordial meeting. In fact, the only discernible evidence of individuality is the written style of the letter. The letter is an opportunity to parade one's education and impress both secretary and recipient(s), by one's *tournure* (expression).

The French clearly indulge in what, by Anglo-Saxon standards, is excessive formality. French business correspondence seems to prize inordinately complex set phrases such as those quoted by Zeldin (1980, 352), *'J'ai l'honneur de vous prier de bien vouloir'* (= please) or *'Il ne saurait être question d'apporter à cette demande une suite favorable'* (= no). These *formules* do not add to the core message and, if anything, actually serve to conceal it. Thus, for example, in the correspondence one of the present authors had with a French firm, he was led to expect a favourable response until, upon reaching the fourteenth line of the letter (see Figure 6.3), it was finally stated that a visit to that company would not be allowed.

It would seem that the French sometimes indulge in voluntary long-windedness. One *cadre* admitted as much by saying, *'on prend plaisir à tourner autour du pot'* ('we relish beating about the bush'). Certainly, they do not always seem anxious to get to the heart of the matter. This would seem to bear out the traditional portrayal of the French as a people overly concerned with style, sometimes attaching more importance to means than ends, to form than content. It would apear that the American managerial values of practical utility, efficiency and performance have not been fully integrated into the French managerial model.

Yet this lack of directness is also an indication of French humanitarianism. Their elegant meanderings display respect for the individual and a desire to avoid inflicting unnecessary loss of face. The coded nature of French business correspondence gives it a sense of abstraction – which renders the most virulent attack impersonal. Similarly, a request which is turned down is made far more palatable if the sender takes the trouble to compose a courteous and personalized refusal – the brusqueness of the negative message is attenuated by a veneer of grace and humility which provides both sender and recipient with a certain psychological refuge.

This preoccupation with form has additional implications. Most importantly, it serves to uphold the distinction between those who know the rules and those who do not. Since the former are generally the products of higher education it helps to reinforce educational élitism in business. Admittedly, awareness of written protocol is only one barrier among others, but it supports the claim of the educated to hold high positions in organizations. Simultaneously, self-taught le 21 janvier 1987

Monsieur le Professeur,

Vous voudrez bien ne pas me tenir rigueur du retard avec lequel je réponds au courrier que vous m'avez adressé en décembre dernier avec la recommandation de M. CARRON de LA CARRIERE, Ministre Conseiller chargé des affaires économiques et commerciales à l'Ambassade de France en Grande-Bretagne.

Ce délai me permet cependant de vous répondre en meilleure connaissance de cause car mes collaborateurs ont pu ainsi étudier votre proposition avec une attention réellement bienveillante, ainsi que je les y avais invités.

En réalité, nos structures d'accueil pour les étudiants doivent faire face à de nombreuses demandes et nous tentons de satisfaire le plus grand nombre d'entre eux. Malheureusement aujourd'hui, nous ne voyons pas la possibilité d'accueillir votre élève le temps suffisant pour entreprendre valablement une étude en profondeur sur les méthodes de gestion pratiquées dans notre entreprise.

Croyez que je regrette de ne pouvoir vous apporter l'aide que vous sollicitiez et je vous prie d'agréer, Monsieur le Professeur, l'assurance de mes sentiments très distingués.

Monsieur Peter LAWRENCE.
cc : **Monsieur G. CARRON de LA CARRIERE.**

Figure 6.3 Elegant meanderings in a letter of rejection.

individuals are discouraged in their bids to infiltrate this graduate preserve simply because they are not *au fait* with the written niceties of business etiquette. Emphasis on the need for correct written expression in business communication mirrors and lends weight to the French conviction that educational credentials are the proper means for determining managerial eligibility.

The power of written expression as a means of weeding out 'undesirables' was suggested by the decision of one *autodidacte* (self-taught) PDG to install telex machines throughout the group – on the basis that such a system would help to cut through the verbosity which impeded intra-group communications. A different interpretation of this decision was provided by a less than charitable graduate *cadre*. He confidentially suggested to us that it was in fact motivated by the PDG's desire to conceal his inability to compose a good business letter.

Further evidence of the importance of educational qualifications for business legitimacy can be found in the business card. These bear the name of the *grande école* attended (its fame permitting) and are therefore vital in establishing the status relationships, since there is widespread consensus on the implicit pecking order of schools. Thus, the ritual exchange of business cards enables each party to know which role to play and leaves them in no doubt as to who has the upper hand.

Feeding rituals

Meals

According to *The Financial Times* (21 May 1986, 20), in Finland, the focal point of informal business discussion is the sauna. Its French equivalent is the restaurant. The two have a great deal in common. Both are ambivalent public/private places. Both serve to diminish hostility whilst fostering intimacy by increased physical proximity. Moreover, inhibitions are lowered: in the one case by absence of clothes and in the other by the consumption of alcohol.

The importance of business lunches as an arena for extended business discussion was emphasized by a free guide (resembling a travel brochure) received unsolicited by a commercial director at one of the companies in our study. This brochure listed all the hotels and restaurants available for seminars and *repas d'affaires* both in France and in France's more exotic overseas territories. Confirmation of the French expectations regarding hospitality can be seen in the way British managers shudder at the costs of entertaining in France.

Eating is a convivial affair; the French enjoy talking about food in much the same way as the British find diversion in the weather – these are topics which unify a nation. People with nothing else in common can quite happily rhapsodize about what has been eaten, what is being eaten and what will be eaten. And this preoccupation with food has infiltrated the organizational setting, so that business expressions are replete with gastronomic references.

Every business language borrows food imagery to some extent; most have some sort of equivalent of 'bringing home the bacon' (*'gagner son pain'/'défendre son bifteck'*). But what is distinctive about French managers is the *degree* to which they plunder the gastronomic world for imagery. They do not confine themselves to set phrases but invent their own variations and frequently have spontaneous recourse to food vocabulary in their expressions. Take, for instance, the PDG who contemplates introducing merit-based salaries with the justification, *'Il y aurait davantage de biscuits pour ceux qui les méritent'* ('There'll be more cookies for those who deserve them') – this is by no means a set expression, but he uses *biscuits*[1] as a variation on the recognized association between confectionery (*le gâteau, le nougat, la tarte, le miel*) and rewards ('just desserts').

Some of the better known expressions include:

1. The top brass are *les grosses légumes* (big vegetables) or *le gratin* (cheese topping) and a sinecure is *un bon fromage* (a mature cheese).
2. A contract that clears a healthy profit *fait des choux gras* (yields large cabbages) and one which sustains losses *bouffe de l'argent* (gobbles up money).
3. Likewise, a *cadre* involved in negotiations rounded off his sales pitch with the aside, *'J'ai vendu ma soupe'* ('I've sold my soup') – it only remained to see if they were interested, *'si la mayonnaise prend'* ('if the mayonnaise was setting').
4. On the other hand a favourable situation which deteriorates is said to *tourner au vinaigre* (turn sour) or *se gâter* (going off). Or, if negotiations appear to be leading nowhere (paying 'homage' to German cuisine), *ça patine dans la choucroute* (we're pedalling in sauerkraut) – possibly a sign that a compromise is needed and that the time has come to *mettre de l'eau dans son vin* (dilute one's wine).
5. Finally, an interesting example of linguistic imagery 'materializing' was provided by a group of *cadres* celebrating the early retirement of a colleague. Among the departure gifts they included a squeezed out lemon mounted on a stand – a visual joke evoking

---

1 The euphemistic allusion to biscuits is indicative of the lingering reticence to talk of money per se.

> the popular reference to a 'washed out' *cadre* as *un*
> *citron pressé* (a squeezed lemon).

This 'appetite' for gastronomic expressions is a mark of the central role of food in business negotiations – so synonymous are they that it becomes almost inconceivable to talk business outside the meal times. As one sales director explained:

> '*Il arrive qu'un rendez-vous soit remis de plusieurs*
> *semaines faute d'avoir pu trouver un déjeuner de*
> *libre avant.*' ('It is not unknown for a meeting to be
> postponed for several weeks simply because of a
> failure to find a free lunch hour.')

In France, *la table* is regarded as the best means of promoting healthy relations since it has a number of obvious advantages over the more formal organizational setting. For a start, business can be conducted graciously, at a leisurely pace, and diluted with social conversation to ensure both parties are at ease – and by getting away from operational pressures one can be more attentive. After all, it is not easy to conduct a discussion in an office where one's attention can be distracted by the sight of some unanswered telex, or else one can be interrupted by a secretary needing an urgent signature, and however much one insists on no disturbances, some calls or individuals invariably find their way through. Even without these unforeseen interruptions, the background bustle of organizational life can prove unconducive to negotiation. So the prime advantage of eating out is the peace and tranquility it affords.

By distancing themselves from the immediate pressures of work the protagonists are able to think more clearly. Managers who may have some inhibitions about negotiating in front of their peers (even behind soundproof glass) will find it easier to adopt a bolder *persona* outside the confines of the organization. Self-presentation is easier and anxiety is lowered by eating. The atmosphere that reigns in a restaurant is more propitious to reflection and creativity.

What is more, moving away from the organizational setting means leaving behind all the files relating to the case – without his 'heavy artillery' to fall back on, the manager requires a perfect understanding of the case. This means that preparation will have to be better resulting in better informed and more coherent argumentation.

As mentioned earlier, the physical proximity in the restaurant facilitates psychological proximity. In a restaurant the two parties shift from a desk-width apart to within touching distance – in other words, from a work relationship to a social relationship. This facilitates communication, both psychologically and physically. The actors can see and hear each other perfectly and non-verbal communication is less 'showy' and stylized.

The restaurant can also be used to achieve an early psychological edge. The host *cadre* can give an inflated impression of his organizational standing by choosing a restaurant noted for its fine cuisine (rather than its décor, in France). This impression of status can be reinforced by a cordial greeting from the proprietor and by the means of payment (the more discreet, the better – the epitome being to leave casually immediately on finishing thus indicating an open table). All these signals suggest that the *cadre* is a 'regular' and enhance his social and organizational kudos.

Since business lunches are so important, *le savoir manger* (knowing how and what to eat) is deemed an indispensable string to the manager's bow. This implies an awareness of etiquette; a French meal should be composed of well delineated parts and ingested with well defined liquids at specific points. The host is expected to determine the structure and contents of the meal – and this influence over meal format can be used in such a way as to spring surprises on his unsuspecting guest. The host is able to induce drowsiness and sap the adversary's intellectual faculties, leaving him open to attack. The mere reaction to the 'plate arrival' gives some measure of the level of vulnerability. Attention becomes riveted on the dish; even if immersed in deep conversation everything becomes secondary as the dish is sighted (reminiscent of a cat sighting a mouse). To avoid dropping one's guard at this point requires considerable willpower.

Of course *le savoir manger* also demands a capacity to cope with alcohol and to stave off its debilitating effects. This was supported by a commercial director; he confessed to resorting occasionally to consuming a tin of sardines prior to important negotiations in order to delay the absorption of alcohol. French managers are not averse to using their international reputation as *bons vivants* as a means of 'softening up' their adversaries – particularly when dealing with foreign visitors.

Interestingly, it is not only the after-effects of the meal which facilitate acquiescence – the very prospect of a meal can provoke a similar reaction. One store manager from the sample used hunger as a device to curtail protracted meetings. Being rather partial to *les petits déjeuners à l'anglaise* (English as opposed to continental-style breakfasts), he would timetable awkward meetings for late morning and would programme particularly contentious issues at the end of the agenda. By the time it came to discussing them, the interested parties could rarely muster much support from peckish colleagues. Having thus gained the upper hand, the polemic issue of working on a bank holiday was passed relatively unhindered. He was inadvertently putting into practice Maslow's hierarchy of needs whereby satisfaction of low order (physiological) needs takes priority over more ethereal needs.

A lavish *repas d'affaires* (business meal) will last anything up to two or three hours and although lunch hours are supposedly shortening, getting in touch with French managers between 12:00 and 14:30 is still problematic. In fact, the French are conditioned into taking a long lunch-hour from school days when a two-hour break means that they stay relatively late in the afternoon to compensate. (This is a trend which carries over into adulthood and will be examined in the following section.)

Business lunches are loaded with social and political significance. For instance, lunching with the boss is regarded as a real privilege. It is used regularly as a bone to toss to meritorious subordinates for whom alternative forms of recompense (namely financial or promotional) are inappropriate or unavailable. This reward draws its value from the prestige of being seen with the boss. One *cadre* in our study went as far as to suggest that the length of the meal was critical since competing *cadres* would compare the time accorded to one another.

The superior whose attention is so sought after must be cautious in distributing his favours. Accessibility must be limited in such a way as to give subordinates the impression of being privileged to be in attendance. Used sparingly, private lunches can be a powerful means of inclusion in, and exclusion from, social groups. Food in fact plays an essential role in constituting unofficial networks since people are particularly touchy about who sits near them outside the functional requirements of the office environment. Of course, the issue of access would not be considered so critical if it were more available – but in France the right of access to people or information is not a basic democratic principle. Having access is equated with power.

Political guests may also be invited to meals, perhaps in order to placate a disgruntled subordinate, or in order to 'butter up' external parties like clients, suppliers, works' inspectors, or representatives from the employment agency and the town hall. They will be flattered by the time accorded to them and the charade of listening to their preoccupations. Dining with someone is also a mark of respect for that person. As one *cadre* explained:

> '*C'est une façon de reconnaître l'importance sociale
> de votre interlocuteur. Un moyen de partager
> quelque chose qui soit au-delà de la conversation et
> de la cigarette.*' ('It's a means of acknowledging
> someone's social standing, of sharing something
> more than a talk and a cigarette.')

In this respect, it can help to cement an association. Just as a handshake facilitates informal comments *entre quatre yeux*, so the table reduces the physical distance between participants and enhances persuasive power.

Perhaps the most significant social implication of this obsession with food is the way it discriminates against women. They are placed at a relative disadvantage on two counts: first, long drawn-out meals at lunch-time are fine provided one is free to compensate for the loss of time in the evening; secondly, in the organizational context (as outside), it is far less acceptable for a woman to be overweight than for a man. It is harder for a woman to set the pace at lunch-time – a female executive is expected to be slim and elegant. Likewise, her diminished capacity to drink will put her at a disadvantage if she attempts to keep up with the traditional sequence of *apéritif*, two wines and *digestif*.

Such discrimination perhaps contributes to the paucity of women in senior management positions – and is all the more dangerous for being unintentional. Whilst it does not in itself explain their relative absence from the higher reaches of French management, it draws attention to the way in which the work pattern is designed to fit in with a man's lifestyle – and a unilateral change in habits (i.e. working through lunch and leaving early) is useless unless colleagues do likewise.

Coffee and drinks

Contracted versions of the food sharing ritual are discernible in the French penchant for coffee and alcohol. Drinks are, after all, only liquid foods.

Coffee provides a welcome psychosomatic boost to help managers start the day or ward off the soporific effects of a heavy meal – '*un petit jus pour me mettre en route*'. It acts as a gentle prelude to the rigours of work – a sort of ice-breaker whereby everyone gathers round the *cafetière* (percolator) for the *pause café* (coffee break), which serves to prolong the morning handshake and ease people back into work. The informal congregation about the coffee machine in fact facilitates the obligatory *tour de mains* (round of handshakes) since everyone is within close proximity. It also provides an opportunity for a little informal chat that goes beyond the initial contact – and which may or may not be deemed productive.

One company visited regarded coffee breaks as so unproductive that they had removed all coffee percolators save a drinks distributor in the basement – though there was a real percolator '*pour les hôtes/invités de marque*' ('for VIPs'). This effectively proved dissuasive but the time wasted in descending up to seven storeys made the solution less than satisfactory. In addition, people were made to feel guilty if they spent too long in the basement. One *cadre* surmised that the 'prohibition order' was indicative of French narrow-mindedness regarding management work. To 'them', working and offices were synonymous – it was inconceivable that one might actually gain something from the informal contacts made around individual coffee machines installed on each floor: '*En France on ne travaille que quand on a le cul sur une chaise*' ('In France you can only be working if you are sitting down'). So much for Tom Peters' Management By Walking About (MBWA – a phrase coined in '*A Passion for Excellence*').

The early morning/early afternoon consumption of caffeine as a stimulant has its antithesis in the end of morning/end of day aperitif to wind down. The consumption of alcohol in French companies was not excessive but it was certainly regular. It was not uncommon for directors to have their own drinks cabinets and to use them as bait with which to tempt colleagues to *prendre un verre/boire l'apéro* (share a glass) and engage in an impromptu chat just before lunch or prior to leaving in the evening. It provided an opportunity to relax and talk at greater length about the 'strategic' issues for which there is little time in the tumult of operational pressures.

Perhaps this need for informal contact at the end of the day also indicates French aversion to MBWA. Observation suggests that the tendency of *cadres* to keep themselves to themselves throughout the day (with the exception of an American subsidiary, no open-plan offices were encountered in the companies visited) may explain a need for informal contact at the end of the day in order to transmit information. It may be that Americans, with their more interactive management styles, do not require a specific time set aside 'after hours' for more diverse exchanges.

The formal version of the aperitif is the *pot*, which consecrates the most insignificant piece of good news. One sales rep organized a *pot* simply because he had spent a whole year in the job. More commonly they are held in celebration of a personal event such as a marriage or birth. The announcement of these glad tidings is invariably greeted with the ritual call of *ça s'arrose* (it's your shout) and the subsequent breaking out of various cocktails and savoury snacks.

Since this is a social occasion, absences are particularly unforgivable – the boss will generally be invited out of courtesy but his failure to take up the invitation will not go unnoticed and is likely to vex the person in whose honour the *pot* is held. The act of presence, because it is voluntary and non-work-related, is particularly important, and a brief speech on the part of the *patron* (boss) will prove an important mark of esteem. The boss can gain a modicum of goodwill *vis-à-vis* his personnel on these occasions but risks a far greater loss by failing to attend.

Business hours

The ritual of long working days is partly a knock-on effect of the preceding ritual concerning copious meals. Because meals are both time-consuming (they 'eat' into the afternoon) and sleep-inducing, afternoons tend to be more sedate than mornings, with a compensatory effort in the evening. The managers involved in our work shadowing exercise regularly put in eleven-hour days – typically starting around 8.30 a.m. and leaving after 7.30 p.m. Again this is a work pattern to which French *cadres* are accustomed from childhood since the school day generally lasts from 08:30 until 16:30, with a two-hour midday break.

For prima facie evidence of this tendency to work late we need look no further than the television. In most European countries the evening news is screened at 18:00 or 19:00 whilst the French *journal télévisé* traditionally has a 20:00 slot. This is probably a sign that the bulk of the news-watching audience is not home before that time.

The ethos of working late is a curious one. Leaving on time is *mal vu* (bad show) and to do so is to risk accusations of having *un esprit de fonctionnaire* (a civil service mentality) – though the criticism can be warded off by being seen to take work home. This is based on the principle that a *cadre*, unlike a civil servant or a worker, is paid to do a job, not to complete a set number of hours – a notion supported by the fact that *cadres* are not entitled to overtime pay.

Cadres supérieurs are supposed to spend more time at the office. Leaving on time *ne se fait pas* (is not done) even if some allowance is often made on their morning arrival. *Le patron* would not take kindly to his commercial or financial director not responding to his call at 7.00 p.m. And the virus spreads downwards from PDG (CEO) to *cadres dirigeants*, to *cadres supérieurs*, to *cadres moyens*. Not surprisingly, this has generated a certain amount of folklore. One *cadre* recalled a colleague who gave a show of conscientiousness by having two overcoats – one to wear and one on permanent display on the coatstand, thereby signalling his presence when the boss walked past his office early in the morning and late at night. Another spoke of a colleague who would take his car to work and go home on the bus.

The compulsion to leave late was seen by several *cadres* to have degenerated – so that they would stay behind, often to no great avail, simply *pour la forme* (for show). Staying late irrespective of the real need for it has an element of play-acting about it. There is a certain amount of self-pity, of playing up to the image of the *cadre* as an overworked, overburdened individual without a moment to himself – *le malaise des cadres* (the unhappy lot of the *cadre*) is a frequently cited syndrome. There is something comforting about being hard done by in a culture where success should not be flaunted.[1]

Quite apart from this self-pitying aspect, there is also an addictive side to staying late – *cadres* are conditioned into it. The upshot of all this is that they find themselves unable to 'kick the habit'. Several *cadres* confessed that they were reluctant to go home early because they were irritable and unable to relax – so they preferred to stay at

---

1 The stereotypical joke about the cyclist and the Rolls-Royce owner is indicative of the French attitude to success. The American cyclist wishes he too owned a Rolls while the French cyclist wishes the car owner had to ride a bike – it does not do to stand out in France.

work where the pace had slackened than to go home and risk annoying their wives and children.

Of course, this had a double edge to it since the wives were fed up of taking second place to work. This problem was particularly acute in the exacting hypermarket retail trade, which boasted a high proportion of actual or prospective divorcees. One of the latter explained that his wife would almost rather he were adulterous than '*la tromper avec le boulot*' ('play second fiddle to work').

One public relations officer was particularly sceptical about the value of staying late at all costs. He felt that it promoted inefficiency – work would be dragged out to fill out the available time. And although one benefited from the absence of distractions (telephone calls or subordinates), the *cadre* was by the same token bereft of secretarial help, making some work impossible. Another cadre confirmed, '*On ne travaille pas toujours à fond le soir*' ('We don't overexert ourselves in the evening'). It is seen rather as an opportunity to wind down and reflect on the day's events.

If, as certain (mainly American) specialists maintain, working outside normal hours is an indication of poor organization – of the individual or the company – then French managers or companies are models of disorganization. Some speculated on the possiblity of changing the 'obligation' to work late and adopting a quasi-American approach of working more consistently hard but finishing on time. However, this was little more than wishful thinking since a unilateral change in working practices would not solve anything. It would only serve to put them, as a company, out of synchronization with their associates. In actual fact, they confessed, they had locked themselves into a recurrent cycle of inefficiency from which they could not break out (shades of Carlson's 'administrative pathology'[1]).

Whilst ostensibly French *cadres* long for regular hours they realize that the intensity of work which would necessarily accompany the change would not suit them. They are conditioned into supplying a long intermittent effort rather than a shorter, more sustained effort. One female executive neatly summed up the difference in approach by saying:

> '*En France il y a du temps mort et on sort à 20:00 –
> en Amérique on sort à 17:00 mais mort.*' ('In France
> there is quite a bit of dead time and we leave at 8.00
> p.m. – in America you leave at 5.00 p.m. but dead
> beat.')

---

1 The term 'administrative pathology' was coined by Sune Carlson in '*Executive Behaviour*' (1951). It refers to the inability of managers to devote more time to strategic matters because of their involvement in operational problems – which might have been pre-empted had they engaged in more reflection.

She went on to enumerate some of the ways in which time was wasted – specifically on the telephone and in meetings which seemed to drag out because 'on se perd en paroles' ('we get lost in words'). She tentatively ascribed this disregard for time to the Latin mentality (a scapegoat for everything from money taboo to a lack of pragmatism) and their tendency to 'vivre dans le désordre' ('live chaotically').

Working long hours clearly implies a certain lack of respect for time. The Anglo-Saxons have ingeniously wedded time and money in the adage 'Time is money'.[1] But this philosophy seems anathema to the French, who do not share the American obsession with time as a measure of efficiency or as a serious constraint – On finira quand on finira (We will finish when we finish) is a French version of the Latin philosophy, mañana. The French show a patience for, and appreciation of, the historical flow of events, a belief that problems can be put off and left to resolve themselves. For instance, Gérard Vincent quotes Henri Queuille (three times President of France in the space of only two years, 1948–50) who had this to say about decision-making:

> 'Il n'est aucun problème, si complexe soit-il, qu'une absence de décision ne puisse résoudre' ('Any problem, however complex, can be solved by failing to take a decision.')
>
> (In Santoni, 1982, 127.)

This view of time 'the great solver' is reiterated in an old proverb (borrowed from the Chinese and naturalized) which goes:

> Au dessus de l'art, déjà estimable, de faire faire les choses par les autres se situe l'art, bien plus remarquable de laisser les choses se faire toutes seules. (Beyond the fine art of getting others to do things, is the even worthier art of allowing things to do themselves.)

The sentiment was even echoed spontaneously by a cadre who was convinced:

> 'Mieux vaut ne rien faire que de décevoir.' ('Better to do nothing than disappoint.')

The need to stay late has a number of significant implications which are worth exploring in more detail. First, it is worth reiterating the way in which it militates against the advancement of women. Their careers

---

1 In English, time (like money) is a commodity which is 'spent' as opposed to the French 'passer' – this reveals a more relaxed attitude to the passage of time.

are subtly (if inadvertently) undermined by the expectation that *cadres* should not leave 'on time'. The solution is either to put up with irregular hours and all the concomitant family problems (including self-reproach) or else to leave on time and miss out on what is potentially the most crucial part of the day. One female *cadre* complained that this was when the real decisions were taken – so family commitments effectively barred her from playing her rightful role in the decision-making process. While long hours are not solely responsible for the low incidence of women in the higher reaches of management, they are indicative of a work pattern which seems more 'hostile' to the integration of women than that of most Western cultures (noticeable, for instance, in the relative absence of flexitime).

What is worse, as far as women are concerned, is that the requirement to stay late is not uniform – it increases with rank *(noblesse oblige)*. Thus, the hours spent are more or less proportional to organizational standing. Each *cadre* is supposed to see his subordinate arrive and, more importantly, see him leave. There is a plausible explanation behind this if we take account of the French tradition of centralization and un-willingness to delegate. Let us take as our starting point the assumption that the more senior a person the more onerous their responsibilities will be and, without delegation to alleviate them, the larger their work-load. Thus, centralization of authority and decision-making auto-matically result in a cumulative progression of the workload through the echelons. If this is the case then working late is not necessarily a sign of disorganization but a form of organization based on unequal allocation of tasks.

Holidays

Oddly enough, since it occurs only once a year, the main holiday is also something of a ritual. For a start, it invariably lasts four or five weeks. The French refer to their *mois de congé* (month off) as if holidays in smaller units were inconceivable. This 'compulsory' duration is to some extent imposed by works' shut-downs – for instance, when the large car manufacturers shut down for one month (in August) there is little point in staying open for many companies. Thus a whole host of suppliers, subcontractors and intermediaries must follow suit. There is a knock-on effect which provokes what one PDG (CEO) referred to as *'la mise en sommeil totale'* (the hibernation) of the French economic machine.

With the business world partly closing down from mid-July to early September, relations with French companies are difficult. French subsidiaries abroad will find it hard to get hold of people at head office and foreign customers will be unable to place orders with French firms. The holiday period can also prove disruptive for small French firms which are caught flat-footed and embarrassed by a sudden upswing in orders after the holidays. Yet the ritual persists in spite of its penalizing effect on French industry.

A measure of the concentration of the holiday period can be seen in the fact that there is an identifiable period known as *la rentrée* (the re-opening) which applies to politics, education and industry. As one *cadre* put it, 'France starts back to work next week'. The degree of consensus surrounding the subject is also visible in the way *cadres* will naturally assume their peers have had a break. Throughout the month of September *cadres* ringing each other will open the conversation with 'How did the holidays go?', followed by mutual commiseration at having to be back at work, 'c'est dur la reprise' ('the re-start is difficult'). Even circulars to other personnel may make allusion to the holiday. A note on security at l'Air Liquide concluded with a P.S. wishing those about to leave 'a pleasant holiday' and those returning *bon courage*.

The major preoccupation in offices from the month of April onwards is scrutinizing the calendar in order to extend one's holiday using bank holidays and *jours d'ancienneté* (extra days accruing through seniority) judiciously. A successful holiday is one which is in complete contrast to work – it is the reward for the eleven months of effort, constraint and frustration which precede it. But it is precisely this contrast which provokes greater post-holiday depression. In a month one has ample time to change one's lifestyle and the shock to the system is so much greater on returning. Add to that the fact that everyone's holiday coincides and the result is a case of mass depression.

For most *cadres* the summer holiday is not a chance to go somewhere exotic but a *retour aux sources*[1] (back to the land – in a literal and spiritual sense) – usually to a *résidence secondaire* (weekend house) of which the French are particularly fond and which prompted Zeldin's quip 'a Frenchman's second home is his castle' (1980, 205). The *cadre* longs for the freedom denied him throughout the year – yet he does not seek the freedom to do anything, but the freedom to do nothing. As Jean Gandois, the head of Péchiney, explains:

> *Je ne vais surtout pas à l'autre bout du monde. Cela,*
> *je le fais toute l'annee. En été, je vais à la montagne*
> *et dans mon Limousin natal.* (I don't go to the other
> side of the world. I do that all year round. In summer,
> I go to the mountains and to my home region).
> (*Le Point*, 17 August 1987, 50.)

───────────

1 One is tempted to speculate that the importance of regional roots is to some extent responsible for the notorious lack of mobility both within France and, more acutely, away from France. Given that France is so heterogeneous (a geographic and climatic patchwork of regions) one can understand that individuals grow strongly attached to their particular region (or *pays*) and are particularly averse to changing regions.

The whole idea behind holidays is to *recharger ses batteries* (revitalize oneself) and to *faire le point* (think about things) or as Claude-Noël Martin (executive vice-president of the CNPF) puts it, *'j'ai besoin de me retrouver moi-même'* (*Le Point*, 17 August 1987, 50). The French *cadre* generally uses the holiday period to reappraise his career situation. Indeed, he is capable of genuine self-criticism (in an abstract sense) but he does not show the same enthusiasm when it comes to acting upon those perceived strengths and weaknesses. Of those willing to discuss their shortcomings, a particular favourite is, *'je parle trop et je n'écoute pas assez'* ('I talk too much and listen too little').

Future trends

As in most other countries, French business rituals are losing their identity (slowly) under the influence of international business. In terms of formality, some younger *cadres* are adopting more easy-going styles. They have shown impatience with the old formal approach and are setting less store by titles and decorum. For instance, the use of first names, though still much less widespread than in Britain or the US, has become far more usual among the under-forties, especially in the newer professions such as advertising. Similarly, the *tu* form of address is steadily gaining ground at the expense of its more formal equivalent. This is particularly the case among students and teenagers and to a lesser extent among younger *cadres*. Similarly, letter writing is giving way to the more mechanical telex or fax as well as the ubiquitous Minitel.[1]

Another change is the 'Americanization' of meals. Many French executives for reasons of health and time are today putting less accent on the long heavy business lunch as a matter of routine, and will reserve it for special occasions. At other times, they will opt for a *brasserie* or even a snack bar. The American-style working breakfast, often in a hotel dining-room, has also now come into vogue.

According to surveys, the French are now going on holiday nearer to home and for less time but more often. Long week-ends and short holidays are apparently sweeping the nation. This is partly the result of a push by companies to get into 'sync' with the rest of the Europe. Notwithstanding this trend, *les grandes vacances* (the summer holidays) have maintained their grip over the French nation – and anyone who disagrees should try their hand at setting up meetings in the August/September period.

---

1 The Minitel, the telephone on a screen referred to in the first chapter. It was, in fact, the British Post Office which dreamt up videotex but it is the French who have created a massive network with the state providing free terminals.

Overview

Paradoxically, the foregoing rituals have as their unifying feature the fact that, by their mundane nature, they go unperceived by those who enagage in them. Nor are they acknowledged by management writers, although they are an essential dimension of business life. Their existence seems glaring to the novice, who is well placed to point out the absence of the Emperor's clothes. It also transpires that what may pass for petty concerns subliminally convey deeper messages reflecting and reinforcing essential characteristics of French management.

One is particularly struck by the formality, restraint and awareness of status differences which would not be out of place in Japan. It has in fact been said that French executives *d'un certain âge* are the Westerners who fit most easily into Japanese business life. Their behaviour has even earned them the label, *les asiatiques de l'ouest*.

The theatrical aspects of French management are probably more developed than in Anglo-Saxon countries which value a more direct approach. The French seem particularly adept at the art of organizational mime which conveys feelings or reinforces relationships without putting either into words. In extending a hand to shake, in their greeting or in electing to meet over lunch they predetermine the relationship.

The French still tend to be rather hierarchical and ceremonial, even if a new social informality is now emerging among younger people. The fact remains that the French continue to put value on doing things in elegant style, and on the formal courtesies and forms of address.

▎Chapter Seven

Those who set the tone

> 'Peut-être appreciés personnellement, les patrons
> sont critiqués collectivement.' (People generally
> like their bosses on an individual basis, but dislike
> them as a group.)
>   (Conversation with John du Monceau, Directeur
>   Général des Titres de Services, Accor.)

In much the same way as *cadre* does not quite mean manager, so *patron*, the subject of the present discussion, has broader connotations than its translation as 'boss' or 'employer'. According to Priouret (1968, 14), the term *patron* gradually superseded that of *maître* (master) under the Second Empire (1852–70). It has its roots in the Latin *pater* (father), which suggests patriarchal overtones – and, in spite of the advent of less loaded terms like *chef d'entreprise, industriel, employeur* or *Président-Directeur-Général* (PDG or CEO), it remains the most widely used designation of the company head. The term is a catch-all that includes the chiefs of owner-managed and professionally managed companies, in the public and private sectors. It is also used to designate intermediary bosses (somewhat on the lines of the English 'governor') since, as one maintenance manager explained, *'Pour l'ouvrier spécialisé, c'est le contremaître son patron'* ('As far as an unskilled worker is concerned, the foreman is his "boss".')

Reputation

Employers in France have traditionally suffered from a poor public image. They have been criticized for making money by exploiting others (*sur le dos des autres*). Zola's *Germinal*, published in 1885, provides a useful indication of the prevailing attitude towards *le patron*. In this novel, one of the characters (Deneulin) weighs up the various ways of making money and concludes, *l'argent que vous gagnent les autres est celui dont on engraisse le plus sûrement* (Zola, 102 – 'making money through others is the surest way of making fat profits'). The phrase endorses the popular view of profit as synonymous with profiteering. And, as Ehrmann points out, Zola's portrayal is by no means exceptional:

> For a country where literary incarnations still
> command wide popular appeal, it is significant that
> in the French novel there seems to be not a single
> example of an outstanding entrepreneurial pioneer;
> where they appear at all, they are slightly ridiculed
> rather than pictured as heroes.
>
> (1957, 210.)

In popular circles, for those brought up on a staple diet of Marxism and Catholicism, the standard view of the *patron* was of a parasite, *un buveur de sang*. If this 'blood-sucker' happened to be successful he was labelled *un aigrefin* (swindler); if he had the misfortune to fail, he would be dubbed *un incapable* (Weber, 1983, 42).

As if this initial prejudice were not enough, the image of employers was further tarnished by accusations of open collaboration with the enemy in World War II. Some of the disgraced employers were punished with expropriation. For instance, Louis Renault who, immediately after the June 1940 armistice, ran headlong into economic collaboration with the Germans, found his company confiscated (the same fate befell Berliet, the lorry manufacturing company) in the wave of nationalizations[1] which followed the War. As Ehrmann puts it:

> The government no less than the man in the street
> was convinced that the employers' record during the
> most difficult hours of the country had been at best
> undistinguished, in many cases despicable.
>
> (1957, 103.)

Even de Gaulle joined in the 'boss-baiting' with a sort of catch phrase '*Où étiez-vous, messieurs?*'[2] (Harris and de Sedouy, 1977, 54) with which he regularly taunted representatives of the embryonic employers' union, the Conseil National du Patronat Français (CNPF). But whatever the extent of employer collaboration, there is a strong argument for suggesting that they had actually failed their country prior to World War II when conservative and uncompetitive practices contributed to the weak economic base of France – one factor in the country's collapse in the face of German might.

---

1 Also included were Air France, the coal-mines, electricity and gas, and the larger insurance companies and clearing banks. Much of this was done in an anti-capitalist spirit with de Gaulle's backing.

2 Analogous to, on the German side, the evocative title of Heinrich Boll's novel, *Wo warst Du, Adam?*

From this all-time low at the end of the War, French employers have achieved an impressive turnaround in societal esteem – to the point that children will now announce with pride that their father is a PDG (CEO), when the fact was concealed for fear of retribution only a decade ago. The reversal of image is rooted in France's entry into the EEC in 1958. This prompted an important change in corporate behaviour since it opened up the French market to foreign competition, at least formally, and signalled the end of a long history of economic protectionism dating back to the fifteenth century. Ardagh drew a parallel with the effect of the Occupation – suggesting that the German menace (economic rather than military) had once again catalysed the French into action, 'This time before defeat and without bloodshed!' (1982, 37).

Further progress was made as a result of the 1968 uprisings, which emphasized the need for a change of style in corporate leadership – a point driven home by the fact that the strike had been the bitterest in the autocratic, old-style firms like Citroën. Ardagh points out that:

> May '68 brought in a new questioning of the
> old assumptions about authority, and it sounded
> the death-knell of a certain rigidly autocratic
> French style of command, both in factories and
> offices.
>
> (1982, 96.)

The rehabilitation of top management has been enhanced in the 1980s by the so-called cult of managerialism and the tardy emergence of an enterprise culture in France. The process was given additional impetus from an unexpected quarter, namely the Socialist government (1981–86). It is ironic that the revalorization of the *patron* should have been engineered by those who were initially thought to 'have it in for him', as seen in the article entitled '*Faut-il brûler les patrons?*' ('Should we do away with bosses?' – *Le Nouvel Observateur*, 12 December 1981.

In fact, the Socialist decision to varnish not tarnish was based on economic rather than ideological grounds. The entrepreneur had to be encouraged as a potential job creator and locomotive for the economy, ideas which though commonplace elsewhere were accepted only belatedly in France. This socialist repositioning in fact reflects a general shift to the right by all manner of political parties, indicating a greater public acceptance of market economics. Even countries as far away as China have experienced something of this revolution as indicated by Schell's book, *To Get Rich is Glorious: China in the Eighties* (1984). Politics is a useful barometer of the changing attitude to entrepreneurs and business.

The net result of these convergent forces is that corporate heroes have actually come to the fore. As Dean Berry put it in *The Financial Times*:

With business exposed, managers need heroes –
they haven't had any.

(2 July 1986, 18.)

Ways to the top

Three distinct avenues to corporate leadership can be identified in the research literature: inheritance, competence and intelligence. It goes without saying that these qualities are not mutually exclusive, but the terms have been selected to characterize a particular means of access to the top. And in each category below, an individual has been chosen as a representative for that group. He is introduced with a brief personal file and his career used to illustrate the category concerned.

Inheritance

Example. François Delachaux: PDG of a 'micro-multinational' (850 personnel and 12 foreign subsidiaries), founded in 1912 (grandson of founder). Aged 47, with an MBA from the University of Indiana.

The proportion of family-run firms in France is high both quantitatively and qualitatively. In other words, a high number of fairly large concerns are family run – for instance, the Dassault family, which supplies military aircraft to the state, or the Rothschild family in banking (see Chapter 8 for further examples). The French seem particularly attached to the tradition. Power is relinquished to outsiders only as a last resort. Ferdinand Beghin, the last in the line of a sugar and paper emporium (Beghin-Say), epitomized the view, when he stated:

> Je n'ai jamais trouvé dans ma famille de gens
> capables de m'aider! J'aurais été enchanté d'avoir
> des gendres à qui j'aurais pu donner des places
> importantes. (I have never found anyone in my
> family capable of helping me! I would have loved
> to have had sons-in-law to whom I might have
> entrusted important positions.)
> (Harris and de Sedouy, 1977, 22.)

The bourgeois saw success in life in terms of augmenting the capital and reputation of their families. Love meant enabling one's child to be richer than oneself and sacrificing individual whims in order to achieve this. This spirit of 'financial affection' is not dead and continues to perpetuate values like thrift and sacrifice – the supreme duty is still seen by some as the transmission of property to their children.

One of the Peugeot chiefs (a company notorious for harbouring family members) was also quite candid about the *raison d'être* of a business:

> *Contrôler le capital, ça sert à placer les enfants.*
> (Controlling the capital guarantees jobs for one's
> children.)
>
> *(L'Expansion,* September 1978, 139.)

Today, there is a rather more discriminating approach to nepotism, with anyone likely to jeopardize the family business sidelined early. *Le patron de droit divin* (a phrase coined for Eugène Schneider, the one-time flamboyant lord of Le Creusot) is a figure of the past. Those who are deemed a liability to the survival of the business will find their families less indulgent than was once the case. As Ardagh explains:

> Nepotism, hitherto rife, has now waned: many
> *patrons* used to regard the family firm as a way of
> giving sinecures to doltish cousins or nephews, but
> today realize that this spells disaster.
>
> (1982, 42.)

With successive generations, inheritors multiply and the company can become a repository for family members. In the common vernacular, *la famille vit sur la bête, elle lui fait rendre son jus* (the family milks the cow dry) – a case of the company working for the family rather than vice versa. Aware of the dangers of such a policy, the second-generation Delachaux brothers (representatives of the family-run business) decreed:

> *Aucun Delachaux dans l'entreprise Delachaux.*
> *Si la maison doit servir à nourrir la famille, elle est*
> *vouée à sa perte.* (No Delachaux in the Delachaux
> company. If the role of the firm is to feed the family,
> we are bound to lose out.)
>
> (Weber, 1983, 26.)

So, François Delachaux's rise to power illustrates the more realistic attitude to nepotism. In order to preclude the extinction of the business, the 21 second-generation Delachauxes got together in a family council to eliminate all but the single most competent family member from the company – in much the same way as the Michelin family have done. That is how third-generation François Delachaux was elected. The other family members pulled out of the company and went elsewhere to exercise their industrial talents.

Enlightened nepotism as demonstrated here, can yield substantial benefits without incurring the traditional drawbacks. To start with, the heir apparent is inculcated early into the ways of the company. The old adage, *Je possède, donc je sais* (I own, therefore I know), has more than a grain of truth in it. Bertrand Lepoutre, the head of a family business, explained:

Les gosses étaient élevés dans l'idée que telle était la
vocation de la famille. (The kids were raised
on the belief that this was the family's vocation.)
(Harris and de Sedouy, 1977, 68.)

Anticipatory socialization enables the heir to prepare himself to take on the mantle of head. The training period can be intense with no holds barred. Almost certainly, criticism will be meted out more readily and accepted more easily since both master and apprentice have the family's best interests at heart. As Patrick Ricard, the PDG of Pernod-Ricard and son of the founder, explained:

Tout ce qu'a fait mon père, c'était avec l'objectif de
me faire rentrer chez Ricard. (My father's every
action was channelled towards my joining Ricard.)
(*L'Expansion*, 4 June 1981, 108.)

What is more, the argument of lack of motivation is perhaps over-stated since the chosen successor must prove himself in relation to rival siblings, is in daily contact with shareholders and is subjected to the critical gaze of fellow executives who may consider themselves more able. As a comparable American heir once said, 'I had to be holier than the Pope and work harder and more conscientiously than anyone else.' (*Fortune*, 17 March 1986, 25). Clearly, some chiefs will try to establish their right to the 'throne' by an epic display of industry and commitment.

As an alternative to this, the future incumbent may have recourse to educational qualifications or experience in other companies as a means of justifying the heritage. Ideally, the heir should aim for an unimpeachable qualification – on that score, Serge Dassault's stay at Polytechnique makes him an irreproachable choice for taking over his father's aeronautical company. However, not everyone is gifted enough to avail themselves of such a qualification. Marceau notes that INSEAD is often used as an instrumental qualification to shake off the 'boss's son' label. This amounts to converting economic capital into more acceptable educational capital.

This was the case for our example François Delachaux, whose MBA was achieved without a *bone fide* first degree, thanks to America's more flexible educational system and the help of one of his father's old friends. The quest for educational legitimation is so important in France that some parents will gladly pay out to procure a diploma for their offspring. As the son of one PDG freely admitted:

Autant le dire tout de suite, je ne suis pas arrivé à la
force du poignet. J'ai fait quelques études, notam-
ment l'école Violet. L'Ecole des fils qui n'ont

> pas les moyens de faire des études, mais dont les
> parents eux, ont les moyens. (You might as well know,
> I didn't get where I am through hard graft. I studied
> a bit, especially at the Violet Business School. That's
> the school for offspring who don't have the means to
> study, but whose parents do have the means.)
>
> (Miler *et al.* 1975, 145.)

Legitimation through experience is perhaps easier to achieve than legitimation through qualifications, but it does not carry the same weight. It is an easier option since the family will generally have contacts which it can approach *pour placer quelqu'un de la famille* (to take on members of the family). Friendly suppliers, customers or banks should manage to put up with the offspring for a while in the knowledge that the favour might be reciprocated for one of their own. Again use is made of economic and social capital to provide the offspring with an artificial track record to mask heredity. He will be overpaid and overpromoted until he is ready to return to the family fold. This was the tactic employed by the Cointreau heir who benefited from an HEC label, followed by three years with Arthur Young and a brief spell with Elizabeth Arden:

> C'était pour moi un sine qua non d'aller faire mes
> classes ailleurs... avant d'entrer dans le groupe
> familiale. (It was essential for me to get a good
> grounding elsewhere... before joining the family
> group.)
>
> (*L'Expansion*, 4 June 1981, 113.)

Competence

Example. Philippe Loridan (58): Armed with only a *baccalauréat*, he found work in a forwarding agency in Morocco. He returned to France in 1955 to start up the French subsidiary of Treifus PLC, which he has since turned into a resounding success employing 800 people.

Basically, there are two ways in which competence can lead to corporate leadership – either by working one's way up a single or a succession of companies over a number of years, or else by setting up a business which provides immediate access.

Trying to reach the top of an organization from a lowly starting position is a fairly remote prospect in France, unless one works for a foreign subsidiary. These reputedly offer the quickest upward mobility for those without prestigious diplomas or family ties – but these companies also make demands on the individual (relentless pressure, set hours, geographical mobility and inflexible objectives) which are anathema to most French managers. As one woman *cadre* explained:

'Pour un Français les conditions de travail
chez Rank-Xerox sont épouvantables.' ('A French
person will find the work conditions at Rank-Xerox
unbearable.')

Taking the example of Amstrad-France, the company has a young head (35) who does not boast a *grande école* education or family connections – and is a woman to boot. There is no way that Marion Vannier would have made it in a traditional French firm, where diplomas, seniority and masculinity are the keys to success.

This triumvirate of qualities prevails in big business throughout France. According to Michel Bauer, a researcher from the CNRS, instances of company men making it to the presidential chair are rare. The case of François Dalle, Charles Zviak and Lindsay Owen-Jones (see Chapter 8) who spent their entire careers at l'Oréal before being named PDG is exceptional among indigenous companies. In contrast to this, IBM, Kodak, Nestlé, Shell, Philips or Unilever all seek continuity of leadership by appointing individuals whose careers have been with the company. Michel Bauer is campaigning for what he terms the *dérégulation* (opening up) of corporate leadership.

There are various ways of reaching the summit in a system that favours introduction from above (*parachutage*) over access from below. Travelling around as a counter to qualifications was the option taken by Philippe Loridan. Realizing that he would not get anywhere in *'ce pays à diplômes'* ('this qualification-conscious country'), he spent three years in Morocco and gained responsibilities which would have taken ten years to accumulate in France. Having made a name for himself, he returned to France and was able to find immediate employment thanks to his experience. Self-imposed exile proved a means of acquiring the experience which would have been denied him in France. This is in stark contrast to countries like the USA where geographical mobility is part and parcel of the promotion game – in France it is simply the price paid for lack of qualifications.

Another means of rapid promotion is of course to set up one's own business. It is ironical that the nation which spawned the word *entrepreneur* (Jean-Baptiste Say in 1800) should have been traditionally so weak in that domain. In a much-quoted work by David Landes (1951), the author blames unenterprising businessmen for holding back French growth in the nineteenth and early twentieth centuries. According to him, the bourgeois family values hampered economic growth by emphasizing social success over individual profit or industrial expansion. Innovation and success in business were held in low esteem and risk-taking was shunned for fear of bankruptcy, which amounted to absolute dishonour in the social system which prevailed.

As a result of the bourgeois influence, business creation was still frowned upon until a few years ago. Even today surveys show that relatively few *grande école* graduates seriously entertain the idea of 'going it alone'. A poll of nearly 1000 graduate engineers by *L'Usine Nouvelle* (19 March 1987), revealed that only 34 per cent were even contemplating self-employment at any time in their careers, and their answers suggested that for most this was only an outside possibility. Apparently, that particular road to business success is deemed too risky for all but the most adventurous. There seems little point in trading in the security of a well-paid job for the struggle of self-employment and the derisive label of *parvenu* or *nouveau riche* should one succeed. The plea for recognition was made explicitly by the head of one small firm:

> *Que la bataille soit dure, les adversaires coriaces et l'arbitre impitoyable, d'accord, mais qu'en cas de succès on ait le droit au tour d'honneur et non-pas au guet-apens.* (That the battle be tough, the adversary tenacious and the referee pitiless, fair enough, but if we win we could at least expect congratulations not hostility.)
>
> (De Closets, 1982, 137.)

In view of the traditional reception of business success it is hardly surprising that the only people likely to opt for this are those who are 'in a rush' to succeed and find enterprise creation the best short-cut – or else those whose qualifications, class, sex or race preclude career success by more conventional means. A more detailed discussion of the new attitude to business creation follows in the section 'The new breed of managers'.

Intelligence

Example. Jacques Calvet: born in 1931 and a product of Sciences-Po and l'Ecole Nationale d'Administration (ENA). Successively, senior civil servant, Chairman of the Banque Nationale de Paris, and since 1984 head of the private Peugeot-Citroën car group. He has managed to check the plunge of a group on the verge of bankruptcy.

L'Expansion (20 November 1980) included a feature on the CEO of an advertising agency which was entitled, 'L'itinéraire modèle d'Yves Cannac' ('Yves Cannac's perfect career'). The reason his was considered an ideal career was that he was a graduate of l'Ecole Normale (very prestigious), the *major* (laureate) of l'ENA (even better) and had spent ten years in state service to boot. What more appropriate pedigree for the head of France's number one advertising agency, l'Agence Havas.

Yves Cannac's career pattern is exceptional in content, but is by no means unusual in format. Jacques Calvet (Peugeot) boasts a similar *curriculum vitae* – after graduating from l'ENA, he took up various positions in the French administration, notably as the Directeur de Cabinet of Valéry Giscard d'Estaing when the former President was Finance Minister (1970–74). He made his transition to the business world via the public sector where he was appointed Deputy Managing Director of the Banque Nationale de Paris (BNP) in 1974. By the time he joined the Peugeot group in 1982, he had risen to Chairman of BNP.

A cursory glance at the backgrounds of most heads of large industrial concerns reveals a similar story. This is in stark contrast to Britain where, of the twenty biggest companies, sixteen have bosses who have spent virtually all their careers with the company (*Economist*, 5 March 1988, 69). In France, it would seem that the state has taken over the responsibility for training individuals to assume leadership positions. As Michel Bauer, a researcher at the CNRS put it:

> *Il semble normal, en France, d'accéder au sommet en étant non seulement étranger à une entreprise, mais également étranger au monde de l'entreprise.* (It seems perfectly natural in France to be named head of a company without prior knowledge of that business or indeed of the business world in general.)
>
> (*L'Express*, 1 January 1988, 33.)

France's largest public and private groups alike are headed by products of *la haute administration* (the higher reaches of the civil service). In the nationalized and semi-nationalized companies, the appointments are politically motivated. Thus it was that the French Socialist electoral victory in May–June 1981 was accompanied by the biggest reshuffle of corporate leaders ever carried out in a Western capitalist country (in Stokman *et al.*, 1986, 184).

The appointment of former state officials as heads in the nationalized sector is perhaps understandable. What is less obvious is their occupancy of similar posts in private companies such as Peugeot or Moët-Hennessy, as well as companies like Péchiney, Rhône-Poulenc and Saint-Gobain whose management by senior state officials pre-dates their nationalization in 1982. The ubiquitous presence of senior state officials in the private and state sectors makes the conventional distinction between public and private industry less relevant in France since both types of company will be run in similar ways. Inevitably, this raises the question of competence – what do private companies see in these individuals?

It would seem that the attraction is primarily instrumental. The civil servant is courted for his contacts rather than his talents *per se*. In the French context, where relations with the state are more important to a company's well-being, it is desirable to be on good terms with the authorities. As Alain de Cointet put it:

> *Dans une économie aussi largement administrée,*
> *recruter des fonctionnaires issus de l'X ou de l'ENA*
> *permet d'entrer en dialogue beaucoup plus*
> *facilement avec ceux qui administrent.* (In such an
> interventionist economy, recruiting top flight civil
> servants who have graduated from Polytechnique or
> ENA facilitates discussions with the government.)
> (*L'Expansion*, 20 January 1980, 215.)

As ex-civil servants they are accustomed to being on the receiving end of discreet pressure and are initiated in the ways of politics. They are responsible for building and maintaining the bridges between the company and the state. This does not mean they are bound to win out, but their case will not go by default of not being heard.

Besides this capacity to open doors with the state, and bearing in mind that they are inevitably products of l'ENA or l'Ecole Poly-technique, what else can these ex-state officials offer a company? Not much, if we are to believe Roger Martin, the ex-PDG of Saint-Gobain:

> '*En sortant de Polytechnique, je savais tout mais*
> *rien d'autre*'. ('When I left Polytechnique, I knew
> everything but nothing else'.)

There is a grain of truth in this statement in that these élite graduates lack specific expertise. However, the quip fails to do justice to the reasoning power, the depth and rigour of the study process, addiction to hard work, and the tradition of honesty inculcated into those heading for state service. These individuals are sought after because their intellectual probity is second to none. The compliment *une belle mécanique intellectuelle* (a fine intellectual apparatus) is often employed to describe them.

Finally, if the alleged resistance to change (referred to by Michel Crozier in *La société bloquée*, 1970) is real, this provides another good reason for systematically appointing outsiders in preference to insiders. When a company wants to make sweeping changes, the task is best handled by an outsider. Insiders tend to be hamstrung by obligations towards individuals who have helped them on the way up. Perhaps, in France's 'stalemate society', this has proved the most effective way of implementing change.

The new breed of managers

The previous section outlining the various means of access to top management deliberately played down the setting up of one's own business – justifiably so since, until recently, there was little incentive or consideration for those who did so.

All that has changed under the combined influences of managerialism and Socialist exaltation of entrepreneurs. The acceptance of managerialism is largely attributable to *In Search of Excellence* by Peters and Waterman. Its French version achieved quite spectacular success with sales of 100,000 copies in just three years – that, in a country where a business book was deemed a hit if it sold 5,000 copies in a year.

In parallel with France's love affair with American business gurus, the Socialist régime (1981–86) endeavoured to promote the entrepreneur as the new saviour of the economy. In many respects, this turnaround could only be achieved by a Socialist government whose a priori hostility to employers lent authenticity to its message – if they say employers are all right, they must be. Had the same notion been put forward by a right-wing government it would certainly have been viewed with suspicion.

In the space of a few years, the self-made individual has become a folk hero, replacing philosophers and writers as France's new gurus. As Gérard Mermet puts it:

> *Après les maîtres à penser, les maîtres à agir.* (After the men of thought, the men of action.)
>
> (1986, 254.)

As one PDG saw it there has been a subtle change of emphasis in business philosophy:

> '*Il s'agit maintenant de lutter pour et non pas contre quelque chose*'. ('We now fight to achieve something rather than to resist change'.)

The socialist rehabilitation of profit and entrepreneurial values were helped substantially by the success of one particular individual, Bernard Tapie. He more than anyone can be credited with the restitution of the entrepreneur. His case is worth investigating since it is inherently interesting and highly revealing of the French need to personalize the new movement in order to exorcize anti-capitalist prejudices. It is difficult to find an article on the new French managerial values that does not acknowledge Tapie's influence.

Described as the 'superstar' of French business, Bernard Tapie is in his mid-forties, the son of a fitter, a graduate of *une petite 'grande école'* and an unsuccessful crooner in the 1960s – pure Hollywood melodrama. He heads a conglomerate of companies which include La Vie Claire, the leading French health food chain, Wonder Batteries (a joint venture with Francis Bouygues), Look Ski Appliances, the Marseilles Olympique football club (à la Robert Maxwell), as well as the fashion house Grès and Kicker shoes.

His business empire, built up from scratch in nine years, employs 10,000 people and has a turnover of Ffr5 billion (about £ 500 million). He has specialized in buying up bankrupt companies for a symbolic Ffr1 and turning them into profitable concerns – without even trying to capitalize on the much vaunted synergy. Instead he exploits the French legislation which allows the receiver to issue a 12–24 month freeze on the company's debts from the moment of filing the winding-up petition. While his managers streamline the staff and start working on new products, Tapie buys back most of the debts from hard-pressed creditors.

His knack for turning all manner of lame ducks into golden geese is such that there is actually a waiting list of companies in distress hoping to be acquired by his conglomerate. His selection criterion is simple: it must be the company's management, not its products which are at fault.

> *Il détecte les sociétés dont les déboires sont*
> *imputables à la mauvaise gestion. Ce qui permettra*
> *de rétablir leur rentabilité en resserrant les boulons.*
> (He seeks out those companies whose setbacks are
> the result of mismanagement – which will allow
> them to return to profit by tightening up a few nuts
> and bolts.)
> (Baumier, 1984, 109.)

So powerful is his effect that simply being associated with him is often enough to redress the falling share price. As Vincent Beaufils of *l'Expansion* points out:

> *La présence même de Tapie, par son action*
> *médiatique, est à elle seule un facteur de bénéfice.*
> (The mere presence of Tapie is, in itself, worth
> several percentage points.)
> (*L'Expansion*, 23 October 1986, 62.)

He is anti-establishment and pokes fun at the archaic approach of most French employers. His blunt style and taste for hype have not made him a favourite in traditional French business circles. His style is perhaps best captured by a commercial for one of his products. It shows an energetic businessman striding purposefully through his office pursued by journalists, politicians, secretaries, Japanese factory managers, Arab oilmen, American salesmen, union leaders and assorted business figures while he relentlessly flings orders to a harried assistant. As one pursuer after another falls to the floor exhausted, the voice-over asks: 'But what makes him run?' Whereupon the businessman reveals a cavity in his back, containing a pack of 'Wonder' brand alkaline batteries. As his assistant pulls them out, he also collapses with a wink at the camera.

The star of that advertisement is Bernard Tapie himself (à la Victor Kiam), plugging one of his own products. The whole presentation is typical of his cocky, go-getting style with '*un sens extraordinaire de la mise en scène*' ('an uncommon appreciation for theatrical effects'). He is a master of self-promotion, combining the high profile of Richard Branson (Virgin Records' irrepressible chairman) with the business style of Chrysler's popular CEO Lee Iacocca. Christine Mital of *l'Expansion* described him as:

> *Le patron à grand spectacle qui réconcilie les Francqis avec l'entreprise, la fortune, la réussite et l'esbroufe.*
> (The epic boss who is reconciling the French with industry, wealth, success and showing off.)
> (*L'Expansion*, 11 September 1986, 45.)

He has become.a symbol for the new business-minded, money-oriented France of the late 1980s: the self-made entrepreneur who creates jobs, does not beg for state subsidies, and is proud of his wealth, success and hard-edged business approach. He has managed to make a hero out of the *nouveau riche*, a traditional figure of fun in French theatre.

He is endlessly selected in opinion polls as the individual young people would most like to meet or emulate. A poll in 1985 actually found him to be the ideal holiday companion of 48 per cent of French women, ahead of the film stars Yves Montand and Alain Delon, whilst 36 per cent of French voters would like him as Prime Minister. He is generally regarded as the best known French personality outside the political world.

Tapie's cue has been taken by many who have tried to follow in his footsteps. The management press is hunting out all the brightest, most personable young entrepreneurs and turning them into folk heroes – Vincent Bolloré, 35-year-old, with '*le look du gendre idéal*' ('the appearance of the perfect son-in law') and a meteoric rise behind him makes ideal fodder for the voracious cover features. His opinion is regularly canvassed – '*Les recettes de Vincent Bolloré* (*Challenges*, March 1987); '*Saint Bolloré – gagner pour nous*' (*l'Expansion*, 22 October 1987.) Such individuals are merely the tip of the iceberg.

The management journals regularly present new sets of entrepreneurs who have succeeded *à la Tapie*: *l'Expansion* (11 September 1986) introduces us to, '*Quinze stars*' ('Fifteen stars'); *Le Point* (14 April 1986) reveals, '*Comment faire fortune en 1986*' ('How to make a packet in 1986'); *Le Nouvel Observateur* (4 February 1983) lets us in on '*Le secret des Gagneurs*' ('The winning formulae of the successful'); *Tertiel* (September 1987) details, '*Le who's who des clubs d'entrepreneurs*'; and *l'Expansion*

(10 September 1987) presents 'Le club des gagneurs' ('The winners' club'). When the journals are not highlighting a cross-section of successful entrepreneurs, they will focus upon individual bosses (preferably under 40) and question them on their recipes for success.

The journals are bolstered by a quantum leap in the number of business books with a similar thrust: Les héros de l'économie (Superstars of the Economy), Ces patrons qui gagnent (Bosses Who Win) . . . etc. Their aim is to draw up a photofit picture of what it takes to succeed in order to provide budding entrepreneurs with role models and inspiration (if little else). The portrayals conveniently play down money, qualifications and contacts but emphasize youth, imagination, courage, effort and perseverance. Their central tenet is that 'n'importe qui peut faire fortune' ('anyone can get rich quick'). The new buzz words quoted by Le Point (28 July 1986, 66) are all success-oriented: les décideurs, les battants, s'investir, assurer (deciders, battlers, commitment, self-confidence) – words which have traditionally been in poor taste in 'aristocratic' France.

In short, public opinion is now favourably inclined towards business and businessmen. However, the backbone of this new ethos has not been tested and there are real doubts over its survival in the event of a major crisis. Because Bernard Tapie has been so instrumental in forging the new enterprise culture, their fortunes are permanently linked. Consequently, his personal failure might have devastating repercussions on the fate of French capitalism as a whole.

In his bid for success, Tapie has not endeared himself to everyone and even his peers (les patrons) include many detractors who resent his 'stardom'. There have been several unkind rumour campaigns to the effect that his business empire is built on debt. Tapie himself admits to debts of Ffr1 billion, but his group turns in a profit and benefits from an A-credit rating from the Crédit Lyonnais. Notwithstanding Tapie's reassurance, his critics have a point. His entire 'system' is based on confidence and growth – a stumble might quickly reveal an inability to refund his group's debts. The embodiment of new, French-style capitalism in one man is at once a strength and an Achilles heel. Christine Mital expressed her fears that the bubble could burst:

> On tremble à l'idée qu'il lui arrive quelque chose: l'image du capitalisme en prendrait un coup dont il ne se relèverait sans doute pas! (Perish the thought that anything should happen to him: it would deal a hefty blow to our perception of capitalism and it is doubtful that it would recover!)
>
> (L'Expansion, 11 September 1986, 45.)

It would seem, then, that le phénomène Tapie is a precarious one. And, beneath the vociferous support, French capitalism is in fact highly susceptible to a reversal of values. Oddly enough, much of the danger comes from the *patrons* themselves – outwardly, they join in the chorus of openness or mouth the latest buzz-words, but privately they resent the invasion of American-style values. Paul Evans, professor of organizational behaviour at INSEAD, the European business school based just outside Paris, strikes a cautionary note:

> Things have only changed on the surface . There
> is lots of talk, and a mood of change, but
> deep-set social and political changes have not yet
> occurred.
>   (*The Financial Times*, 2 July 1986, 18.)

Perhaps because of the very rigorous intellectual training which French chief executives typically receive, they have difficulty in subscribing to the view of management as a fairly straightforward activity – in the Tom Peters' KISS (Keep It Simple Stupid) tradition. There seems to be resistance to the notion that managerial work includes some that is routine, some fire-fighting, juggling, walking about, some 'man-handling' of recalcitrant circumstances (and people), some speedy irrational decision-making, and some inspired acts of adaptive implementation; individuals chosen for their brains are not necessarily best suited to carry this out. Maybe the French overcomplicate management but this seems consistent with a more complex view of human behaviour than that proffered by the Americans.

So behind all the media hype fronted by American-style managers, there is an undercurrent of scepticism, which top managers generally refrain from expressing in public, since to do so would be tantamount to subverting progress. As one PDG put it:

> '*Ça serait considéré une tare pour un patron
> de ne pas adhérer à ce movement.*' ('Not to endorse
> managerialism would be viewed as a real defect
> in a boss.')

The current obsession with American gurus and the 'go-getting' spirit is so powerful that it would be foolhardy to criticize it out loud. Yet in private conversations, a number of managers speculated that the cult of managerialism and the public interest in management were a flash in the pan (*un phénomène de mode*) and fully expected values to go round full circle. They were simply waiting for the whole thing to blow over and for 'normal service' to be resumed.

One is reminded of the way the French embraced management by objectives or quality circles in theory, but have failed to implement them successfully. Perhaps these are simply manifestations of what Ardagh regards as a national trait:

The French have a tendency to fall in love intellectually with new ideas and then not to bother too
much with their application; in some firms, new
American jargon and gadgetry barely conceal the
persistence of old French habits of rigid hierarchy
and routine.

(1982, 42.)

Homogeneity?

In the light of the preceding discussion it may seem odd to discuss the
homogeneity of French bosses. Allusions have already been made to their
divergent career patterns – in particular the distinction between owners
(sometimes called *le patronat réel*) and salaried heads (*le patronat de
gestion*). Notwithstanding this fundamental duality, a number of
common traits are worth highlighting.

United we stand

To start with, bosses are united under the banner of a single union
(in contrast with five separate worker unions), the Conseil National du
Patronat Français (CNPF). The organization was conceived after the
Liberation as a means of facilitating contract between employers and
government – and in the hope that it might help retrieve some of the
employers' power and self-esteem, damaged by the Occupation. The
head of the confederation is usually referred to as *le patron des patrons*
by newspapers.

But the notion of collective body goes beyond a single union. The
patrons are clearly perceived by the media as an entity sharing common
political, economic and social views:

> *Edmond Maire réhabilite les patrons.* (Edmond
> Maire legitimizes bosses.)
> > (*Le Nouvel Observateur*, 13 March 1986, 19.)

> *Les dix patrons les plus durs.* (The ten toughest
> bosses.)
> > (*L'Expansion*, 19 September 1985, 90.)

> *Pour gagner, changez vos patrons.* (If you want to
> win, change your leaders.)
> > (*L'Express*, 1 January 1988, 33.)

> *Comment les patrons prennent congés.* (How bosses
> take their holidays.)
> > (*Le Point*, 17 August 1987, 50.)

Métier: patron. (Profession: boss.)
(*L'Expansion*, 7 November 1985, 51.)

The idea is reinforced by books with titles such as *Les patrons face à la Gauche* (*The Impact of the Socialists on Bosses*), *Paroles de patrons* (*The Bosses Speak Out*), *Les patrons* (*Bosses*), *Comment devient-on un grand patron* (*How to Become a Big Boss*), *Ces patrons qui gagnent* (*Bosses Who Win*), *La fin des patrons* (*The End of the Bosses*) and so forth. As with the *cadres*, the media tend to treat them as a discrete group in spite of their self-professed heterogeneity.

But whilst bosses are themselves reluctant to acknowledge a common bond which transcends questions of ownership or background, there are indications that it does exist. According to Harris and de Sedouy, François Ceyrac the former head of the CNPF, was particularly adept at hitting this unifying chord, each time he addressed the bosses:

> *Cette disposition bien française, un peu maurras-sienne, qu'accompagnent en general le goût du beau langage, pour ne pas dire des belles-lettres et une certaine méfiance vis-à-vis des modes et de la modernité, François Ceyrac en use et en joue a chaque occasion.* (François Ceyrac forever plays upon the peculiarly French penchant, rather in the manner of Charles Maurras, for stylish not to say sophisticated language and a certain suspicion of fashion and novelty.)
> (Harris and de Sedouy, 1977, 46.)

This view was corroborated by a PDG who, as an *habitué* of CNPF meetings, had seen many a skilled orator unite the various factions of employers with a few well-chosen words. According to him, all you had to do was evoke a few of their *bêtes noires* (pet hates) – union leaders, civil servants, politicians, intellectuals – to elicit Pavlovian indignation from all quarters.

So, in spite of the emergence of the new entrepreneurial culture, the legacy of vilification against bosses has left its mark – and for many of them the solidarity born of adversity remains a source of considerable unity. This reaction is the product of several decades of perceived persecution and misunderstanding – and the struggle to gain public approval. Bosses seem particularly preoccupied by the no-win situation in which they have found themselves in the past. Harris and de Sedouy quoted a number of bosses on the matter:

> *Si nous réussissons, nous sommes des exploiteurs; si nous échouons, des salauds doublés d'incapables.*
> (If we succeed, we're exploiters; if we fail, we're bastards – useless one's at that.)
> (1977, 8.)

> *Aujourd'hui, être patron, c'est peut-être aussi accepter*
> *de se sentir 'mal aimé'...* (Being a boss today is also
> about being disliked.)   (1977, 23.)

> *Les dirigeants? depuis le temps qu'on leur colle*
> *mauvaise conscience!* (Bosses? how much longer
> must they be made to feel guilty?)   (1977, 36.)

> *S'ils font des bénéfices, ce sont des salauds; s'ils*
> *ratent, se sont des imbéciles et il faut s'en débarrasser.*
> (If they make money, they're bastards; if not, they're
> idiots and we should be rid of them.)   (1977, 36.)

The consensus view on the part of bosses was that they were despised by the general public, or at very best regarded as a necessary evil – we need bosses, *'comme il "faut" des gendarmes ou des putains!'* (Harris and de Sedouy, 1977, 74 – 'in the same way as we need policemen or whores'.) Even if their image has changed in the last few years, the disdain is still fresh in their collective memory and there is no telling how long the present euphoria will last. The bosses remain bonded by the solidarity borne of adversity – and in their own mistrust of the fickle public.

Types of capital

Another feature which unites the corporate rulers, whether owners or salaried heads, is their possession of one or other form of capital: economic (money), educational (qualifications) or social (connections). The theme of social inequality in France is very well documented – the hobby-horse of a number of French sociologists. Alain Girard was one of the earlier contributors to the debate:

> *Tout se passe comme s'il existait une véritable trans-*
> *mission professionnelle de génération en génération.*
> (It's as if professional status could be handed down
> from generation to generation.)
>
>   (Girard, 1965.)

A similar argument was put forward by Bourdieu and Passeron, who argued in *Les héritiers* (1966) that the French bourgeoisie had hit upon a system of 'social reproduction' whereby the various forms of capital could be passed on from one generation to the next – thanks largely to the nature of the education system.

Around the same time, a statistical study by researchers at INSEAD revealed that of the heads of France's 500 largest firms in 1966–67 42 per cent had fathers who were themselves company heads and 25 per cent could boast at least two generations of chief executives. According to Marceau this tendency to social closure was reinforced by endogamy, that is marriage within similar social circles (1977, 134).

These findings are confirmed by the more recent work of Pierre Birnbaum – and also by Claude Thélot whose book on the subject bears the appropriate title, *Tel père, tel fils (Like Father, Like Son)*. In fact, the social reproduction argument is further enhanced by the fact that individuals with different political convictions take a similar stance.

The three forms of capital identified above are by no means mutually exclusive – more often than not they are cumulative. For instance, the PDG whose offspring are not bright enough to reach one of the *grandes écoles* may well deploy social and economic capital in order to send his children to foreign universities – rather than opt for a French university with its 'second-rate' image in relation to the élitist *grandes écoles*. The value of a foreign higher degree (preferably from an American university) will go some way to offsetting the lack of a highly prestigious French diploma.

Such a conversion strategy is fairly typical since educational capital is by far the most precious form of currency – presumably because of its cleansing effect on the less meritorious social or economic capital. Inherited power is concealed beneath a veil of merited power thanks to a highly competitive and overtly objective (based on maths) public secondary and higher education system. Bourdieu and Passeron (1966) argue that the *grandes écoles* transform inherited privilege into 'merited' privilege.

As Birnbaum *et al.*(1977) explain, this system is not guaranteed to work for a particular individual (that is where the element of merit comes in), but on a class-wide basis it does ensure the reproduction of the ruling class. That does not mean that the individuals at the top are incompetent, but simply that their accession was in part based on considerations other than strictly rational and objective ones – and, in some cases, which carried more weight.

Another example of the way one form of capital will help procure other forms of capital is that of those already in possession of educational capital. The graduate who comes from a well-to-do family stands a better chance of rapid accession to top management than his working-class counterpart. As Vincent puts it:

> *Si on a un père bien placé, on obtient des avantages*
> *qui sont évidents, soit par la position même du père,*
> *soit par la position des amis du père.* (Having a
> father in a position of authority is a source of obvious
> advantages, either directly through his actual position,
> or indirectly through that of his friends.)
> (in Santoni, 1981, 143.)

The various forms of capital will be inherited, invested, accumulated, multiplied (through marriage) and converted so that, in Jane Marceau's words, 'to him that hath, more shall be given' (Howorth and Cerny, 1981, 118). Or, as Bourdieu and Passeron put it, 'capital attracts capital'.

Whatever one's mode of access to the *patronat* (top management), the notion of predestination is strong. Yvon Gattaz, the former head of the CNPF, went as far as to say that the desire to be a boss was 'congenital', (Zeldin, 1983, 193). This view of bosses as a hereditary class is corroborated by Gaillard's book *Tu seras président, mon fils (A Chairman You Will Be, My Son)*. It is rare in France to succeed from nothing, without any of these trump cards. Characters like F. Scott Fitzgerald's *The Great Gatsby* are nowhere to be seen in French folklore. It would seem that Detoeuf's (a progressive boss of the 1930s) quip still holds true:

> *En France, pour réussir, un seul secret: avoir déjà réussi.* (The secret of success in France is to have succeeded already.)
>
> (in Santoni 1981, 174.)

One is reminded of a saying attributed to Bob Hope about banks only lending money to those who can prove they don't need it.

Activities

The notion that top managers all round the world partake in the same sort of activities is true to a certain extent – but there are differences of emphasis which unite bosses from a particular nation and may distinguish them from their counterparts in other countries. In the case of French bosses, the distinguishing features seem to derive from the nature of the relationship with the authorities, and from a certain taste for ritual.

In terms of activities, there is common ground between all manner of bosses. For instance, parallels can be drawn in terms of their dealings with the authorities. Whether these are at national level or at local level, French bosses find themselves involved with the state to a far greater extent than their Anglo-Saxon counterparts.

In France, when there is lobbying to be done, the onus generally falls upon the individual at the top. Partly this is by virtue of their educational background, which will stand them in good stead with like-minded civil servants. But status also enters into it, since the state officials will find the attentions of a PDG more flattering than those of one of his 'lackeys'. However, when the qualifications of the PDG are somehow inappropriate, a more suitable corporate representative may be sought out.

For instance, confronted with a rather thorny issue, the head of a provincial production plant, an engineering graduate, elected to send his second-in-command, the *directeur administratif*, to meet the local *préfet* – this in the knowledge that the *préfet* would be an *énarque* and in all probability, a graduate of *Sciences-Po* (the favoured preparation for l'ENA). In the administrative director's own words, 'The conversation 'somehow' got round to *Sciences-Po* and the period we were there – and the dialogue was much easier after that.'

At a local level, the head of a production plant or small business will be considered *une personalité locale* and his presence is often requested at official functions. Relations with the mayor and the town council will be attended to, so that favours do not fall on deaf ears later. For instance, a hypermarket manager in our study wanted to use the municipal stadium for the corporate football team's home games. With the town council making an unnecessary fuss over the matter, the head discreetly reminded them that the local handball team was sponsored by the company. Needless to say, access to the facilities was granted.

Another example from our study involving reciprocity was demonstrated in a Communist-dominated municipality. Late one afternoon, at about 5 p.m., the Communist mayor, with whom relations were strained to say the least, telephoned the head of the business. He explained that he was in a fix since he had invited a number of guests from England (neo-Marxists according to the PDG), and the factory they had intended to visit had gone on strike – so finding a substitute factory was a matter of some urgency. The PDG gave his approval and the· visit went off without a hitch. Later that year, the poor results of the company's divisions meant that 50 people had to be laid off, so the PDG contacted the mayor. He outlined the situation and explained that the last thing they needed was a stirring up of public disapproval. The mayor *'qui avait la haute main sur la CGT'* ('who had control over the Communist-based union, the CGT') reassured the PDG that he need not worry and stood true to his word.

At a national level, the same sort of preoccupations were evident on a larger scale. For instance, the national management of the same hypermarket which had negotiated access to the municipal stadium were trying to persuade those concerned to reframe the legislation on pharmaceutical products – and lift the chemists' monopoly on their sale.

Another company, selling luncheon vouchers, was involved in lobbying the authorities for greater tax relief on their service where the profit margins were melting away. Of course, when secured, these concessions would benefit the entire industry, not just the company in question. But there was a rather convenient division of labour since the company's main rival happened to be a co-operative. So, if a left-wing government was in power, the head of the co-operative would 'go and see his socialist friends' – if the right were in power, it was the turn of the company's PDG *'d'aller au charbon'* ('to go to work'). In the face of this *force majeure* the two competitors collaborated to achieve the best possible deal for the industry.

In a similar vein, the head of a leading pet food company was exerting pressure on the treasury minister to place their product in a lower VAT bracket[1], on the basis that pet food was a necessity, not a luxury. Irrespective of the success of this request, the pleading was designed to raise parliamentary awareness of the company's performance and shatter the illusion that *'c'est une activité facile qui rapporte gros'* ('it's an easy way of making money'). The real aim was to legitimize their business so as to pre-empt 'some half-wit parliamentarian from demanding that we be included in the uppermost VAT bracket.'

Another feature of French corporate management is the need to comply with certain duties, either by law or by custom. It may be worth highlighting a few of these which distinguish the French employer from his Anglo-Saxon counterparts, at least in degree. The company head will generally attend the works' council meeting *(comité d'entreprise)*. His presence will also be expected at internal ceremonies such as handing out of medals (which range from the basic *médaille du travail*, through *meilleurs ouvriers de France*, to the highly-prized *Légion d'honneur*[2]). Other internal appearances include best wishes for the New Year and cocktails for special (and not-so-special) occasions such as departures. The PDG will also be called upon to attend a number of statutory assemblies with the unions or with employers' organizations. One gets the impression that the French chief has more official duties foisted upon him than his Anglo-Saxon counterparts – and what with *la réunionite* (meeting-itis) of which the French are so fond, the boss's day seems almost entirely preplanned.

Finally, in the list of distinguishing activities is one which is new to the French boss, namely the art of media communication. With the new public interest in business, bosses suddenly find themselves the subject of considerable media attention. They are increasingly accountable to the general public and their views are eagerly canvassed by reporters. This is proving just as time-consuming for small bosses with the regional press as it is for large employers with their national counterparts – since the former, though less solicited, do not have a specialist in public relations at their disposal to take some of the burden off them.

The new leader must be *un homme de la communication* (a communicator) – and the bosses are aware of this new imperative since many are taking courses on how to present themselves effectively on TV. One specialist consultant in this field explained to the authors that he had seen the number of heads seeking advice multiply ten-fold

---

1 France has three basic VAT rates (33 per cent, 18 per cent and 5 per cent) together with a special category for cars (28 per cent) so as to keep the French automobile manufacturers internationally competitive.

2 Where the PDG is himself the recipient of the *Légion d'honneur* it may be pinned on him by the Minister for Industry. At Accor, those not privy to attend the ceremony in person, were cordially invited to watch it live on closed-circuit TV.

in the last decade. Indeed, his appraisal of the situation was endorsed by the fact that even large management consultancies (such as the CNOF) had been forced into providing media induction courses in order to satisfy demand and to maintain their blanket coverage of available management development courses. Of course, it may be held that this media exposure is not strikingly different from what goes on in the UK, but this facet of the boss's work should be seen in the French context where it is, on the whole, novel.

Photofit picture
Finally, the ranks of the 'patronat' also bear a number of outward similarities. An annual check-up by l'Expansion of big business in France ('La galerie de portraits des grands patrons') is particularly revealing in this respect. Of the 100 bosses surveyed:

1. 50 are grande école graduates – including 6 énarques and 29 polytechniciens;

2. only 15 have not undergone higher education, and of those only two (each with their own businesses) admit to being autodidactes;

3. in terms of age, 14 per cent are in the 40–50 age group, 38 per cent are between 50 and 60 , and a surprising 32 per cent are in the 60–70 bracket – the remainder are divided almost equally between over 70s and under 40s;

4. not a single woman appears in the sample population, 'l'univers de la grande industrie' ('the realms of big business').

Several conclusions can be drawn from these findings. First, French bosses are highly qualified in international terms – and those who were not privy to higher education prefer to keep quiet about it. Little pride is derived from having succeeded against the odds or being a 'self-made man' – presumably because at least some of those who were bereft of qualifications had other resources to fall back on such as heritage. Secondly, as a group they are relatively elderly, certainly in comparison to the workforce they lead. This is a finding corroborated by Maurice et al. (1986, 274), who point to a number of empirical studies that have shown that French company presidents are older, on average, than their German counterparts. Finally, they appear hostile (whether consciously or not) to the infiltration of women in their ranks. The fact that big business is an exclusively male domain is worth investigating in more detail.

Women bosses

The French business world – and its uppermost stratum in particular – remains to a large extent a male bastion. This is partly the result of the overt chauvinism of the *grandes écoles* which supply industry with its business élite. The foremost school, l'Ecole Polytechnique, did not open its doors to women until as late as 1972. What is more, the annual intake of women at l'ENA rarely exceeds 15 per cent whilst at Polytechnique the 'barrier' is around 10 per cent – this in spite of the fact that the percentages of women candidates are approximately double those figures. The heads of the schools are baffled, but the indications are that the entrance exam somehow militates against female success – thus denying women access to these seed beds of top managerial talent.

Women are perhaps discouraged in the first place because the top *grandes écoles* are founded on 'virile' values – decisiveness, networks, hierarchies, camaraderie and dominance. There is little place for 'feminine' qualities like nurturing, accessibility, intuition or openness. The curriculum too bears the stereotypical masculine hallmark of logic, mathematics and Cartesianism. Boltanski explains:

> *Les valeurs viriles inculquées dans les grandes*
> *écoles conduisant traditionnellement a des positions*
> *d'autorité dans l'industrie, comme l'Ecole des Arts et*
> *Métiers ou l'Ecole Centrale, sont fortement exaltées*
> *et recherchées.* (Qualities of leadership and other
> manly virtues inculcated by schools such as the Ecole
> des Arts et Métiers and Ecole Centrale, whose graduates
> have traditionally assumed positions of authority in
> industry, are highly praised and exalted.)
>
> (1982, 325.)

The traditional hostility towards 'soft' values is also linked with France's attachment to classical management – after all, it is in classical management that our association between man and management is rooted. Was it not Henri Fayol who helped designate management 'a man's job' by equating it with rational and deductive aptitudes such as organizing, commanding and controlling? But even before Fayol imposed his 'macho' view of management, top management in France was dominated by engineering graduates – something which is still true today.

The combined legacies of engineering and classical management have done little to facilitate female access to top management. In fact, the few women who did manage to infiltrate this preserve seem exceptionally gifted: women like Yvette Chassagne who graduated from l'ENA and was the first woman to be appointed in a succession of prestigious civil service posts and recently retired as the head of l'Union des Assurances de Paris, or entrepreneurs such as Annette Roux, the PDG of Bénéteau pleasure crafts (and the only woman on the CNPF's executive council), and Francine Gomez, who inherited and worked wonders with Waterman pens. Cynics maintain that the regular appearances of these women in the management press is an attempt to allay fears of underrepresentation. They are sometimes referred to as *femmes alibis* (token women).

It may be that French women have been socialized into adopting a more passive role than their cohorts in other countries. No doubt the bourgeois values (based on aristocratic aspirations) which are blamed for influencing French businessmen have also marked their wives and daughters. The idea of the wife having to work was considered to reflect badly on the ability of the provider to fulfil his role. And the daughter was seen not in terms of a potential inheritor of the family business, but as bait to attract a 'competent' son-in-law. Alternatively, Francine Gomez (the PDG of Waterman pens) suggests a more endemic explanation for French women's attitude to power:

> Les hommes ont un désir de puissance que n'ont pas les femmes, c'est physiologique. (Men have a craving for power which women simply do not possess – it's physiological.)
>
> (Harris and de Sedouy, 1977, 39.)

Optimists point to the belated emergence of an enterprise culture as a possible way round traditional barriers. Certainly the starting up of small businesses by women has received a lot of publicity, notably in the women's magazines. And institutional backing was provided by the socialists in the form of a Ministry for Women.

This, together with the new managerial emphasis on openness, accessibility and intuition may help to undermine the masculine stereotype of top management. To some extent, the traditional view of management as a logical, mechanistic process is being replaced by a more 'feminine' approach. The new manager is seen as 'un animateur pas un gendarme' ('a facilitator not a traffic cop'), as someone who should be accessible and supportive not distant and directive. The foundations are perhaps being laid for more widespread female involvement. Certainly, courses in management studies are attracting more women – in some business schools they even outnumber the men. It can only be a matter of time before women start to filter through to top management.

In spite of these encouraging signs regarding wider female involvement in management, there is a nagging feeling that the very highest rung may continue to elude them – in much the same way as it continues to elude the under-forties. This is tied to the concept of corporate leadership in France which seems to demand more than mere management ability.

The role of the *patron*

The way the French view their national leaders may give an indication of what they expect of their corporate leaders.

The centralization of authority in the hands of an individual is a long-standing and popular trait in France. The authoritarian central-izers in the nation's history are all glorified and looked upon as heroes – stemming from monarchs like Philip the Fair at the start of the fourteenth century, through Richelieu, Mazarin, Louis XIV, Colbert, the Committee of Public Safety at the height of the French Revolution (1793-94), Napoleon and most recently de Gaulle.

One could posit that the French reputation for individualism requires strong leadership to galvanize them into collective action – as de Gaulle did both during and after World War II. The umbrella of his presti-gious paternalism helped to provide a national focus in the period of turmoil and moral confusion after the Liberation. The French are prepared to entrust one man with absolute authority, provided he is remote and cannot act directly upon them. They have a taste for the personification of power and show deference towards it.

Today, General de Gaulle's absolutism is in many ways replicated by François Mitterrand's style of government. In fact, the history of the Fifth Republic (1958–   ) is replete with 'monarchic' leaders who apparently adhere to the philosophy *L'état c'est moi.*

Before reaching office, for instance, François Mitterrand pronounced the following indictment of Giscard d'Estaing:

> *Déjà pourvu des grands pouvoirs que lui confère la*
> *Constitution de la Ve République et héritier d'usages*
> *et d'abus qui en ont élargi le champ, il s'est emparé*
> *de ceux qui lui manquaient... L'exécutif c'est lui..., le*
> *législatif, c'est lui..., le judiciaire c'est lui.* (As if the
> tremendous powers invested in him by the constitut-
> ion and amplified by custom and malpractice were
> not enough, he has seized those which he lacked...
> he is the executive..., the legislative..., the judiciary.)
> (*Le Monde*, 11 February 1981.)

This from the president dubbed '*Un roi socialiste* ('a socialist monarch') by Konrad Müller (1983), his own biographer.

Another, manifestation of the elevation of selected individuals can be seen in the way that former political leaders tend to embody political philosophies. Sympathizers are referred to as *gaulliste, pompidolien, giscardien, chiraquien, barriste* (in the way reserved in Britain for mon-archs or long-standing leaders: Victorian, Thatcherite, Churchillian).

The tradition of omnipotent political leaders is echoed in corporate circles. And company law replicates the French constitution by con-ferring absolute power upon a single person.

France has a singularity in terms of company law: the *Président-Directeur-Général* (PDG). Based on the *Führerprinzip* model imposed by the Vichy régime in 1940, French corporate management has the peculiarity of placing in the hands of an individual what, in most countries, is shared out: deciding on, executing and controlling a policy. The PDG is what Britons would regard as 'chairman of the board' and 'managing director' rolled into one. His role is in even sharper contrast to that of the *primus inter pares* German *Vorstandsvorsitzender* (a chairman of the executive committee). This point was brought home by the PDG (CEO) of a small firm visited, who claimed:

> *'Je peux tout faire sauf vendre la société'.* ('I can do what I please with the exception of selling off the company.')

This concurs with Horovitz's view of French businesses as 'one-man shows' (1980, 64), which is nicely captured by Sempé's illustration (see Figure 7.1), and is further reinforced by an article in *l'Express*, stating:

> *Le patron règne en maître absolu, quitte à être black-boulé sans préavis par le conseil d'administration qui le désigne.* (The boss rules like a feudal overlord, unless there is a spontaneous vote of no confidence from the administrative council which elected him.)
> (*L'Express*, 1 March 1985, 33.)

Tenure appears almost completely assured (barring political interference) irrespective of age, longevity and even to some extent performance. The status of the PDG is sharply differentiated from that of the rest of top management, which helps to explain why bosses are so revered in France.

> *Il faut voir, en particulier dans les grosses entreprises nationales, l'apparat et le phenomène de cour qui entourent les précieux PDG, avec huissier personnel, ascenseur privé et collaborateurs directs qui servent du 'Monsieur le Président' gros comme le bras a celui que des Americains appelleraient tout simplement 'Bob' ou 'Bill'.* (It is difficult to imagine the pomp and circumstance which surrounds the CEO, particularly in large, national companies. What with his own 'orderly', private lift and a cortège of immediate subordinates who earnestly address him as 'Sir' when Americans would simply call him 'Bob' or 'Bill'.)
> (*L'Express*, 1 March 1985, 33.)

Figure 7.1 The perceived role of the *patron*. (Extract from Sempé's album *Vaguement competitif* (Denoël, 1985.)

These are clear manifestations of the difference between the PDG and those around him – rather like a yucca tree, which grows strong while killing off everything around it.

Other signs of the demarcation between the PDG and his staff can be seen in the apparels of power. By Roger Alexandre's reckoning, a chief is identifiable '*à l'épaisseur de la moquette, à la cylindrée de la voiture, au nombre de plantes vertes...*' ('by the depth of the carpet pile, by the horse power of the car, by the number of potted plants...'). What is more, the PDG's intellectual aloofness is reflected in his physical remoteness. France does not favour a 'hands-on' approach to management and the PDG is invariably out of harm's way:

> *Où met-on le chef, où situe-t-on le pouvoir? Au
> sommet, naturellement. Au plus haut, au presque
> inaccessible, là où l'humanité a toujours placé les
> dieux, les héros et les confitures.* (Where should we
> place the chief, where should we locate the power?
> Why at the top, of course. At the very highest, least
> accessible point, that spot which men have always
> reserved for gods, heroes and jams.)
>
> (*L'Expansion*, 19 May 1985, 72.)

The coalescence between God and the boss is actually formalized in a number of set expressions, '*plus on est près du bon Dieu, mieux on se porte*' ('the closer you are to God, the better off you are'). Similarly, '*le patron de droit divin*' ('divine-right boss') is a phrase which is in popular usage to describe those who acceed to power by birth. On another occasion in our study, a perplexed *cadre* emerged from the boss's office muttering, '*les voies du Seigneur sont impénétrables*' ('the Lord works in mysterious ways') – again denoting the PDG's supremacy.

Since one individual is endowed with so much power, the status of PDG has tended to inflate proportionately. As Dyas and Thanheiser put it:

> *Etre PDG* (to be a president) is referred to as belonging
> to a caste apart, regardless of the size of the operation
> being run. The respect is given almost more to the
> ability of a president to exercise absolute authority
> than to the actual power to influence. And *de PDG*
> (as in *voiture de PDG*) has become an adjectival
> phrase to describe a high status item somewhat as
> the word 'executive' is used in the US.
>
> (1976, 246.)

There is also a measure of self-fulfilling prophecy in this 'one-man show' image. The perceived status and authority associated with the title of PDG affect the behaviour of both title holder and those around him. Dyas and Thanheiser (1976, 246)) quote a French *cadre* who speculates that simply being named PDG has an impact on behaviour, bringing out the autocratic tendencies – the sort of outlook typified by *l'Expansion's* 'Ten toughest bosses' (19 September 1985). In its bid to identify the nation's top despots, *l'Expansion* took statements from those who worked alongside them. This is a typical selection:

> '*L'autorité est du style quasi militaire. Quand il
> convoque, c'est pour dans deux minutes*'. ('It's not
> unlike a military regime. When he calls you in to see
> him, you don't play hard to get.')

> *'Il est au courant de tout, y compris des problèmes personnels, il a des sous-marins partout.'* ('He permanently knows what's going on, including personal problems – he has spies everywhere.')

> *'Ultracentralisateur. Les meilleurs cadres deviennent des exécutants. Il signe tous les chèques à la main.'* ('The ultimate centralizer. The very best managers are reduced to puppets. He signs every cheque by hand.')

> *'Quand il s'est fait son opinion personnelle, il ne sait plus écouter.'* ('Once he's made his mind up, you might as well talk to a post.')

> *'Il faut être disponible à tout moment. Les coups de téléphone à des heures impossibles, ça pleut.'* ('You must be available at all times. Telephone calls come raining in at all hours.')

The notion of the all-seeing, all-knowing boss is fairly widespread in France. This makes it difficult for the bosses themselves to ask the advice of their subordinates since, as one *cadre* explained, the *patron* is supposed to have a monopoly on ideas and solutions:

> 'Il est parfois mal vu pour un PDG de consulter ses collaborateurs au sujet d'un problème dont il est censé, par sa position, connaître la solution.' (It is generally bad show for a PDG to consult his staff about a problem to which, by his position, he should know the answer.')

Nor are subordinates encouraged to offer up alternative solution on matters where *'le président considère détenir la vérité'* ('where the CEO's word is gospel' – *l'Expansion*, 19 September 1985, 92). As one of Francis Bouygues' staff put it:

> *'Chacun avait le droit de prendre la parole, mais peu de téméraires osaient le contredire.'* (Everyone was free to express themselves, but few were reckless enough to disagree with him.')

Boses are perhaps encouraged in their despotism by the very fact that they have been traditionally disliked by the French public, which leads them to take a 'devil-may-care' attitude to the popularity of their management style. It may be that their authoritarianism stems from the fact that they are disliked (and consequently do not care) rather than vice versa. This view was suggested by a number of comments:

> *Je ne veux pas qu'on m'aime je veux qu'on m'obéisse.*
> (I want people to obey me, not like me.)
> (Harris and de Sedouy, 1977, 84.)

> *De toute façon il est détesté, le patron. Le problème n'est pas d'être aimé, mais d'être respecté et suivi.*
> (Anyhow bosses are hated. The aim is not to be liked, but to lead and to be respected.)
> (Harris and de Sedouy, 1977, 94.)

But the signs are that this approach suits the French – that they actually admire them. Why else glorify them by searching for the nation's toughest boss?

The PDG is effectively at liberty to do as he pleases – something which manifests itself in the way that bosses behave towards their subordinates. The conduct of one particular boss from our sample is worth highlighting since by Anglo-Saxon standards it would appear rather unusual.

The boss in question had an obsession with picking people up on minor faults – correcting their French on a number of occasions: not 'prendre la porte' but 'passer par la porte', not 'aller au coiffeur' but 'aller chez le coiffeur' (rather like correcting someone on 'different to' or 'equally as' in English). He also castigated a woman for chewing gum and a cadre for talking with a cigarette in his mouth. He was no doubt caricatural in the extremity of his behaviour, but the trait was visible among other bosses in the sample. Another boss insisted on correcting a cadre who used 'ennuyant' rather than 'ennuyeux', and invariably drew attention to missed subjunctives. These are not, in fact, signs of disrespect for the personnel since the same boss who was such a stickler for savoir faire claims he would never take the liberty of sitting at a subordinate's desk – he refuses to exploit his authority.

Perhaps the motive behind correcting subordinates is that the patron sees himself as responsible for the education (au sens large) of his workforce. On the positive side, for instance, the pedantic boss described above, made a point of complimenting one cadre – after checking in the dictionary – for employing an adjective never before heard by the boss. He congratulated another cadre 'pour une lettre bien tournée' ('for a stylishly written letter'). Perhaps such behaviour is to be expected since it is conventionally the boss's education that sets him apart from his subordinates. Therefore to correct a grammatical mistake is a means of reaffirming one's intellectual superiority and, by the same token, one's right to lead.

Is there an explanation?

The desire to entrust one person with absolute power is a trait identified by Crozier in his classic analysis, *Le phénomène bureaucratique* (1964). He starts with the basic premise that the French are individualistic. Consequently they will not tolerate dependence relationships which impinge upon their freedom of action. Yet the collective action requires some form of leadership. So, an omnipotent conception of authority has emerged whereby the locus of the power is sufficiently remote to preserve the independence of the individual. Crozier characterizes the French model as:

> Preferring to submit to impersonal rules and to
> appeal to a superior authority than to fight and
> compromise in its own right.
>
> (1964, 251.)

Individuals are quite prepared to accept the arbitrary decision of a distant leader since it provides direction but guarantees independence. Such a perception of decision-making might seem alien to the Anglo-Saxon mind which believes that decisions should be taken at the point of action. But the French approach compensates for loss of detail with enhanced objectivity.

On a national scale, this willingness to bow down to a greater design can be seen in the French system of *planification indicative* (five year plan) which was successful for several decades while long-range planning was a meaningful exercise. The French approach is perhaps epitomized by the senior civil servant who explained:

> In the final analysis, the best decisions are the ones
> that are made when one is able to be at some distance
> from reality.
>
> (Crozier, 1982, 222.)

▎Chapter Eight

Corporate culture

'It's very difficult for me to explain what is distinctive about the company – the singularities are a part of my mental furniture.'
(Conversation with M. Lafforgue, Directeur Général Technique, l'Oréal – 8 April 1987.)

Corporate culture is a difficult thing to pin down. Yet it is an aspect of organizational life which an outsider is perhaps better placed to appraise than insiders, who grow oblivious to corporate idiosyncrasies.

In this chapter, we have picked out four companies for a closer look in terms of their corporate culture. The choice is based on spontaneously cited examples of what are considered typical French companies by French managers we have talked to. Although each of the four companies is distinctive, it is hoped that a number of common threads may emerge – and that these elements may provide some clues as to the national identity of French companies.

Michelin

A recent book parodying the careerist tactics that offer the best chances of success in particular French firms included a fairly comprehensive selection of the top French firms (including two of the companies cited later). But, by the book's authors' own admission, one conspicuous absentee was Michelin – the reason being:

'...que l'organisation cultive avec une redoutable efficacité le goût du secret.' (...that the company has an extraordinary capacity for the art of secrecy.)
(Wickham and Patterson, 1983, 206.)

Our desire to understand Michelin has also been affected by the company's renowned secrecy! Affirmations about the firm here are derived from interviews with senior personnel but have not been confirmed by informal contact with junior personnel or by periods of direct observation, as in some of the other companies mentioned. Even with this limitation, however, the standing of Michelin certainly justifies a discussion of its culture.

It is generally agreed that secrecy is a definite feature of this company. Outsiders are immediately confronted with it since interviews are conducted in a meeting room which acts as a no man's land between the company and the outside world. But this is no reflection on the status of the visitor since even General de Gaulle was forced to leave his presidential cortège at the entrance when he came to visit the company in 1959.

It is a company which makes appearances in the specialist or trade press but is rarely sighted in the management press. The role of the journalist is seen as being fundamentally opposed to the interests of the company:

> 'Votre métier est de percer les secrets. Le nôtre est
> d'assurer l'avenir de la Maison.' ('Your job is to
> penetrate secrets. Ours is to safeguard the future of
> the Company.')

Anonymity has become a way of life, and the tone is firmly set by the discretion of François Michelin, the grandson of the founder. So contagious is the desire to avoid le vedettariat (stardom) that even the person in charge of public relations prides himself on only having been quoted on two occasions, and that was by mistake. Still more surprising, there was talk of the same head of public relations naming a porte parole (spokesperson) of his own – but the idea was finally turned down on the grounds that it would degenerate into a sort of cascade effect.

Of course, efforts to stay out of the limelight tend to fuel speculation. And exaggerated rumours persist simply because the company refuses to be drawn into public denial. One example is the lingering myth that presence at mass was compulsory for the personnel. While it is true that François Michelin is a devout Catholic, the rumour itself is totally unfounded. In a way the company is a victim of its own secrecy – and its head, François Michelin, all the more enigmatic for keeping a low profile. He is a man of few words, who holds by the Chinese proverb, 'Tu es prisonnier de la parole que tu vas lâcher' ('You are a prisoner of your next word').

He claims that his behaviour is the result of corporate socialization: 'Ce que je suis c'est la Maison qui l'a fait' ('Michelin made me'). François Michelin sees himself as no more than an inheritor of the tradition initiated by his grandfather:

> ...la grande ombre d'Edouard Michelin, sa
> clairvoyance, son mépris de l'opinion publique.

(...the almighty spectre of Edouard Michelin, his
vision, his contempt for public opinion.)
(Internal publication, May 1945.)

The founder's influence is undeniable, but the present head does not
do himself justice. By shunning publicity when others are clamouring
for it, François Michelin has done far more than simply perpetuate a
legacy. Media interest in business has reached such a pitch in the 80s
that staying out of the limelight has to be a conscious decision. The
company regularly has to turn down offers of free publicity, including
one from the American Institute of Management which sought to
present the company in a book on management success stories.

François Michelin's attention is turned inwards rather than outwards.
He sees his responsibility as being to ensure that people fulfil themselves: 'Que chacun devienne ce qu'il est'. He uses simple imagery to
get this message across:

> Imaginez que vous ayez trois verres sur cette table.
> Un grand, un moyen, un petit. Le rôle d'un patron,
> c'est toujours de faire en sorte que chacun des verres
> puisse se remplir d'eau au point de déborder.
> (Imagine three glasses on a table – one small, one
> medium, one large. The boss's role is to see to it that
> they are permanently topped up.)
> (Freydet and Pingaud, 1982, 203.)

Oriental affinities

The simplicity of his language is just one aspect of a corporate culture
which has oriental overtones and which has prompted the description,
'la plus japonaise des entreprises françaises' ('the most Japanese
French company'). It is worth exploring this comparison since the
company exhibits several traits traditionally associated with Japanese
companies.

Many of François Michelin's speeches include messages that would
be considered trite or hollow in other companies or from other heads
but are not in his case. Take his conditions for success, expressed in
the company's brochure:

> Au fond, ces conditions du progrès expriment
> l'essentiel: rester jeune et ouvert sur la réalité des
> hommes et des choses. (Simply stated, progress is
> dependent upon our staying youthful and open to
> the reality of men and things.)

Another example was François Michelin's speech when awarding the
médaille du travail to a number of workers:

153

> *Derrière le contrat qui vous lie à la Maison et qui lie*
> *la Maison à chacun de vous, il y a un contrat moral,*
> *un contrat de confiance qui nous lie les uns aux*
> *autres avec nos clients et qui est le vrai fondement*
> *de l'ouvrage.* (Underpinning the contract which ties
> you to the company and which ties the company to
> every one of you, there is a moral contract which ties
> you to each other and to our customers. That is the
> real basis of our work.)
>
> (*L'Expansion*, 1979, 104.)

Two further points emerge quite forcefully from the above speech: first, a concern for the customer, and secondly, a heavy dose of paternalism.

While the company is not overly concerned with public opinion, it is clearly committed to its customers. As François Michelin himself explains: *'La seule mission d'une entreprise, c'est de servir ses clients'* ('A company has only one mission – to satisfy its customers'). Senior managers spoke convincingly about the fact that they were fundamentally answerable to the customers who are literally trusting them with their lives every time they purchased a Michelin tyre. What is more, it is the customer, not François Michelin, who really pays their wages.

There is more than a hint of paternalism in the reference to a moral contract between the individual and the company in the short passage quoted from *l'Expansion* – an idea reinforced by the use of the noun *maison* to designate the company, which has the same overtones as 'house' in English used in, for example, the fashion business or publishing. Another obvious manifestation is the workers' reference to *Monsieur François*. This is typical of family concerns in which it has been necessary to distinguish between various members of the family.

Paternalism at Michelin has been a powerful and long-lasting force. But it has still been steadily eroded as a result of state intervention. For instance, holiday camps, the Christmas tree, leisure spending have all been put in the hands of the Works' Committee. And control over corporate schools was relinquished to the state, albeit as late as 1967. This is regarded in Michelin as a *déresponsabilisation* of bosses who need no longer concern themselves with the welfare of the workforce. Nonetheless, at Clermont-Ferrand (the heart of the company) there is still a Michelin hospital, a sports complex and a chain of stores which bear witness to the company's sense of pastoral responsibility.

Michelin also displays certain Japanese values in its personnel policies: recruitment, promotion, training and employment. In terms of management recruitment, Michelin rarely seeks to fill a specific vacancy: *'Nous cherchons des gens qui fassent carrière'* ('We are looking for people who want a life-long career with us'). A 'Michelin Man' was described to us as, 'self-motivated, self-respecting and self-sufficient'. He should also be able to cope without an enveloping hierarchy or a *titre ronflant* (pompous title). The consensus was that Michelin Men are made, not born, but that there is certainly an element of predisposition. The recruitment policy is biased towards young entrants who, as the head of personnel put it, '*ont une formation mais pas de déformations*' ('who are qualified but not corrupted').

More recently, there have been a few problems with experienced *cadres* who have joined the company. Until the 1960s the company relied on home-grown talent, notably from the region of l'Auvergne, a rather dour region in central France. But expansion and internationalization provoked a call for new blood with broader experience. Inevitably, the steadfast values of the company have provoked occasional culture shocks among individuals who were not *type Maison* (company men).

Recruited usually at an early age, immersed in the corporate culture, there is a sort of clubbishness about the company. Managers will talk fondly about the career progress of people who were on the induction course at the same time as them. An essential part of the induction programme is to learn humility (very Japanese), which can prove a hard pill to swallow for the more extrovert who are quickly brought back down to earth. One divisional head was quite adamant that it was one of the rare companies where '*on peut gagner en s'appuyant sur les faits*' ('you will win if your argument is founded'), and where one would ultimately fail by trying to *vendre du vent* (pull the wool over people's eyes).

In terms of career development, the company seeks to fit the job to the person rather than vice versa. Individuals are given a free rein as well as the concomitant *droit à l'erreur* (right to foul up), to accumulate what responsibilities they feel capable of taking on. As one *cadre* quaintly put it, people are like the Michelin Man of the well-known advertisement – they are allowed to inflate their jobs to their natural limits. A job definition is determined by the particular aptitudes of its incumbent. This notion was epitomized by the experience of the head of Public Relations. He started off promisingly in the prestigious R & D section of the firm but it became clear that his personal skills would make an ideal communications person out of him. He took on the post in a small way and turned it into a significant force in the company: '*le poste a grossi avec lui*' ('the post grew with him'). This is empire building with a difference – it is not a negative force. Horizons are not blocked and *aucune rente n'est acquise* (no position is for keeps).

The familiar race for inflated titles is minimized at Michelin since there are none. Managers will introduce themselves modestly as Mr X, Michelin.[1] Officially, even François Michelin has no more of a title

---

1 The absence of formal titles – with the exception of financial director and plant manager – can prove quite disconcerting for outsiders who like to be able to situate their opposite numbers, and some concession to titles has therefore been made in order to accommodate outsiders.

than anyone. He is modestly known as the *gérant* (manager) in the corporate vernacular. Even corporate heroes such as the inspired worker who invented radial tyres are not glorified in the company folklore. On the other hand, workers' suggestions are considered seriously and rewarded appropriately – the implication being that anyone may make a useful contribution but everyone is on an equal footing. François Michelin rejects the spurious distinction which opposes *patron* and *salariés* and points instead to a common goal:

> *Tous ceux qui travaillent chez Michelin ont un*
> *même dessein: fabriquer le meilleur produit possible*
> *pour le client.* (All those who work for Michelin
> have a common goal: to make the best possible
> product for the customer.)
> (Freydet and Pingaud, 1982, 206.)

Another feature reminiscent of Japanese business is the commitment to life-long employment. We have already seen how recruitment and promotion policies are geared towards life-long careers through careful selection and acculturation of entrants. The same applies to the organizational structure which was put forward as being a web, as opposed to the more familiar rake or pyramid. It is claimed that the company lives without an organizational chart. In a way, the company has a biological aspect with each cell fulfilling its natural function. Of course, there are grey areas where responsibilities are not clear. But it is this natural slack which helps to preserve life-long employment – thanks to what the French call *voies de garage* (sidings for burnt out managers) or, on a grander scale, *fonctions de délestage* (functions or departments which have been put out to grass).

Finally, in terms of Japanese similarities, the company exhibits caution, patience and meticulous planning in its approach to exporting and production abroad. They are willing to export for decades before committing themselves to manufacturing on the spot. Nor does the company suffer from the traditional French weakness of impatience when results are not forthcoming. Instead it shows a willingness to devote time and money to establishing links, preparing the ground and sealing a contract.

Gallic pragmatism

The company philosophy is based on a certain pragmatism which manifests itself in *le culte des faits* (the quest for proof, or as Harold Geneen of ITT called it, the search for unshakeable facts!). There were several references to the importance of truth and the need to support one's case with hard facts. One *cadre* explained that the company gives a priority to facts rather than financial, political or 'custom and practice' considerations. The implication is that the truth will out.

What holds true at interpersonal and interdepartmental level is equally true at corporate level. The company is not given to 'discours intoxicants' ('inflated opinions') or predictions about new products, profits or likely performance. Information is not released unless the company is capable of backing it up. Indeed they prefer to underestimate targets in order to avoid unnecessary speculation. François Michelin's language is devoid of the hyperbole normally associated with corporate figureheads. On the contrary, his is 'un langage d'une banalité stupéfiante, ('a language devoid of pretension'). Yet it is meaningful to those imbued by the Michelin spirit. Further proof of corporate integrity can be seen in the decision by the Algerian government not to nationalize the company. Michelin justifiably derives much pride from the fact that it was the only foreign multinational spared that fate – a real tribute to its moral rectitude.

This no-nonsense approach is perhaps a manifestation of the company's provincial roots, and more specifically its origins in Auvergne. It is one of the few companies which persistently shuns the bright lights of Paris. While the likes of Peugeot claim to retain their provincial identity with a nominal presence in Sochaux, Michelin's bosses are actually based in unglamorous Clermont-Ferrand. They have not renounced the company's provincial origins.

The region of Auvergne is believed to exercise a profound influence on corporate values. Certainly the company mirrors the cautious, thrifty, sober and conservative attitudes that characterize that region. What is more, the French provincial disdain of Paris as depraved and superficial is reflected in the company's refusal to succumb to the lure of Paris. So in spite of the company's global expansion it remains staunchly based in Clermont and its officials still eschew the salons of Paris. As one cadre put it, 'When they tell you it's raining in France, they mean it's raining in Paris.' Perhaps it is thanks to the fact that it remains little known to the authorities that it escaped the nationalizations which befell half a dozen big industrial firms (including Elf-Aquitaine, Saint-Gobain and Thomson) under the Socialist (Mitterrand) régime in February 1982.

Oblivious to accusations of parochialism, François Michelin steers well clear of the crowd of civil servants, bankers and industrialists who consort to run France. A divisional head explained how François Michelin shuns the fallacious trappings of power. He illustrated the point by saying that François Michelin would not have to ring twice to have an audience with a Minister. Yet he refuses to indulge in that sort of egotistical power-mongering. So, while Michelin might resemble Dassault, the aeronautic pioneer, in many respects, he is totally different when it comes to relations with the state.

The company has a very strong production orientation. For instance, the Factory is given a capital letter, like 'la Maison, le Patron ou le Client'. In fact, 'the Factory' is used as a generic term implying the company as a whole rather than the place of work.

Technically speaking, Michelin has no reason to hide its light under a bushel. It is one of the few companies in the world that has single-handedly transformed an industry by a revolutionary invention, namely the radial tyre (1946). Its reputation for innovation and quality products is second to none, as reported in a survey in *l'Expansion* (3 December 1987).

There is no skimping on research. The company reputedly devotes 5 per cent of its turnover to R & D. By doing this irrespective of financial wellbeing, it has managed to retain its technical advantage over competitors. Indeed, part of the reason for the recent opening out of Michelin was to let the public know that poor performance would not impinge on research programmes. The development of the public relations department was a 'proactive' move designed to attenuate possible fears that a downturn in performance would lead to R & D cut-backs.

Michelin frequently develops products related to wheels and the vehicle suspension system, but it sells the technologies to others (again, *à la japonnaise*), preferring to concentrate on tyres. The company sees no need to diversify any further than the guides and maps. These were shrewd developments since they guarantee a permanent association between the company's name and the idea of travel for pleasure. The decision not to emulate Goodyear and Firestone in wider diversification (to cushion the volatile automobile market) is based on François Michelin's philosophy that diversification is not the company's problem but that of the shareholders. François Michelin displays a shrewd awareness of what the company is selling – the fundamental need to travel. And he realizes that to date, there is nothing better than a tube of rubber enveloping a mass of air under pressure to get about on land. That is the *raison d'être* of Michelin.

There is a very real affinity with and respect for the raw material. Rubber is venerated as a quasi-mystical substance and one which lends itself to corporate analogies. François Michelin himself claims the company is like a tyre ('*Nous sommes pneumatiques*') – supple and resilient. The company is also compared to its emblem (the Michelin Man) in its resolute determination to swallow all obstacles placed in its path.

This association between company and emblem was carried to its logical conclusion in London's Fulham Road where Michelin House was built in 1911. The tyre showroom broke new architectural ground by using the façade to advertise the product. The Michelin building embodies the bravura and ebullience of Mr Bibendum (the Michelin Man) himself. To employ the company engineer, Mr François Espinasse, who may or may not have been an architect, to design the building was a brave stroke. The result was a building which was not only functional but also incorporated the selling of tyres and the promotion of an image.

Another Michelin trait is the importance of freedom. First and foremost, this means independence from state interference. But secondly, it means steering clear of 'the Parisian virus' which, according to François Michelin, merely cuts people off from reality. And finally, for the head himself, it means voluntary exclusion from the French employers' organization.[1]

The company values its independence, not to say isolation. Michelin's is a closed world whose workings are difficult to grasp. Indeed the more one delves into it the more one wonders how it works. And yet ... Michelin is a testimony to the fact that a different management philosophy from the traditional US blueprint can work – not only in France but also in the US, where Michelin has five production plants as well as research and testing centres.

Strangely enough the *avant-garde* technology goes hand in hand with practices that some might describe as archaic. The company was characterized by a senior manager as having one foot in the nineteenth century and one in the twenty-first century. This manager intimated that they were trying to eradicate the nineteenth century side, yet without it, the company would not be Michelin.

The company is run in a dedicated, unpretentious way which is deeply rooted in its provincial origins. There is a strong sense of what the company values – modesty, a respect for facts, personnel and customers. Clear ideas and consistent language, *'Langage simple, idées fortes'*. Its members speak intelligently and convincingly about what makes this organizational anachronism tick.

Michelin is perhaps the ideal representative of French corporate culture – or at least it would be if it were not so exceptional. It embodies both extremes of what typifies French companies.

L'Air Liquide

L'Air Liquide is a family firm producing industrial gases. It is the world leader in its field and boasts large market shares in Europe, North America and Japan.

In its own way, l'Air Liquide is even more self-effacing than that paragon of discretion, Michelin. Of course, it has the advantage of manufacturing an industrial rather than a consumer product. But in addition to this, it does not shun publicity in quite the same obsessive way that Michelin does, and therefore avoids undue attention.

In its long history the company has always done its best to stay out of the limelight – to steer clear of litigation with either customers or

---

1 Feeling let down by the alleged irresponsibility of the Confédération Nationale du Patronat Français (the French Employers' Organization) in 1968, François Michelin decided to opt out of the organization.

personnel. As a matter of policy the company refuses to lay people off for economic reasons – the only proviso being that individuals accept transfers. Anyhow, in view of its impressive profit record, the company would probably be prevented from making anyone redundant by the 'Inspection du travail' (equivalent of the Department of Employment in UK). So, although l'Air Liquide bears the battle scars of lost markets, failed initiatives and missed opportunities, it gives an impression of immunity from injury. The company has earned an unparalleled reputation for stability.

This has made the company a firm favourite with investors. Its shares are highly respected in the investment fraternity who look upon them as *une valeur de fond de portefeuille* or *une valeur de père de famille* (blue chip investments). These are the corporate equivalent of granny bonds – they will provide shareholders with a steady income year in year out.

Primarily for this reason, the company boasted by far the largest private share ownership until the recent spate of privatizations. It has over 300,000 faithful shareholders. Their influence has a considerable impact on the company's actions and in many respects determines the corporate culture.

The atomization of the company's capital means that the group is theoretically vulnerable to the sanction of the market. The shareholders can decide to vote with their feet if they are not happy with the management. So the company is particularly attentive to its shareholders. This is rather unusual for French companies, which are generally unsympathetic to gains not earned through effort. But the PDG, Edouard de Royère, is quite adamant that the shareholder takes priority:

> *Chez nous, les actionnaires passent avant le banquier. S'il y a une bonne affaire à réaliser, c'est l'actionnaire qui doit en profiter.* (Here the banker takes second place to the shareholder. If there's a good deal in prospect, the shareholder must be the first to benefit.)
>
> (*L'Expansion*, 16 April 1987, 64.)

On the other hand, provided the company retains the goodwill of its shareholders, it is in a stronger position than companies with a more concentrated ownership. Some consider that the company can partly thank its shareholders for avoiding nationalization in 1982. Had it not looked after its small shareholders properly, l'Air Liquide might have suffered the same fate as the nationalized companies whose disillusioned small shareholders offered little resistance, succumbing easily to the state pay-off. Another feature of the share ownership which promotes solidarity is the absence of differentiation. The company has avoided several categories of share, which might prove divisive and frustrating. It has opted instead for a system which entitles shareholders to financial benefits but limits their decision-making participation.

Stability incarnate

Many of the corporate characteristics emanate directly (perhaps subconsciously) from the image of stability which the company seeks to project.

Visually speaking, this stability is apparent in the sartorial temperance at Head Office. The aim is not to stand out (contrast with l'Oréal), but to maintain a low profile. The same reasoning lay behind the company's recent decision to sell the company jet, which gave an unnecessarily flashy impression to customers and personnel alike. The trappings of corporate success must be toned down in an era where money is one of the few remaining taboos. Again this shows considerable sensitivity to the image projected and is somehow reminiscent of the frayed curtains, threadbare carpets and ink stained desks in the solicitors' office – comforting signs which give the impression of low fees and inspire the confidence of their thrifty clientele.

The company does not value the showy approach of some of its counterparts: for instance, the head of Saint-Gobain (Polytechnique graduate but modest origins) was regarded by one senior *cadre* as excitable and lacking in *savoir faire* in comparison to the sober Edouard de Royère (PDG of l'Air Liquide and a member of the French provincial aristocracy). The austerity is also visible in the attitude of the PDG who, according to one senior manager, is barely happier when the shares go up unexpectedly than when they go down. What he wants to see is measured progress based on performance, not speculation – it is precisely to quell volatility that, according to one shareholder, '*la société fait tout pour lisser ses résultats*' ('the company does everything to smooth out its results'). It is this sort of attitude which prompted *l'Expansion* (16 April 1987), to describe the company as having, '*Un management aussi discret que peu remuant*' ('a management whose discretion is matched only by its aplomb').

For the same reason, political activism is not appreciated when it interferes with professional life. The upper echelons are particularly sensitive to the development of a *hiérarchie parallèle* which might undermine *la hiérarchie naturelle*. For this reason, when informal discussion groups (*droit d'expression des salariés*) were introduced by the Socialists, the company took the precaution to impose the *chef hiérarchique* as session leader rather than run the risk of having a political activist elected as group leader (the theme is further discussed in Chapter 9 on labour relations).

The family nature of the business also contributes to the stability. With only three bosses in over eighty years, one could hardly hope for greater continuity. Of course, the massive reigns of Edouard de Royère's two predecessors (Paul Delorme 1902–45, and his son Jean Delorme 1945–85) have left their imprint on the firm. So in spite of his long apprenticeship as the firm's second in command, Edouard de Royère has had some difficulty stamping his own personality on the company.

He is also faced with the problem of modernizing the image of the company, 'de rompre un long silence' ('to break a long silence') without shocking public opinion or his predecessor who has been given an honorary post as Président du comité général consultatif.[1] As the head of public relations told me:

> 'Fifteen years ago, the company was like a black box
> – no one knew what was going on inside. But now
> there is pride in the company's achievements.'

This contrast in exposure was underlined by the fact that l'Air Liquide now subcontracts the measurement of column inches and TV seconds allotted to the company to determine their value in terms of publicity. The Head of Public Relations pointed out that, until recently, this would have been a useless exercise owing to the company's secrecy and the absence of media exposure.

Jean Delorme, the present PDG's father-in-law, would not hear of being talked about in the press or being photographed (à la Michelin). But de Royère would like to dispel the company's rather staid and comfortable image 'd'une grosse entreprise tranquille, sans relief et bien nourrie' ('of a large company which is aloof, characterless and slightly overweight').

Curiously, for a company which is so familiar to investors, the company remains little known to the general public. The decision to set up a public relations department was not really intended to remedy the fact – it was more for the benefit of the shareholders. In the light of media interest in corporate affairs, l'Air Liquide could not afford to stay hidden, since this might be interpreted as a sign of inadaptability. If the company showed inability to move with the times on the communications front, shareholders might equate this lag with inadaptability, backwardness or, worse still, skeletons in the cupboard. And with the company so susceptible to rumours something had to be done.

So, like Michelin, l'Air Liquide's concession to expose itself was a proactive move primarily destined to allay shareholder fears. Still, the Head of Public Relations was not entirely convinced that the media revolution was anything more than a passing fad. These sentiments were echoed by Edouard de Royère himself, who showed

---

1 Thus bearing out the old French chestnut – 'Once a president, always a president' (of some committee or other).

scepticism about the current 'love affair' between companies and the media:

> '*Je ne crois pas qu'il suffise d'un coup de pub pour obtenir la confiance des actionnaires.*' (It takes more than a bit of advertising to gain shareholder confidence.)

And he added that it had taken l'Air Liquide several decades to gain the trust of its shareholders.

The caution displayed by the company – in exposing itself and its profits, in avoiding negative publicity – is a deep-rooted trait which finds physical form in the head office. When it was built, in 1932, the building was designed to double up as a hotel should the existing business turn sour. This may have been a wise precaution on the part of the founder, but it has left a legacy of mazy corridors and isolated offices.

The physical geography of the building does not lend itself to easy communication – either spoken or physical. What is more, the sumptuous, marbled décor (reminiscent of a museum or ministerial office) seems to militate against any sort of informal contact – the only coffee point, for instance, is in the basement. While this is an extreme example, it does highlight French attachment to classical management principles and the rejection of spontaneous exchanges, or what has been dubbed 'management by walking around', as a legitimate means of communication. The French attitude to work is based on the ideal of intellectual effort.

The coldness of the architecture seems to have repercussions on the personnel. Wickham and Patterson (1982, 324) refer to the company thus:

> *L'Air Liquide n'est pas réputé pour la cordialité des relations que l'on entretient avec ses collègues.*
> (L'Air Liquide is not renowned for promoting friendly relations between colleagues.)

The climate is certainly rather reserved when it comes to interpersonal relations, a fact corroborated by the systematic use of the *vous* form of address[1] which plays a protective role for those in authority. Whilst one of the present authors was there, a secretary was at a loss to communicate the Christian name of one of her immediate superiors in order to book a flight. Similarly, considerable importance was attached

---

1 The tu/vous distinction and the preference for first names or surnames discussed in Chapter 6 proved useful litmus tests when attempting to determine the nature of interpersonal relations.

to being on first name terms with the PDG. Only five or six people were privy to it, and it was deemed 'une marque d'estime extraordinaire' ('real recognition')[1].

The company appears strong on vertical differentiation – quite literally, since the importance of managers at head office could be determined by their position along the plumb-line linking earth to the sky. The PDG was at the summit and the typing pool in the basement – which gave new meaning to the careerist's quip pour être plus près du Bon Dieu (to be closer to God).

Having reached the desired 'altitude' (same floor as the PDG), thoughts turn towards geographical proximity. It was ironic that the Public Relations manager, whose role as company impressario brought him into constant contact with the boss, would never be given an adjoining office for fear of upsetting the numbers two and three. The PR manager described himself as an 'offshore' cadre (i.e. outside the direct hierarchy) and therefore an unsuitable candidate for such choice spot. Instead he was on the same floor – but 'côté cuisine' alongside the secretaries. Even if the regularity of contact logically warranted a closer office, the proposition was inconceivable from a prestige point of view. Protocol dictates that the general must be surrounded 'par son état major' ('by the top brass') – even if the radio operator is his most valuable ally.

Whist the preceding description tends to burlesque the situation, these are latent but very real concerns. For all their egalitarian claims, the French seem to cherish pecking orders and the perks that go with them. Here we have the underside of the hexagonal constellation of values (discussed at the end of Chapter 1). To indicate the meteoric rise of a mutual acquaintance, one plant manager explained to another, 'il a un parking au siège' (he has a parking space at Head Office). There was also a hint that political games were being played at Head Office, where one progressive young manager had suddenly become more cautious: 'Il n'y a pas longtemps il fonçait, jusqu'à ce qu'on a commencé à lui glisser des peaux de banane' ('He used to rush headlong, until they started slipping him a few banana skins').

As regards careers, the favoured route to the top is allegedly research. This is perhaps understandable in view of the research orientation of the company. Quality research and the ability to find concrete commercial applications for new products are deemed the group's main assets. Though a promising young centralien who had started in research claimed that research was a dead end – adding 'pour avancer dans cette boîte il faut se frotter au client' ('to make headway in this company you have to move into the commercial side'). It is noticeable, though not necessarily significant, that he referred to boîte (meaning

---

1 One is reminded of Pierre Daninos (1960): 'A ma connaissance, il y a quatre person-nages qui ont droit aux fleurs "comme le patron"' ('To the best of my knowledge, there are four people who are entitled to have the same sort of flowers as the boss').

firm), which is colder than the more homely *maison* employed by Michelin personnel.

Another promising route was said to be expatriation. It is understandable that mobility within the group is valued since the majority of the company's activities and personnel are abroad. What is more, the management of its international implantations is regarded as an essential apprenticeship for taking on the group's more prestigious French operations. And mobility is seen as an important means of diffusing the corporate culture, *'véritable ciment de l'ensemble'* ('a real corporate stiffening agent') promoting group coherence.

It also helps if one is a graduate of l'Ecole Centrale, though all three top engineering schools (Polytechnique, Mines and Centrale) are well represented as is the top business school, HEC. Edouard de Royère (*Valeurs Actuelles*, 21 July 1986, 32) explicitly denied the popular rumours that there are *mafias* within the company by stating that the upper echelons were not recruited as a result of their qualifications:

> *Les membres de la direction générale ne sont pas*
> *recrutés en fonction de leur diplômes au sein de*
> *chapelles particulières.* (Those on the board of
> directors are not selected on the basis of qualifica-
> tions obtained from particular establishments.)

Clearly, there is some confusion about the best recipe for success at l'Air Liquide. But the fact that the PDG feels compelled to comment on them tends to suggest there may be an element of truth in the rumours. Still, it is a company which is committed to life-long employment (with a qualification of mobility) and which encourages *promotion interne*.

Independence is another key word for the company. Like Michelin, l'Air Liquide is determined to stay clear of the state in spite of obvious attractions:

> *'Bien sur, nous pourrions être tentés de céder à telle*
> *ou telle pression des pouvoirs publics, par exemple*
> *en matière d'investissements.'* (Of course we could
> be tempted to succumb to pressures from the state,
> for example where investments are concerned.)

This independence is of course based upon a solid financial base, which allows the company to snub the state. It has enjoyed spectacular post-war growth – without state assistance. According to their Head of Public Relations, the company's policy is to be *'une bonne citoyenne'* – to put new legislation into practice quickly, and never to ask for subsidies or *'passe-droit'* ('favours'). In exchange for steering clear of the state, the company does not expect the state to interfere in its running. As with Michelin, this is believed to have contributed to their avoidance of nationalization in 1982 - since the company was an unknown quantity. Indeed one plant manager jokingly speculated how much the company had paid the Socialists to stay off the nationalization lists.

On the matter of the future the question was raised about prospective successors to Edouard de Royère, 'Do his sons work here?' we ventured. 'Not yet', let slip a senior manager. He added that the logical successor would have been Jean Delorme's own son (rather than his son-in-law) but in spite of his intelligence he was politically imprudent, had played his cards badly and now found himself permanently '*à l'écart*' ('sidelined') – in a Singapore diving equipment subsidiary.

L'Oréal

Like l'Air Liquide in industrial gases, l'Oréal is the world leader in cosmetics. Like l'Air Liquide it has an enviable financial and export record. Like l'Air Liquide it has known only three heads since it started in 1907. Like l'Air Liquide its penultimate head has been forced into retirement having reached the statutory age limit but retains an honorary position as advisor.

But, while the two companies share similar track records, they are very different in character. For instance, l'Air Liquide's low-key approach is in stark contrast with l'Oréal's polished image. For the last two years l'Oréal has been voted top in the corporate image stakes by the readers of *l'Expansion* (3 December 1987). Company reputations were judged on six criteria – and Oréal won two individual categories (quality of management and capacity to innovate) as well as the overall title – ousting the illustrious IBM from that position in the process.

The company bears the hallmark of the product it sells – appearances matter. On a superficial level this can be seen in the sophisticated and artistic décor at head office and in the sartorial elegance of its personnel. Yet, the characteristic percolates much deeper than this – Wickham and Patterson (1983), cynical observers of French careerist manoeuvres, go as far as to suggest that it colours managerial behavior. At a number of levels substance plays second fiddle to style.

For example, the production plants out in the provinces – establishments conventionally associated with purely functional goals – pay real attention to 'window dressing'. The offices are pleasantly decorated, the plant manager smartly dressed, and the corridors carpeted. Even the production line was marked by '*le souci de l'esthétique*' ('a concern for aesthetic values'). Production managers would enthuse about the visual merits of glass protection over metallic protection on the machines: '*Ça donne à la ligne une allure géniale*' ('It makes the production line look wonderful').

There was a concern for making the workplace more pleasant for the benefit of visitors and personnel alike. The customization of machinery was encouraged and bright colours were used to liven up normally dull workshops. There was what one production manager termed 'un côté cinéma' ('showy aspect') to all this, but there were also sound practical reasons. The judicious use of glass protective screens on the machinery meant that workers could see what was happening on the production line. The pleasing appearance of the workshop made workers more inclined to keep it clean and tidy.

However, the point about image consciousness was brought home most forcefully at a meeting held to discuss the external redecoration of the factory. The meeting was a presentation of the various types of wall covering available for the façade. For nearly an hour the discussion revolved around the visual impact of the various coverings as typified by phrases like: 'on pourra faire des trucs marrants' ('we'll be able to do some fun things'), 'un brin de fantaisie' ('a touch of inspiration'), 'rendre la façade vivante avec la lumière' ('make the façade lively with light'). One form of covering was even deemed 'plus fin, plus noble' ('more refined and noble') – not the sort 'qu'on retrouve partout' ('you see everywhere'). Not until the very end of the hour-long meeting were practical considerations like resilience or cost brought up – again the preoccupation was with appearance rather than function.

L'Oréal's culture has been heavily influenced by two men: the founder, Eugène Schueller and his successor and penultimate PDG, François Dalle. Between them they 'ruled' for nearly 80 years (and Dalle now heads the Comité stratégique, regarded by some as a sort of golden cupboard, un placard doré). They incarnated the two driving forces of the company, namely research and marketing.

Research was the great strength of the founder Eugène Schueller who invented the first artificial hair colourings. This tradition has been reinforced by the subsequent PDG, Charles Zviak, whose entire career at l'Oréal was in fundamental and applied research. He spelled out this commitment in slightly melodramatic terms in the company brochure:

> Il était une fois une entreprise qui avait choisi la
> qualité et les moyens d'obtenir cette qualité: elle
> avait choisi la recherche. (Once upon a time, there
> was a company which had chosen quality and the
> means of achieving that quality; it had chosen
> research.)

> L'essentiel, c'est de chercher, toujours chercher. Les
> idées viennent quand on a la volonté acharnée de
> promouvoir l'entreprise à la pointe de la qualité,
> à la pointe de l'innovation. (The main thing is to

seek, ceaselessly. Ideas will come if the company is
wholeheartedly devoted to staying at the sharp end
of quality and innovation.)

L'Oréal is continually innovating and coming up with new products.
So research is critical to the company's success – but to capitalize on
that research requires marketing dexterity. The man responsible
for giving l'Oréal this appetite for marketing was François Dalle, a
particularly fervent admirer of *'le marketing à l'américaine'*. When he
took over from Eugène Schueller in 1957, he introduced marketing
techniques borrowed from the likes of Procter and Gamble – and these
had a considerable impact on the unsophisticated French consumer.

For instance, when l'Oréal launched its now famous tetrahedral
shampoo container (*shampooing-berlingot*) it revolutionized French
social habits. Novel packaging, clever promotion and low price turned
the product into an instant success. It also transformed the French into
the world's most devoted hair washers – this in spite of their otherwise
poor reputation (among developed countries) for personal hygiene.

It was Dalle who coined the phrase *'Saisir ce qui commence'* as a
corporate rallying call. This dictum reflects the company's obsession
with being at the centre of things. The company's main concern is
not to miss opportunities. Missing the boat on the trend in 'natural'
products was a particular disappointment – despite the fact that the
company has now made up for lost time. This was a severe blow to the
corporate ego which prides itself as being a trend-setter, not a follower.

Before handing over the reins to Charles Zviak in 1984, knowing
that the latter was due to retire in 1988, François Dalle nominated a
successor, Lindsay Owen-Jones. His background, like Françqis Dalle's,
is in marketing. With hindsight, Charles Zviak was an interim PDG
who 'minded the store' until François Dalle's *fils spirituel*, Lindsay
Owen-Jones, came of age. (Dalle himself was nominated by his predecessor, Eugène Schueller.) Lindsay Owen-Jones, or O.J. as he is known,
was 40 at the time of his accession and a graduate of Oxford University.
So the company looks set for another lengthy reign, as well as a slight
shift back towards marketing.

When questioned about the strengths of l'Oréal, Lindsay Owen-Jones
paid tribute to the company's commitment to research and marketing,
but went on to underline the quality and motivation of l'Oréal's
management – something he attributes to being picked early:

> *Nous avons la chance, pour la très grande majorité
> d'entre nous, de faire notre notre vie à l'Oréal. J'y
> suis entré pratiquement, comme tous mes camarades,
> directement à la sortie de l'Université et, à 40 ans,
> j'ai presque 20 ans de l'Oréal derrière moi.* (The vast
> majority of us are fortunate enough to build our

careers at l'Oréal. I entered the company, like all my
colleagues, straight from university and now, aged
40, I have had nearly 20 years as a company man.)
(*LSA*, No. 1057, 15.)

The same was true of Charles Zviak and his *état-major* (council), most
of whom have been with the company all their working lives. The
company clearly places a high premium on loyalty. This was obvious
from the slightly derisory way a plant manager referred to his young
second in command – with a tally of four companies to his name:

'*C'est un carriériste. Il n'a pas de maison – comme
un escargot.*' ('He is career-minded. He has no house
(firm) – just like a snail'.)

This commitment to life-long employment has several repercussions – notably on recruitment and promotion policies, management
training and on the handling of 'burnt out' *cadres*.

Sources of recruitment

As one might expect of a company that places a premium on ideas and
initiative, l'Oréal cannot afford to recruit from a single source. It must
cast its net wide so as to avoid the problem of too many like-minded
individuals stifling creativity. So, as one personnel manager put it, '*par
volonté de pluralisme*', the company recruits from both tiers of higher
education – universities and *grandes écoles*.

This is rare for a large group, particularly a successful one which
could recruit exclusively from the cream of the *grandes écoles* if it
wished. L'Oréal sees itself as a sort of 'equal opportunity employer' as
far as university students are concerned. This fact was corroborated by
the presence of university people in a number of key posts, not least
Director of Management Development. However, the insistence with
which the claim '*nous n'avons pas peur des universitaires*' ('we're not
scared of university people') was reiterated, tended to draw attention to
their second-class status in France – the point would not have to be
made if there were parity between the two sides of higher education.

Lindsay Owen-Jones sees motivation, rather than qualification, as
the main recruitment criterion:

*Il faut faire un choix entre ceux qui recherchent
l'appartenance à l'Oréal parce qu'ils y voient une
façon de s'exprimer dans une organisation déjà
dynamique, et ceux qui cherchent avant tout une
sécurité, qui ont envie d'être portés par la vague.
Nous avons besoin de porteurs, et pas de gens à
porter.* (We must distinguish between those who see

l'Oréal as a means of expressing themselves in an
active company, and those who seek security first
and foremost, and want to be carried by the wave.
We need locomotives, not wagons.)

(*LSA*, No. 1057, 15.)

L'Oréal appears less than sympathetic to the old school tie allegiances
(*les mandarinats*) which often dominate French companies. Perhaps
this reflects the university backgrounds of its leaders. The company has
nothing against *grande école* graduates, but it expects them to set aside
their schooling when they join the company. As François Dalle put it:

> *Nous souhaitons seulement qu'étant chez nous, ils*
> *gardent le moins possible l'esprit de l'école d'où ils*
> *viennent. Nous souhaitons qu'ils perdent cette*
> *forme d'orgueil que donnent les grandes écoles.*
> *Nous voulons des hommes disponibles, et non pas*
> *a priori supérieurs.* (We simply hope that once
> admitted, they don't retain the spirit of the school
> to which they belonged. We hope they lose that
> sort of conceit typical of *grandes écoles*. We need
> people with adaptability, not a superiority complex.)

(Priouret, 1968, 115.)

Internal promotion
As with recruitment, individuals are judged on their merits and on
their performance 'on the job' rather than by their educational credentials – though François Dalle qualifies this by saying:

> *Sous cette réserve que nous attachons beaucoup*
> *d'importance à la culture et la formation que*
> *représente un diplôme.* (Bearing in mind that we
> attach a great deal of importance to the culture and
> training which qualifications represent).

(Priouret, 1968, 111.)

When a post comes up, there is always a conscientious *tour de piste*
(lap of the track) before the company looks outside for talent. They are
proud of their internal promotion tradition. Even *autodidactes* have a
chance of 'making it', provided they play their cards right. One *cadre*
explained that you could make it through the tradesman's entrance
(*la petite porte* as opposed to *la voie royale*) but, you have to 'navigate'.
This was meant both literally (that is, you have to be geographically
mobile – such is the price for a paucity of qualifications), and meta-
phorically (in other words, you have to be politically adept and
manoeuvre judiciously).

While there were no clans based on educational allegiances, one *cadre* suggested that there were divisions by generations – '*Il y a l'équipe de Dalle (60–65)*', then a gap of twenty years to the 40–45 age range, and then a ten year gap including the 30–35-year-olds.

Of course, internal promotion also necessitates some commitment to management training in order to prepare *cadres* for changes in responsibility. The company was instrumental in setting up a co-operative training establishment, the CEDEP (Centre Européen d'Éducation Permanente), in 1971 on the INSEAD campus at Fontainebleau. This centre is staffed by INSEAD professors and provides the company's top and middle management personnel (along with *cadres* from a restricted number of companies) with high quality management development. The stated aim of this establishment was to provide member companies with a 'critical mass' of managerial talent, speaking the same language and with the same objectives to enable the companies to act coherently and break through the *pesanteurs sociologiques* (all forms of sociological inertia).

Being sent to the CEDEP is invariably regarded as an important sign of career development – indeed it often confirms a forthcoming promotion. As a result, it is valued more for instrumental reasons (confirmation of prospects) than for its intrinsic worth (knowledge imparted). Those selected described it as:

> '*Un peu répétitif mais très valorisant*' ('a little repetitive but a great personal endorsement').

> '*C'est la super récompense*' ('it's the supreme reward').

> '*C'est un événement professionnel*' ('it's a professional watershed').

> '*Un sine qua non pour l'avancement*' ('a pre-requisite for promotion').

The course clearly acts as confirmation of the company's faith in a particular individual – it acts as implicit confirmation of one's career prospects. But because of the small quota allotted to each company in the association, the waiting list *de gens CEDEP-able* (of possible candidates) is long. Strict rules govern eligibility and the appropriate mix of ages, functions and hierarchical levels allowed on to the prestigious course. There is a touch of hierarchical apartheid since learning is considered a potentially embarrassing situation – *on se dévoile* (you bare yourself) and seminars involve *relations intimistes* (intimate relations). To mix levels would be to risk erecting psychological barriers to communication. L'Oréal is also careful not to award a diploma with the course – presumably to deter individuals from using it as a springboard to leave.

Burnt out *cadres*

A policy of life-long employment implies dealing with individuals whose relative contribution to the company is diminishing – what American managerial parlance has labelled the 'Bobo' (burnt out but operating) syndrome. The grounds for keeping on these individuals are often humanitarian: out of tolerance, respect or recognition for having helped the group through difficult times. Alternatively, more practical reasons may be invoked for their retention: to help nurture young talent, to preserve the collective memory of the company and pass on the corporate culture. Or as François Dalle put it:

> *L'ancien peu rendre des services avec son*
> *expérience, dans un domaine différent de celui où*
> *il est resté jusque-là.* (Senior managers can put their
> experience to use in an area which is new to them.)
>
> (Priouret, 1968, 116.)

François Dalle goes on to explain why he considers the problem of dealing with ageing *cadres* as one of his foremost preoccupations:

> *Je suis attaché à ceux qui ont fait leur vie dans*
> *l'entreprise, parce que cela correspond à mon*
> *tempérament. Il s'agit là d'une simple correction;*
> *on ne peu pas être ingrat avec ceux qui ont contribué*
> *à faire la maison. Mais être fidèle, c'est aussi notre*
> *intérêt; si l'on sacrifiait les anciens, les jeunes*
> *n'auraient pas confiance dans l'entreprise.* (I am
> attached to those who have spent their working
> lives with the company, because I can identify with
> it. Being grateful to those who have helped build
> the company is simply a matter of fairness. But it is
> also in our interests to stand by them; if we sacrifice
> the older managers, the younger ones will have no
> faith in the company.)
>
> (Priouret, 1968, 116.)

In other words, Dalle expresses the concern that if l'Oréal fails to 'take care' of its ageing *cadres*, it risks deterring young *cadres* from even joining the company!

So the company is left with the problem of what, in practical terms, it should do with its loyal servants. L'Oréal is fortunate in that it is large and successful enough to accommodate a fair amount of excess weight in the so-called *voies de garage* already mentioned for Michelin.

This slack remains invisible because of *un certain flou* (a slight blur) in the organizational chart. This vagueness would seem to confirm Wickham's and Patterson's characterization (1983, 220) of the company as being *très intuitive, à l'organisation un peu anarchique* ('very intuitive, and rather anarchic in its organization'). By their reckoning, territories and responsibilities are ill-defined, re-negotiated daily, with politics and careerism rife. L'Oréal's personnel are reputedly impulsive, *brouillon* (opaque) and perhaps a touch courtesan. As one plant manager explained, ideas must be sold to the right people and support canvassed in the right areas *'avant d'aller présenter son projet au 10ème'* ('before taking a project to the top floor'). Wickham and Patterson (1983, 332) also note that *'certaines décisions seront prises alors qu'elles n'ont apparemment fait l'objet d'aucune délibération officielle'* ('certain decisions will be taken which have not apparently been the subject of official deliberation').

This analysis was borne out at plant level where decisions from head office were often greeted with incomprehension. Explanations from the head office were typically lacking and production plants were presented with a *fait accompli*: *'le comment mais pas le pourquoi des choses'* ('the "how" not the "why" of things'). This proved demotivating for those on the receiving end and prompted criticism along the lines:

> Les économistes de la division manquent de
> méthode, de logique et d'objectifs. (The
> divisional economists are short on method, logic
> and objectives.)

This criticism seems to point to a certain subjectivity in decision-making – the implication being that even the managerial ethos is coloured by the *paraître* (seeming) and *être* (being) ambivalence of the product. *Cadres* at all levels would pride themselves on their ability to assess a situation without empirical evidence – and there were numerous references to *le feeling* or what used to be called *le pif* (the nose). It would seem that, at l'Oréal at least, intuition is deemed a legitimate basis for action.

The professed penchant for intuition, together with the *'coloration féminine du produit et du métier'* ('the feminine nature of the product and the job'), make the actual paucity of women all the more shocking. One female *cadre* suggested that whilst the company boasts *'une grande ouverture'* ('great openness') towards sex and race, the reality is that it is *'pas très en avance sur le restant de la France'* ('not very far ahead of the rest of France'). She went on to explain that research and marketing are fairly open to women since these involved limited responsibility in personnel terms, but production and sales are strictly out of bounds. Only recently have there been any female sales representatives – a real irony for a product range aimed primarily at women.

The company operates a decentralized philosophy. *'C'est une culture qui fait confiance aux hommes'* says one plant manager who receives a budgetary envelope to allocate as he sees fit. The plant manager himself is referred to as his own boss, with a big B. *'C'est lui qui fait la pluie et le beau temps de ses cadres'* ('He determines the lot of his *cadres'*) since it is he who evaluates them and awards bonuses – though, as might be expected, the evaluation is oral, since writing is deemed to promote vindictiveness.

The company also boasts the hackneyed *droit à l'erreur*, though one *cadre* suggested this was only possible because of the high profits. In other words, it is easy in their position to allow people to pursue far-fetched ideas. The result is a virtuous circle where, *'il faudrait être idiot pour perdre de l'argent'* ('you'd have to be stupid to lose money').

As with the companies previously described in this chapter, l'Oréal is a company which boasts total independence from the state. As Dalle put it:

> *Nous n'avons rien à leur demander.* (We have
> nothing to ask of the state.)
>
> (Priouret, 1968, 120.)

The fact remains that rumours suggest that there may have been one or two instances of state indulgence on legislation enabling l'Oréal to maintain competitiveness – and these rumours are lent credibility by François Dalle's long-standing friendship with François Mitterrand. Baumier (1986, 54) describes François Dalle as: *'Un des rares, parmi ses proches, à tutoyer François Mitterrand'* ('one of the few, in François Mitterrand's circle, on familiar terms with him'). And, as one rather cynical PDG suggested:

> So many industrialists say they want government
> off their backs when what they really mean is that
> they want government in their laps.

In terms of self-image, the company sees itself as a beacon for French companies in general, and as an advert for 'the French way of life'. The company brochure refers to:

> *A travers les liens multiples que tissent l'entreprise,*
> *ses produits, ses hommes, s'inscrit une certaine*
> *image de la France.* (Through the multiple ties
> made by the company, its products and its people, a
> certain image of France emerges.)

However, behind its international success, l'Oréal faces unsuspected problems in finding French *cadres* to look after their international operations. As François Dalle put it:

> *Nos cadres supérieurs et nos directeurs veulent*
> *bien, pour nous dépanner, aller un mois ou deux*

en *Amérique du Nord ou du Sud, ou en Asie, ou en
Afrique, mais pas au-delà.* (Our senior managers
and directors are perfectly willing to go out to North
or South America, Asia or Africa for a couple of
months to help us out – but no longer than that.)
(Priouret, 1968, 114.)

The corporate culture, like the company's image, is *soigné*
(well-groomed). Each year the top fifty individuals in the company (*la
première couronne*) get together to reflect on the group's culture
and the values to be encouraged. The trick seems to work since the
personnel spontaneously refer to the distinctive culture of the
company – *le monde de l'Oréal, l'homme oréalien,* or *une grande
famille* – phrases which one might expect from an IBM-er. Clearly
working for l'Oreal is an identity not a label.

Carrefour

Carrefour is in the vanguard of successful post-war French companies
alongside groups such as Accor, Club Meditérranée, Bouygues or BSN.
Carrefour is different from the companies already discussed in this chapter
in that it is a retailing, not a manufacturing, company and was launched
in the early 1960s rather than around the turn of the century.

Its founders, Marcel Fournier and the Defforey family have been
responsible for introducing several innovative concepts to the French
retail sector – most notably the hypermarket and *produits libres*
(no-name products). Over the past quarter of a century, Carrefour has
developed into one of the leading food retailers in Europe – a success
which has been built on a number of tenets.

Decentralization
The cornerstone of the firm's operating philosophy has been the
decentralization of management. Although financial control is highly
centralized, and the performance of individual stores is closely
monitored, in most aspects of operation the company is decentralized.
Each store is operated as a profit centre and the store manager has
complete responsibility for the performance and operation of the
store which must meet sales objectives established annually by
the company.

It is worth noting that this philosophy runs counter to received wisdom on responsibility. Goldsmith and Clutterbuck (1984, 29) maintain
that whilst decentralization is a hallmark of successful industrial
groups, retailing operations rely on centralization. In support of this
thesis they cite Sainsbury's and Marks and Spencer, which maintain
central control over design, presentation, stock and pricing.

The decentralization of authority is intended to provide scope for flexibility, allowing store managers to respond to local factors and environmental conditions. The store managers are encouraged to think of the stores as their own businesses – a notion made quite explicit by the head of Carrefour-France, *'Nos directeurs doivent être plus que jamais des chefs d'entreprise'* ('More than ever, we expect our store managers to behave like heads of their own companies'). This was confirmed in the field, where one store manager explained to me that the buck stopped with him, that this was the reason for his security consciousness – it was his money that he had to fork out – and he underlined the view further by referring to *'mon magasin'* ('my store').

Ironically, perhaps, the best testament to the level of discretion enjoyed by store managers is that independence is not a hard and fast rule. Store managers are at liberty to contravene the decentralization philosophy and get together in small groups so as to improve their competitiveness. Further proof of this delegation of responsibility can be seen in the size of the head office staff which numbers only about 20, including secretaries, chauffeurs and caretakers. In terms of communication, too, little more than 10 per cent of the overall budget is devoted to the national campaign. The latter merely serves to set the tone and avoid *une cacophonie d'initiatives* which would leave the customer *dépaysé* (confused).

This commitment to decentralization does not stop at store manager level. Within the store, the individuals in charge of particular sections are free to decide which goods they wish to carry and are responsible for negotiating additional discounts with suppliers. The aim is to personalize all that is on show to the customer.

Of course, the greater the level of decentralization the harder it is to maintain a sense of corporate identity. Until recently, coherence was achieved via an oral tradition. Corporate values were passed on in an *ad hoc* way through meetings and informal contacts. Standardization was given further impetus by the systematic rotation of store managers. (Only three of the 71 store managers have been *en place* for more than three years.) These methods are still used to communicate corporate beliefs but they have been supplemented with a formal expression of corporate culture.

In 1979, Carrefour introduced a small book entitled *Politiques* – a sort of corporate manifesto which sets out objectives and policies as well as expounding the corporate philosophy:

> *La pérennité, l'indépendance et la croissance*
> *régulière de CARREFOUR sont fondées sur les*
> *hommes. Tous, chaque jour, s'efforcent d'apporter*
> *une réponse plus harmonieuse aux attentes*
> *multiples des partenaires de l'entreprise.* (The future,

the independence and the regular growth of CARRE-
FOUR are based on people. Together, each day we
must do our utmost to satisfy more fully the many
expectations of the partners of the company.)

These are regarded as the terms of reference for any initiative, or as
the Head of Carrefour France put it, '*C'est l'élément le plus fédérateur
de la culture originale de notre groupe*' ('it is the most unifying element
of the group's unique culture').

In theory, the existence of such a document takes the responsibility
off the store managers for spreading the corporate gospel. They merely
have to refer their personnel to the booklet when the need arises. For
instance, when documents are drafted at a local level, store managers
will urge the writers to use the existing terminology in order to promote
written standardization.

Yet the oral tradition seems to persist. Store managers proved very
adept at peddling the corporate message using concrete incidents as
they occurred. For instance, one store manager would make a point of
conscientiously stopping to pick up litter on the floor of the store. The
implications of this action were twofold. On the one hand, it confirmed
the idea that he thought of the store as his own ('*nous ne sommes pas
des fonctionnaires*' – meaning that they are not civil servants devoid
of personal involvement), and on the other hand he was effectively
saying to colleagues that no one is too big to bend down and pick
up rubbish. In the same vein, on his way through the store to lunch
(sacred) with a number of *cadres*, he made a point of stopping to
answer customer queries (to reinforce the notion of service). Afterwards
he pointed out to his colleagues that some of their personnel still
walked off in the opposite direction when they saw a customer heading
for them. He implores them to '*faire passer le message*' ('pass on the
message') to their teams.

His example was quickly picked up and applied down the line. In
one instance, a section was getting a little carried away with its
displays. This prompted the head of the sector to rehash a message
passed on to him that very morning by the store manager, namely: '*Il
faut raisonner client, pas professionnel*' ('we have to reason like
customers, not retailers'). This was in response to a self-consciously
clever display that only served to confuse customers and impair their
judgement. The sector manager then went on to remind his team that
the company philosophy regarding customers states: '*Le client doit
garder le libre arbitre*' ('The customer must have freedom of choice').

This respect for the customer is reflected in another Carrefour
peculiarity, the inverted organizational pyramid. This is a vivid, if
somewhat gimmicky, image whereby the customer is on top and the
top brass at the bottom. Not everyone was convinced about the reality
or desirability of this claim. Some sceptics criticized its feasibility:

'*Une pyramide à l'envers ça se casse la gueule*' ('An inverted pyramid is bound to topple'). Others, at section level, failed to carry the logic through and had their own (sector level) pyramids 'the right way up'. But irrespective of these drawbacks, it is a symbolic statement and provides a visual reminder of customer supremacy:

> *C'est lui qui paie les salaires, lui qui permet*
> *d'investir, lui qui paie les dividendes aux*
> *actionnaires.* (It is they who pay our salaries, they
> who allow us to expand, they who keep our share-
> holders satisfied.)

The inverted pyramid also helps to promote the check-out personnel as those in the front line. They are in constant contact with the customer and provide the first and critical link in the feedback process – prime communicators of customer needs. What is more, the inverted pyramid serves to reiterate the central tenet of decentralized responsibility by emphasizing the way in which the success of the group depends upon its lower level personnel.

Of course contact with the customer is not the sole prerogative of check-out personnel. Even the store manager eats in the same canteen as the customers. This enables him to see things from the customers' perspective and to eavesdrop on their conversations. The very nature of the work brings the managers into constant contact with the customer and there is an immediate response to new initiatives. Because of this immediacy, action was valued. There was little point doing two years' research, when a makeshift improvement could be implemented straight away and fine tuned according to customer reaction.

As mentioned earlier, there is tangible evidence of the commitment to the customer. Respect for the customer's freedom of choice translates into wide aisles to ease circulation around the store, objective information round the store and an absence of pressure to buy at the check-out. Further evidence of customer orientation can be seen in the shift away from the original 'move more merchandise' conception towards a more qualitative approach. The customer is no longer offered 'rock bottom prices', but a wider choice of goods instead. This reflects Carrefour's move away from consumerism and towards what the company labels 'humanism'. Customers are actively involved in the selection of products through in-store questionnaires and 'round tables' in which they offer constructive criticism.

The image of Carrefour as the leading innovator in French retailing is one of which the company is understandably proud, and the group has taken steps to preserve this reputation. As TV advertising by retailers is prohibited in France, Carrefour has had recourse to less traditional methods, notably the monthly '*Carrefour Journal*' produced individually for each of its stores (once again confirming commitment to decentralization). This eight-page news sheet, which accounts for 20 per cent of the group's advertising expenditure, is delivered free to nearly a million households.

But there are other means of getting round the advertising bar. One way is to get reported on in the media – rather in the same way that betting shops in the UK will take advantage of free editorial to get round advertising restrictions[1]. In this respect, the launch of the *produits libres* range of generic products in 1976 proved an important publicity and marketing coup for the company.

But Carrefour is not averse to grabbing media attention in more notorious ways. In 1979, Carrefour first tangled with the thorny issue of the legality of comparative advertising when the group launched an 'economic indicator' to reinforce the discount element of the Carrefour operation. The comparative advertising campaign encroached upon a grey area of the law, and prompted a series of law suits from furious competitors. The campaign is thought to have cost the company four million francs in legal fees, but made a lasting impact on customers: '*Ça a fait parler de nous*' ('it got people talking about us').

At a local level the emulation can take many forms. One interesting initiative was that of a store manager who managed to gain prime-time (national news) TV exposure and newspaper coverage (see Figure 8.1) by introducing condom dispensers into his store. This shrewd manoeuvre was justified on the grounds of responding to the AIDS scare. But the introduction of these vending machines was calculated to cause a stir in Catholic France, where the subject remains taboo: '*on gesticule pendant 20 minutes*' ('people gesticulate for 20 minutes') before daring to buy the offending item. This initiative demonstrated the store manager's presence of mind and his eye for a coup, but also confirmed his independence since he did not have to seek Head Office clearance (even on potentially damaging publicity) before inviting the film crews to his store.

Other off-beat examples include a store manager who succeeded in getting the Carrefour logo displayed on all the street maps in the locality by offering to pay for their printing. Another store manager employed what can only be described as 'preventive advertising' in his fight against local rivals. Following a decision to try to attract more occasional customers, signposts were put up to syphon off traffic from the nearby motorway. However, the route signalled was neither the shortest nor the quickest – it was simply the least competitive!

All this suggests that there is little love lost among retailers. Partly this is due to the transparency of any new initiative. Competitors have easy access (as customers) to the store and are free to steal any

---

1 For example, William Hill betting shops gained world-wide media coverage (which they could not buy) by offering odds on who shot JR, on the name of the Royal Baby, and more recently on Chris Bonnington's chances of finding the Yeti.

(a) Préservatifs dans les hypers: Carrefour tire le premier

Il fallait s'y attendre. La vente des préservatifs dans les grandes surfaces va commencer. C'est le magasin Carrefour d'Ivry, en banlieue parisienne, qui annonce le premier ses intentions en la matière. Dès samedi prochain, il mettra à la disposition de sa clientèle un distributeur automatique de préservatifs installé dans le rayon parfumerie-hygiène. La boîte de 6 sera vendue 10 francs. Un petit prix aux grandes conséquences.

(b) Préservatifs en libre service

Les hypers continuent leur offensive sur les produits de santé. Mammouth adopte la méthode douce: le référendum à propos des préservatifs. Le super-marché qui d'habitude écrase les prix pose à ses clients – par voix de presse et téléphone – quatre questions: pensez-vous que les préservatifs soient encore un sujet tabou? Parmi les réticences à l'achat, quelles sont, de votre point de vue, les plus importantes? Une manière de tester les réactions de ses clients avant de lancer la vente des capotes en libre service.

Le magasin Carrefour d'Ivry-sur-Seine est plus « hard » : depuis vendredi, un distributeur automatique permet à ses clients de mettre une boîte de préservatifs dans leur caddy. En toute discrétion. Une simple pièce de 10 francs et la boîte (de six) est à vous. Pratique, rapide et discret: il n'y a pas à présenter l'article à la caisse.

Dès le mois prochain, deux cents autres machines devraient être installées. Délicate attention: sur le distributeur automatique, on peut lire: « *L'hygiène et la protection sont une preuve d'amour.* »

(c) *Les préservatifs ne se cachent plus*

OBJECTIF: FAIRE « CAPOTER » LE SIDA

Une première en région parisienne... Depuis hier, le magasin Carrefour d'Ivry (94) met à la disposition de ses clients des distributeurs de préservatifs.

Ça ressemble à un distributeur de confiseries... Mais rien à voir ! Deux distributeurs de préservatifs ont été installés, hier après-midi, dans le magasin Carrefour d'Ivry. Le premier a été installé dans les toilettes publiques et le second – c'est plus original – en plein milieu du rayon forme et santé où cohabitent savons, shampooings et produits de beauté.

Ce nouveau produit répond au nom de « Prépharma ». Il vous suffit de glisser une pièce de dix francs dans la machine pour faire l'acquisition d'une boîte de six préservatifs. « Ce produit, déjà proposé chez nous en libre-service, explique un des responsables du magasin, ne l'était pas encore en distributeur. Ces machines offrent des garanties d'anonymat aux consommateurs et respectent leur pudeur. »

Les clients, certes un peu surpris par l'intrusion de ces distributeurs, n'ont pas manifesté de façon intempestive.

En revanche, une bande dessinée, diffusée dans l'Ile-et-Vilaine, le Val-d'Oise et le Bas-Rhin, dans le cadre d'une campagne d'information sur les maladies sexuellement transmissibles, a provoqué la colère des parents et des associations. Intitulée « le Dernier des tabous », cette brochure, éditée à trente mille exemplaires, a été jugée tour à tour « trop crue », « choquante », « antireligieuse ».

Face à cette levée de boucliers, la Direction générale de la santé a demandé aux préfets de suspendre la distribution de cette B.D. litigieuse qui n'avait pas reçu l'aval du ministère de la Santé.

Rémy HIVROZ

Figure 8.1 Publicity surrounding the introduction of condom vending machines at Carrefour; (a) *Le Matin de Paris*, 20 February 1987; (b) *Le Journal du Dimanche*, 22 February 1987; (c) *Le Parisien Libéré*, 21 February 1987.

distinctive advantages since these cannot be patented. As a result of this visibility, *espionnage* is difficult to counter which means that the best (only?) form of defence is attack.

This can take two forms: first, store managers will encourage their staff to display the same sort of curiosity as the Japanese when they visit competitors in order to cull ideas. And secondly, the company must constantly innovate – a real task of Sisyphus, given that nothing escapes copy. But Denis Defforey, the PDG (CEO), takes this philosophically and points out, 'It is always good to be imitated, because when one of your competitors imitates you, he does not innovate' (*LSA* No. 666, 1978). So the company retains its competitive edge.

In spite of the company's reputation for innovation, retailing continues to suffer from long-standing French antipathy towards commerce ('*ce sont des vendeurs de sardine*' – 'they are sardine sellers', is the traditional graduate line). Nor is the notion of service especially well developed in France. As the Head of Carrefour France puts it, '*l'idée de donner du service à d'autres n'est pas toujours très bien perçue*' ('the idea of serving others is not very highly thought of'). Consequently, the company finds it difficult to attract the high fliers from the *grandes écoles*, including business school graduates whose training should find an ideal outlet in the retail sector.

Quite apart from these image problems, the company (like retailing as a whole) makes hefty demands of its personnel which tend to deter prospective candidates. The job has to be learnt out in the field doing menial tasks and in stressful contact with the customer. The initial status of *stagiaire* is off-putting for graduates who know they are passing up the chance to be named *cadre* immediately elsewhere. Managers are subjected to long hours (*corvéable et taillable à merci* – constantly on call) and geographical mobility is an essential requirement. Managers can turn down a posting once but not twice.

What is worse, young graduates will be accountable to *une hiérarchie autodidacte* (a hierarchy of self-taught managers) which may jealously guard its privileges and is liable to show hostility towards their qualifications. One Carrefour manager admitted that this was the case in certain groups and alluded to a competitor, Casino, which (in an official brochure) allegedly requested of its personnel, '*Ne pas bloquer les gens plus intelligents que vous*' ('Do not impede those more intelligent than yourself'). However, the manager in question was adamant that no one was held back at Carrefour, '*On ne met pas de bâtons dans les roues ici*' ('We don't trip people up here').

One thing students know is that their qualification will count for little once admitted. The company they are entering has a reputation for self-made individuals – in keeping with the background of its founders. Qualifications will not procure the same sort of steady progress which it might in more traditional firms – *chacun doit faire ses preuves* (individuals must prove their worth).

It is perhaps understandable that grande école graduates who have exposed themselves to risk and won are loathe to do so again when they are guaranteed more comfortable posts elsewhere. Deprived of this source of talent, Carrefour tends to look towards the Instituts Universitaires de Technologie (IUT) as its favourite hunting ground. These IUT offer two-year vocational courses in both technical and commercial subjects (see Chapter 3) and turn out students who are well equipped for careers in retailing, and who do not suffer from delusions of grandeur (or as one store manager put it, 'C'est nous les plus beaux, c'est nous les meilleurs' – 'We're the fairest, we're the best').

However, retailing seems to be gaining its lettres de noblesse. Certainly Carrefour has started to attract talent from the more prestigious establishments. Partly this is on account of a change in retailing. As one cadre put it, 'Le métier s'enrichit' ('The profession is developing') and hypermarkets are now firmly implanted in French society. But it is also a product of the change in student attitudes. Spurred on by the exploits of entrepreneurs like Francis Bouygues and Bernard Tapie, they are prepared to forgo immediate responsibility for greater medium-term responsibilities. They have come to realize that the possibilities are more varied, the rungs fewer and the chances of promotion enhanced – for anyone willing to make the effort.

In fact, it is an essential part of the career folklore at Carrefour that anyone can make it. Of course, the company has changed since the days of unbridled expansion in the early 1970s:

> 'C'était l'époque des armées de Bonaparte: entré
> comme employé chez Carrefour, vous dirigiez un
> magasin quelques années plus tard.' ('At the time,
> it was like Napoleon's army: you came in at a junior
> level and you'd be in charge of a store a few years
> later.')

Although meteoric rises are less abundant, the company is still keen to highlight them (see Figure 8.2). The company newspaper, for instance, focuses on a number of store managers in their mid-thirties who have nothing more than a bac to their name – people who might have reached their bâton de maréchal long ago in other companies.[1]

The company ethos remains imbued with that go-getting spirit. As one store manager put it:

> 'Chez Carrefour, l'ambition n'est pas une tare. Au
> contraire, si on fait ses preuves, tout est ouvert,

---

1 Though for all its meritocracy, the company has a misogynous reputation with only two of the seventy-odd store managers being women.

L'avenir

Chez Carrefour, on peut progresser.

Bon nombre de directeurs régionaux et de directeurs de magasins sont entrés dans la société dix ou quinze ans plus tôt comme employés ou stagiaires.

Trois examples le prouvent:

■ **Philippe Jarry,** 36 ans. – 1972: entré en qualité de stagiaire aux Comptoirs Modernes, y passe huit ans pendant lesquels il sera adjoint au directeur, puis directeur de trois magasins successifs.

– 1980: débute chez Carrefour, à Nantes, comme chef de secteur épicerie.

– 1982: Nantes toujours, mais chef du secteur produits frais.

– 1984: nommé directeur du magasin de Rennes.

● Diplôme: baccalauréat. Passe ensuite deux années à Paris-Dauphine pour apprendre « la gestion d'une entreprise ».

■ **Marc Devaux,** 37 ans. – 1971: débute à Carrefour Villiers-en-Bière, en tant que stagiaire au rayon disques, livres et papeterie.

– 1974: devient chef de rayon ménage, maison et vaisselle, puis chef des secteurs bazar et textile, à VIlliers toujours.

– 1975: muté, sur sa demande à Dijon, où il est chef de secteur non alimentaires.

– 1977: directeur adjoint à Carrefour Portet.

– 1979: directeur du magasin de Pau.

– 1982: inaugure le centre commercial de Labège (Toulouse).

– 1983: passe à la direction exécutive, au service de la direction des relations sociales, où il assure les fonctions de directeur de la formation Carrefour France. Est nommé en 1986, directeur du magasin d'Ecully.

● Diplôme: brevet supérieur d'études commerciales.

■ **Noël Almagiacchi,** 36 ans.

1969: entre à Sainte-Geneviève-des-Bois en qualité d'employé libre service, secteur bazar.

1971-72: service militaire.

1973: retrouve le magasin de Sainte-Geneviève où il devient gestionnaire de stock.

1974: nommé responsable de rayon.

1975: muté à Villiers-en-Bière. Est successivement chef du rayon matériaux, librairie-papeterie et quincaillerie et responsable, pendant 3 ans, de la formation progressive.

1981: passe chef de secteur, au bazar puis au produits frais, à Villiers toujours. Egalement chef de file du bazar.

1985: directeur de Carrefour Moulins.

Figure 8.2 Pen-portraits of Carrefour career successes. (Extract from the company publication *Notre Entreprise – Carrefour* (Bilan economique et social 85), p. 9.)

> sans aucune restriction.' ('At Carrefour, ambition is
> nothing to be ashamed of. On the contrary, if you
> prove your worth, all doors are opened, without
> exception.')

The implication is, of course, that overt ambition is perhaps frowned upon in more traditional French companies.

Further evidence of this work ethos is the attachment to long hours. These are inherent to retailing but the trend is taken to extremes at Carrefour, where un certain snobisme is associated with working longer than colleagues. In terms of the physical stamina required, one store manager took a humorous dig at the underperforming textile department by suggesting the introduction of a perspiration indicator. He was convinced that no one in textiles 'aurait le dos mouillé' ('would have a damp back') at the end of the day. And he threatened them with a short 'work-out' in one of the high-turnover sections.

Given this commitment to work, it comes as no surprise that stress is an occupational hazard. Two senior managers complained of hyperactivity – one told me, 'Je tourne en rond le dimanche – je suis insupportable' ('I don't know what to do with myself on Sundays – I'm unbearable'), while the other confessed that he dare not go home early for fear of irritating his family.

It is a job which elicits involvement but which requires sustained mental and physical effort. The stress factor means that no one has yet retired as a store manager – and few of them reach 50. Another manifestation of this ambition can be seen in the obsession with self-improvement. There is healthy rivalry within the group with each store trying to improve its displays and service in order to climb in relation to sister stores in the Carrefour turnover rankings. In contrast to this, store managers were perfectly willing to show round their counterparts from sister stores – and would conscientiously point out features of interest, allowing their counterparts to record them on a notepad or a miniature dictaphone.

This ambivalent rivalry/co-operation could also be seen at departmental level. Competition is instilled between the sections by the daily printouts of sales figures which pit the performance of each sector against that of corresponding sectors in other Carrefours. As well as keeping a running check on actual performance as against forecasts and previous year's performance, there is a rolling comparison daily with the corresponding day the previous year.

In spite of constant comparisons between the sections and jibes about poor performances, intrastore co-operation was high – one sector which was being refurbished suggested to the electrical appliances sector that it could usefully employ the unwanted chairs to sit customers down while the rather lengthy order was attended to. There was little evidence of back-biting or power feuding. Indeed, interpersonal relations were unusually forthright and informal. *Cadres* were on first name terms, they wore shirt sleeves and ties rather than suits, and used the familiar *tu* form of address. The standardization of the furnishings, too, were also signs of an egalitarian culture – and were in marked contrast to the considerable vertical differentiation evident in French industry as a whole.

By French standards Carrefour is classless – the ubiquitous qualification hierarchy that dominates French manufacturing industry is diluted. Graduates rub shoulders with the *autodidactes* – though it is fair to say that *grande école* graduates are thin on the ground. Social and educational backgrounds appear to have limited impact on promotion chances/expectations. Carrefour's commitment to training and staff relations is another essential feature of corporate policy. The development of personnel in support of the corporate ethic of the Carrefour group: 'Carrefour's future, independence and steady growth are based upon people.'

The personnel policies are in keeping with this respect for the personnel – five weeks' holiday, bonuses for holidays, end of year and attendance, and a share in the profits.

In terms of pay policy, the company is at the forefront of the move to undermine sacrosanct French salary structures. Carrefour salaries have three components related to inflation, company performance and individual performance, for the entire personnel – this is undermining more conventional seniority-based increases, epitomized by the French Railways (Société Nationale des Chemins de Fer – SNCF). In 1987, a proposal that wages should partially depend on merit so incensed French railway workers that a nationwide strike was called.

Considerable effort and resources have been channelled into personnel management, and Carrefour pride themselves upon their staff relations and training programme. The company invariably exceeds the legal requirement, since it regards training as a guarantee for the company's future. In 1987, for example, 4 per cent of the wage bill was spent on training in comparison to the 1.1 per cent legal requirement.

By pioneering French-style hypermarkets, Carrefour has out-Americanized the Americans. The company has taken the retailing techniques championed by Bernard Trujillo in his 3M seminars 30 years ago, and extrapolated the logic. France is now in the unique position of being able to export to the Americans a formula it originally imported from them.

Of course, part of the reason that hypermarkets did not develop in the US was that the American environment was too competitive – hypermarkets would never have got off the ground there. Carrefour itself has found it necessary to opt out of the more developed markets in Europe and focus its attention on less developed markets such as Spain and Latin America – which in fact more resemble the state of French retailing at the time when Carrefour was launched.

Common threads

Whilst the companies described earlier in this chapter are different in many ways, there are some resemblances. These common features function as a *'point de départ'* – on the one hand to generalize about French companies as a collective entity, and on the other to contrast these four internationally successful companies with the majority of other French firms – they will be the exception which proves the rule.

It is also worth pointing out the divergence between Michelin, l'Air Liquide and l'Oréal on the one hand, and Carrefour on the other. It may be argued that Carrefour typifies the new wave of French companies which have a less traditionalist outlook. This contrast mirrors a similar split in the French corporate landscape. We can use the theme of secrecy to exemplify the point.

With the exception of Carrefour, the chosen companies were remarkably coy by British or, even more, American standards. All were very selective in their approach to publicity and shunned Carrefour's 'all publicity is good publicity' maxim. Even l'Oréal, whose outgoing image would suggest easy access, proved very difficult to penetrate. Indeed, at each of the companies visited there were expressions of surprise at our having made it. For instance, the senior manager who vetted a request from one of the authors at l'Oréal speculated that some difficulty must have been encountered in gaining access to French companies *'qui sont assez spéciales dans ce domaine'* ('which are quite peculiar in that department').

There is no reason to believe that the chosen companies were exceptional in this respect and the findings concur with Ehrmann's view of France as 'the country of "counter-publicity"' (1957, 211).[1] Incidental corroboration in the form of newspaper headlines also suggests that it is a common trait among French companies. A recent issue of *Tertiel* (no. 28) whetted readers' appetites with its cover feature, *'Le PDG le plus secret de France'* ('France's most secretive CEO'). And *The Financial Times* (13 January 1988) did likewise with, 'Paul Betts meets Gustave Leven, the publicity-shy chairman of Perrier'. Horovitz also encountered and noted French secrecy (1980, 46) in his study of management control systems in several chosen countries including France.

This secrecy prone attitude was described by the PDG of a small firm as: *'Pour vivre heureux, vivons cachés'* ('To live happily, we must live hidden'). In the French context, this approach makes sense for a number of reasons. First, secrecy protects the company from competitors – this was a particular preoccupation of Michelin's, which refrains from patenting for that very reason.

---

1 Ehrmann quotes Detoeuf on the matter: 'The Frenchman is not a chess player, but a card player; he chooses games where one hides' (1957, 209).

Secrecy has also been part and parcel of the fiscal game (*la contrainte fiscale*) which companies play with the authorities. More recently, the threat of nationalization has provided renewed cause for remaining an unknown quantity for the state.

However, the primary reason for maintaining 'radio silence' has been to do with the general public. Traditional antipathy towards profit-making may be the motive behind the secrecy of these high performance firms. One PDG explained that '*personne n'aime une entreprise qui crache du fric*' ('no one likes a company that spits [sic] money'). So, *pour avoir la paix* (to be left in peace), successful companies have kept themselves to themselves. We can cite the PDG of the large industrial group, Saint-Gobain, who, on the eve of the company's re-privatization (November 1986), addressed his personnel thus:

> *Chaque jour, de nombreux articles de presse*
> *ou émissions nous placent sous leur projecteur; et*
> *nos concitoyens redécouvrent qu'il existe, dans*
> *notre pays, un groupe industriel – le nôtre – qui est*
> *leader mondial ou européen dans la plupart de ses*
> *métiers...* (Each day, we are the focus of attention
> for press articles or TV programmes; awakening the
> French public to the fact that it harbours, in its
> midst, an industrial group – ours – which is a world
> or European leader in most of its fields.)
> (Jean-Louis Beffa, PDG of Saint-Gobain, in a
> publication for Saint-Gobain personnel,
> November 1986.)

This speech perhaps symbolizes the transition in French attitudes. All of a sudden, a company which, according to its PDG, '*est souvent resté à l'écart des médias*' ('has generally stayed out of the limelight'), moves into centre stage. He found himself introducing the group to an eager French public who, until then, were blissfully unaware of its existence.

Only since the entrepreneur has been billed as the saviour of the economy in the 1980s have companies really felt safe to emerge from their shells. The managerial movement has thrown up a host of individuals like Antoine Riboud, Gilbert Trigano, Francis Bouygues or Bernard Tapie whose business empires are in stark contrast to the closet MNCs which have dominated France. These men actually court publicity – Bernard Tapie popularized the enterprise culture with his prime-time television shows and Francis Bouygues has purchased the recently privatized TF1 (France's number one TV channel). Such extravagances do not endear them to everyone. They are criticized in some quarters as self-seeking publicists who use their companies as vehicles for their personal promotion.

Le vedettariat was particularly condemned in the more traditional companies. One *cadre* explained '*Ils passent pour des truands*' ('They are looked upon as outlaws'), since there is something *louche* (fishy) about anyone who 'makes it' without the benefit of inheritance or qualifications. While people like Tapie are admired by younger generations, their elders are sceptical about what Tapie is up to – rapid success in French terms leaves him open to all sorts of accusations of government collusion (in terms of facilitating necessary redundancies in newly acquired companies as well as reciprocal favours with the former Socialist finance minister, Pierre Beregovoy). The view of the businessman as villain dies hard.

As mentioned earlier, another justification for the secrecy of the companies described was that it helped avoid state interference in corporate affairs, and particularly nationalization in 1982. The fact that all four of the companies should actually boast about resisting state advances is a measure of its persuasiveness – and indicative of a qualitatively different state–industry relationship from that found in the UK or the US.

Looking to the state for help does not carry the same negative connotations in France. One need only look at the way Renault's modernist headquarters on the banks of the Seine announces in huge letters that it is *Renault – Régie Nationale* – a nationalized industry. It is unthinkable that the Rover Group or any British state-owned industry would do the same. Nationalization may be a preoccupation but it is not a stigma. To be nationalized in France is to have the full weight of the state behind you. This can prompt role reversal, with the company, not the state, making all the running. As one journalist put it:

> *Au moindre pépin les chefs d'entreprise sont prêts*
> *à se précipiter dans les bras de l'Etat-papa.* (At the
> slightest sign of trouble chiefs are ready to run into
> the arms of Daddy-State.)
> (*L'Express*, 1 March 1985, 30.)

A fairly accurate indicator of whether a company is under state tutelage is the background of its chief executive. It is a feature of nationalized or semi-nationalized companies that their heads are appointed, usually from outside the group, by the government in office. Needless to say this tends to provoke a real game of musical chairs whenever there is a shift in political power. Such instability is in marked contrast to the unruffled continuity of the four companies examined earlier in this chapter.

Three of the four companies were family-owned or managed. There is a strong tradition in France of relatively large groups being dominated by an individual or family – even Carrefour, with its tradition of open competition, includes Bernard Fournier (eldest son of the co-founder

Marcel Fournier) on its board. Apart from the companies investigated, there are the Dassaults in the aeronautical industry; the Triganos with their Club Meditérranée; the Leclercs, the Montlaurs and the Guichard-Perrachons in retailing; the Ricards, the Cointreaus and the Dubreuils in alcohol manufacture; the Peugeot family in the automobile industry; and the Leroy family in the aptly named Groupe Maison Familiale (small house construction). Even the model entrepreneur and building magnate Francis Bouygues has succumbed to the temptation of naming his own son, Martin, as successor.

French companies have traditionally shown a penchant for 'management by chromosome'. But more recently, this has been tempered by judicious business sense. The case of l'Air Liquide is a perfect example – one of the PDG's sons worked for the company but he was passed over in favour of the son-in-law as the successor to the throne. The automatic handing on of the top job like a family heirloom is a thing of the past. Family companies will do their utmost to keep the business from mains étrangères (foreign hands) by exercising greater discrimination in their choice of successor.

The current approach might be termed enlightened nepotism, whereby family companies exploit its positive aspects whilst limiting its drawbacks. The most important benefit is continuity. The heir to the throne is prepared for the top job from an early age. Even before entering the company, the future PDG is impregnated with the corporate values which are often an extension of family values. Consequently, the baton changes hands smoothly.

A smooth transition of power is important to those who have dealings with the company (i.e. customers and suppliers) who will not wish to have to change long-standing arrangements. It is also of particular interest to the personnel, who will wish to avoid an upsetting change of régime. The case of a somewhat smaller (800 employees), provincial, paper-making company provides an interesting illustration of this point. The company was a struggling family concern which decided to appoint an external PDG 20 years ago. He has managed to turn the business into a minor success story – and now, with retirement looming, he has been unexpectedly approached by his management team. They had had dealings with his son who worked in a local company, and proceeded to recommend to the PDG that he take on his own son with a view to succession (the company had gone full circle).

Such is the desire for continuity that non-family businesses may try to manufacture 'surrogate offspring' who can be entrusted with the running of the company. Generally, these individuals will be picked at a tender age and prepared for the role of leadership. At l'Oréal, for instance, the next PDG is known long in advance. He is variously described as fils spirituel (spiritual son), bras droit (right hand), héritier présomptif (heir apparent) or dauphin (crown prince). Such expressions leave the future occupier *du fauteuil du PDG* (of the CEO's chair) in no doubt as to what is expected of him.

Whether in a family business or not, those chosen must dispel the 'divine right' label by proving themselves more worthy than their peers. The argument that this will demotivate senior *cadres* who have 'no shot at the top' is probably overstated since those with such ambitions will steer clear of companies where predestination operates. On the contrary, perhaps, it acts as a political dampener, since the pole position is out of bounds.

Another feature of the leadership in the chosen firms was its longevity: Michelin and Defforey (Carrefour) had been in place since 1959, whilst l'Air Liquide and l'Oréal had recently changed leaders after 'reigns' of over 35 years apiece [1] – though each of the recently deposed leaders continued to exert influence through their presidency of a strategic committee. In such cases, the firms inevitably become synonymous with their heads – thus provoking a certain personality cult. In fact, if Peters and Waterman are to be believed, these corporately historical figures may account for the success of the companies examined:

> Associated with every excellent company was a
> strong leader... who seemed to have a lot to do with
> making the company strong in the first place.
>
> (1982, 26.)

Evidence for the existence of such a personality cult lies in the widespread devotion to work. Working long hours seemed less a feature of the rules or expectations than a part of the culture in which charismatic bosses reign. People would ring each other at 19:00 fully anticipating an anwer. Such anti-social hours tend to militate against the presence of women in the higher reaches of French management – this, even in retailing and cosmetics where one might have expected a moderate feminine presence.

The exceptional longevity of the PDGs in the companies described in the present chapter was mirrored by the personnel who, except at Carrefour, tend to benefit from lifelong employment. This also requires corporate commitment to internal promotion, expenditure on training and a bit of slack in the organizational chart.

The lack of definition in the organizational chart means that responsibilities are 'up for grabs'. This makes internal promotion easier to handle – unfettered by organizational constraints. able

---

1 Again, this is in stark contrast to the companies under state influence, where ten years is considered a good innings. Michel Bauer, a CNRS researcher, makes the surprising claim that of the 200 largest French firms, only 29 per cent of bosses actually entered the firm before the age of 30 – as opposed to 50 per cent in the US and 74 per cent in Japan (*l'Expansion*, 22 October, 130).

individuals will naturally rise to the top. This vagueness is in stark contrast to American organizational charts which pin-point exactly who does what and who is answerable to whom. Part of the lack of precision also stems from the absence of job descriptions in France. In addition to helping internal promotion, the organizational *flou* (vagueness) enables the company to maintain loyal servants in ill-defined posts.

Another feature of the four companies examined was their very definite product identity. Efforts were directed towards one goal – undiluted by diversification. Even Carrefour which might have been tempted to emulate its American counterparts with vertical integration has passed up the chance. As Denis Defforey put it:

> *C'est déjà assez difficile de connaître son metier –*
> *nous devons avant tout éviter de devenir*
> *un conglomérat. Nous nous refusons à*
> *investir dans l'agro-alimentaire: nous savons*
> *très bien que faire de nos magasins des clients*
> *captifs de nos usines et y vendre nos propres*
> *conserves de légumes serait forcément au*
> *detriment de la qualité et de la productivité.*
> (It's difficult enough getting to grips with
> our business – we must at all costs avoid becoming
> a conglomerate. We have deliberately resisted
> investing in agro-nutrition: we are fully
> aware that making our stores into captive customers
> for our factories and selling our own tinned
> vegetables through them would inevitably impinge
> on quality and productivity.)
> (*Le Nouvel Economiste*, No. 333, 1982, 79.)

L'Oréal too, has avoided emulating its large American competitors and diversifying widely. As for Michelin and l'Air Liquide, they remain strongly attached to innovation in their own fields and to new applications of existing products, but do not venture outside what they know. These are firms which, in Peters and Waterman parlance, have resolutely, 'stuck to their knitting' (1982, Chapter 10). Perhaps, the roots of this commitment to a particular product area lie in the influence of strong 'family' management. While not precluding diversification, traditions which stretch back several generations are unlikely to stimulate it. And as Dyas and Thanheiser explain:

> Personal commitment to a particular product area
> can be particularly strong if the industry involved is
> located within a particular region in which the

founding family has associations and
responsibilities.

(1976, 203.)

All four companies have had considerable success abroad – less
common in France than elsewhere because of its tradition of economic
protectionism lasting up to 1958. By virtue of their own records, these
companies could afford to denounce French faint-heartedness abroad.
Two quotes typify this widespread feeling:

> *Le Français répugne profondément à s'expatrier,*
> *c'est-à-dire à aller vivre longtemps à l'étranger. Il*
> *s'habitue aussi mal à la langue qu'aux usages et*
> *aux manières de vivres locales.* (Frenchmen hate to
> expatriate themselves, that is, to go and live abroad
> for a long spell. They can't get used to the language
> any more than they can to the local customs and
> habits.)
>
> (François Dalle, in Priouret, 1968, 113.)

> *Il faut bien connaître ses clients, les voir et les*
> *revoir jusqu'au jour où ils vous invitent chez eux.*
> *Rien à voir avec les Français qui font trois petits*
> *tours et ils s'en vont.* (You have to know your
> (foreign) customers, see them over and over again
> until the day they invite you home. A far cry from the
> French who look around a while and then go home.)
>
> (Edouard de Royère quoted in
> L'Expansion, 1987, 65.)

At Michelin and Carrefour, too, they were scathing about French
impatience when faced with a new market, in contrast to the more
methodical approach of the Japanese or even the West Germans. As a
returning French expatriate put it:

> 'Les Français ont conservé l'esprit "colon": ils ne
> partent à l'étranger que bardés d'assurances, celle
> surtout de faire du fric.' ('The French still have a
> "colonial" mentality: they only go abroad when
> loaded with insurance cover, and not unless they
> are guaranteed a killing.')

Management recruitment is not generalized. Each company tended
to favour particular sources – specific engineering grandes écoles in
the case of Michelin and l'Air Liquide, and Instituts Universitaires de
Technologie for Carrefour. Only l'Oréal was more or less indifferent to

provenance. The graduate market is highly segmented and companies buy talent which matches their standing and their educational tradition – often mirroring the head's own background. One can tell a great deal about a company's relative standing from where it does its fishing. Starting salaries are less of an indication of prestige since career-minded graduates will seek first and foremost a company where they can *faire leurs armes* (gain their wings) and obtain a useful *carte de visite* (track record) for future employers.

Another unifying feature was the so-called *droit à l'erreur* (right to foul up). It may be that this was a product rather than a factor of success. However, if the claim is founded, then it is unusual in a country where, according to one *cadre*, 'un échec vous poursuit' ('a failure follows you') and 'on en tient longtemps compte' ('it is held against you for ages'). It is also worth pointing out that Peters and Waterman regard tolerance of failure (1982, 223) as a central tenet in their recipe for corporate success.

Finally, the companies examined bear the hallmark of Parisian centralization. With the exception of Michelin which remains staunchly provincial, each company had its headquarters in Paris and its production plants in provinces. This may be a legacy from Napoleon who, for reasons of stability, tried to turn Paris into an administrative rather than an industrial city (distancing the workers to take the revolutionary sting out of Paris). This has produced two distinct populations whose preoccupations, ambitions and lifestyles are totally different. In a way, the provinces have become the corporate equivalent of non-league football, where young hopefuls on their way up to first division Paris cross 'has-beens' on their way out.

It is interesting to note that a number of the features highlighted by Peters and Waterman as critical to organizational success actually manifest themselves in the four French companies scrutinized. However, it would be simplistic to assume that the success of these companies stems from their adherence to the Peters and Waterman blueprint. The companies examined also possessed several distinctive traits which were far removed from the informal processes and intuitive aspects preached by those gurus – it is equally plausible to speculate that it was these which were responsible for their international success.

It would be wrong to suggest that the preceding examples are representative of French corporate culture in general. However, they do display a number of distinctive characteristics which have survived in spite of the increasing internationalization of these particular firms. In theory, what goes for these large, successful companies, which have been exposed to the sterilizing influence of international competition, should apply to even greater degree among smaller French companies.

❚Chapter Nine

A sideways look at labour relations

> *Entre un patronat qui passe pour le plus rétrograde de la communauté européene et des syndicats considérés, dans de nombreux pays, comme des suppots de Brejnev, on se demande comment la France a pu, malgré tout, remporter quelques beaux succès industriels.* (On the one hand France is credited with the most reactionary employers in the EEC, and on the other hand, its unions are widely regarded as Brezhnev's lackeys. Under these circumstances, it's a wonder that France has had any industrial successes at all.)
>
> (Anonymous Eurocrat, in Freydet and Pingaud,
> 1982, 399.)

Labour relations have an inevitable impact on managerial attitudes and behaviour. So, for sake of completeness, we will outline the French system and give some examples of it in action. The aim is not to provide an exhaustive account of French industrial relations, which would need another book in itself, but to shed some light on the way they are viewed by management practitioners. We are using primarily the testimonies of three company chiefs from the larger group of managers who were the subjects of our observation study to convey management's main preoccupations in the area of industrial relations. This tactic makes use of first-hand research; it also provides a realistic picture, albeit a partial and idiosyncratic one, of French labour relations.

Scene setting

The French unions are distinctive from an Anglo- Saxon viewpoint in being divided along political, ideological and religious lines. The biggest union is the Communist dominated Confédération Générale du Travail (CGT). Its main rival is the Confédération Française Démocratique du Travail (CFDT formerly had Catholic affiliations), which has socialist sympathies. In third place comes Force Ouvrière (FO), whose more moderate stance seems to be paying dividends in terms of membership in the late 1980s. Of the smaller bodies, the most important is probably the white-collar Confédération Générale des Cadres, which officially launched the term *cadre* as noted in Chapter 2.

Social progress in French industry has been a fairly slow, step-by-step process, with real breakthroughs achieved only after historic conflicts (1936 and the general strike; 1944–1945 – the end of the Nazi occupation, the Second World War, and the inception of the Fourth Republic; and 1968 with *les événements* – the student uprising and worker strikes). One notable example is the belated acknowledgement of the right of shop stewards to do union work in the firm's time, to have their own offices inside factories and to do canvassing or other such work on the premises. These activities had long been commonplace in, for instance, Britain but were only accorded in France after the uprising of May 1968. Part of the reason for the weak position of shop stewards in the French case is that there are other channels of appeal that will be examined at the end of this chapter.

Company 1: Family firm, based in a communist municipality in Paris

A first clue as to the thrust of the chief's industrial relations preoccupations comes from a cursory glance at the bookshelf behind his desk. Two books stand out from the conventional managerial fodder of 'guru' literature. They are *Les finances du PCF* (The Funding of the French Communist Party) and *Les secrets de la banque soviétique en France* (The Secrets of the Soviet Bank in France) – both by Jean Montaldo. The PDG (CEO) in question considered these essential reading, perhaps for the rather convoluted reason that the Soviets fund the French Communist Party, which controls France's main worker union, the Confédération Générale du Travail (CGT), which in turn dictates the actions of local CGT leaders. As this chief puts it, *'Les représentants de la CGT utilisent un langage et suivent des ordres qui n'ont rien à voir avec les intérêts de la maison'* ('The local CGT's rhetoric and the instructions it obeys are far removed from the interests of the company').

A few examples may illustrate the way in which this senior manager's perception of the unions affected his behaviour in practice:

1. He saw conflicts as falling into two categories: political ones, as when the workers rise up out of solidarity for *'leurs copains du Chili'* (their mates from Chile), and 'real conflicts', but even the latter may be motivated by factors other than the financial ones put forward.

2. The sound proofing of this boss's office door and the anti-tapping device on his telephone were both attributed to the 'red threat' – '*pour ne pas faciliter la tâche aux cocos*' ('so as not to make things any easier for the communists').

3. He subscribed to *l'Humanité*, the Communist daily newspaper, to know what might be afoot. He explained that anyone in a '*point chaud*' (i.e. Communist stronghold) must keep abreast of the national policies which sooner or later will manifest themselves at grass-roots level, since the CGT leaves little scope for local initiatives – again because local initiatives are dictated by national policy. He makes the ironic point that if *l'Huma* were to lose its employer readership, the paper would go bankrupt. He also reckons, tongue-in-cheek, that it is a sign of '*bonne conduite*' ('irreproachable behaviour') to be criticized by *l'Huma*.

4. The manager was on the committees of several employers' bodies and saw himself as something of a local spokesman against the union stranglehold over companies. His charisma and readiness to be opinionated ('*de cracher dans les micros*' – 'to talk to the media') made him a favourite with local journalists. Indeed, he regularly contributed a column to a journal generally condemning the antics of the CGT – and making the most of the opportunity to 'have a go' at some of his favourite targets:

> *Demandez aux journalistes de l'Humanité par*
> *example, s'il n'y a pas de patrons à l'Huma !!!*
> *(surtout à ceux qui viennent d'être licenciés pour*
> *raisons économiques!!!).* (Just go and ask the journalists
> at *l'Humanité* if they don't have any bosses!!!
> – especially the victims of the economic layoffs!!!)

5. In a telephone conversation with one of his management colleagues, a head of division, this manager remembers that he has heard that a neighbour's son is looking for a job, and the 'candidate' has the sort of professional skills they happen to be looking for – and what is more, '*il a des idées proches des nôtres*' ('his ideas are akin to ours'). The chief then spells it out, '*c'est un Polack qui ne peu pas sentir les Cosacks – il pourra nous être utile*' ('he's from Polish stock and he can't stand Ruskies – he may be useful to us').

6. This boss actively 'encouraged' *cadres* to join the Confédération Générale des Cadres (management union mentioned in the scene-setting section above) to ensure *cadre* representation among the works stewards (*délégués du personnel*) and on the works council (described at the end of this chapter). If there were no *cadre* candidate on these compulsory commissions, the way would be open for the CGT to name one of its own members instead. As the chief explains, '*j'ai horreur du vide*' ('I hate to see a void').

This chief was clearly hypersensitive to Communist 'plotting'. His McCarthyite reactions, however, are to some extent justified insofar as the municipality in which the plant is located is a Communist stronghold, which meant he could expect few favours from the local mayor. There was a feeling, however, that he devoted a little too much importance to the Communist threat, to the detriment of his other activities. As one *cadre* put it:

> '*Certains patrons voient rouge partout et accordent trop d'ampleur aux syndicats.*' ('Some bosses see reds everywhere and give the unions more attention than they deserve.')

The personnel manager from this same firm confirmed the fact that the CGT had once been a force to be reckoned with, but since around 1979 it had lost its way (both within the firm and at national level). Its membership no longer consisted of skilled French workers, who were to some extent disillusioned by the rhetoric – '*l'analyse simpliste ne leur parle plus vraiment*' ('the simplistic analysis has lost its appeal') – partly because of the changing attitude towards capitalism and because of a greater understanding of economic interdependencies. This was posited as an explanation for the shift within the firm towards the reformist union Force Ouvrière, which like the Confédération Générale des Cadres, showed awareness of the fact that the company had to be in a healthy position in order to get anything out of it.

With its traditional core melting, the Communist-oriented CGT had been reduced to recruiting among the immigrant labour – the company's CGT representatives were a Portuguese and a Tunisian. This has had a profound influence on the 'culture' of the CGT, since its immigrant followers are less influenced by the Communist ideology – they vote for the CGT but tend not to pay their dues! The head of personnel explained that the immigrants were more demanding in their material expectations, and would simply switch allegiances if they were poorly represented on that front.

The changing nature of the demands of the grass-roots supporters, with their lesser commitment to Communist ideology, has led to occasional divergences between national policy and local practice. According to the personnel manager, at national level the CGT had not signed an industry-wide agreement for five years. Yet at company level the local CGT had been forced to put their signature to wage settlements because their new followers would not have tolerated a refusal – which would be construed as misrepresentation rather than sticking to principles. Thus, using the pretext of 'solidarity' with the other unions, or some other face-saving *clause de style vis-à-vis* the outside, the CGT would 'collaborate with capitalism'.

Company 2: Large provincial plant
(mass production, consumer goods)

The problem of paying too much attention to the unions was a contributory factor in the concerns of the plant manager in this company too. He had recently taken over from a man who had been in the job for 19 years and considered himself something of a 'union specialist' – who liked acting tough and revelled in showdowns. This predecessor had helped to fuel a problem which was actually dying. He had exaggerated the disruptive potential of the unions and had set himself up vis-à-vis head office as the only person capable of dealing with them – on the principle of the *pompier pyromane* (pyromaniac fireman). As the new boss explained:

> '*Les syndicats ont l'importance qu'on leur accorde.*'
> ('The unions are as important as you allow them to be').

The new plant manager had been brought in to stop the rot – and his main problem now was how to revalorize the foremen, who had been spectators in the industrial relations process for 19 years. His predecessor had systematically dealt directly with the union delegates – which meant that the foremen '*avaient le cul entre deux chaises*' ('fell between two stools') – they had lost all semblance of authority and often had to ask the union representatives what was going on. This had provoked a loss of morale *(le malaise de la maîtrise*[1]) and a certain indifference among the foremen. As the boss explained, '*ils ne voulaient plus se mouiller*' ('they'd washed their hands of responsibility'). From their point of view, why should they take awkward decisions when these could be reversed if the personnel representative went to see the head of personnel?

The new boss decided that this situation was unacceptable. And in his own tidied up version of events he proceeded to explain how they had reinforced the 'natural' (organizational) hierarchy at the expense of the 'parallel' (union) hierarchy.

The first stage was to give the foremen the desire to manage and to take on responsibility, since '*ils avaient baissé les bras*' ('they had given up'). To do this, he sent everyone (from himself down to the supervisors) on a three-day training course destined to reinforce the 'natural hierarchy'. Over the three days, they explored their hierarchic relations and expectations. They compared, for instance, the qualities they looked for in their immediate superior, with those they felt their

---

1 The foreman's malaise, as illustrated in this particular case study, seems to be a fairly constant feature of French industry. It is probably more justified than the much vaunted malaise of the *cadre* (discussed in Chapter 2) because the foreman does not benefit from the social consideration allotted to the *cadre*.

subordinates expected.

Next, he tried to 'responsabiliser la maîtrise' ('make the foremen more responsible') by letting them award bonuses, organize and manage their teams, so that a worker with a problem would get used to approaching his hierarchic boss rather than the union representative. As he saw it, he was turning them into mini-PDGs. Indeed, he thought he could detect the change of attitude in their language – saying he had actually heard them explaining to the workers about sticking to budgets.

In some cases, these attempts to empower the foremen had backfired. For instance, there had been indiscretions on the part of some foremen regarding the granting of attendance bonuses and the authorization of time off. 'Il y a eu du laisser-aller' ('there was abuse of the system'), which had prompted the chief to clamp down on certain aspects of the system and put them in the hands of the personnel department.

This merely confirmed the boss's belief that a large proportion of the existing maîtrise (foremen) were indelibly marked by the régime they had known previously and might never be able to assume responsibility properly. Another aspect of this manager's conversion strategy was therefore to try to raise the status of the foremen by recruiting from outside – and not just among workers issus du tas (from the rank and file) as had previously been the case. Increasingly they were looking to take on people with a technical baccalauréat or even two years post-baccalauréat education.

However, raising the recruiting standards was not proving easy since foremen continue to suffer from low status in France. The well-qualified technicians they were looking for preferred office jobs 'comme dépanneur d'ordinateur avec voiture de fonction' ('in computer maintenance with a company car') rather than work in dirty, noisy conditions. The plant manager conceded that the shop floor would never have the same prestige as an office job, but he also remarked that a post of foreman now had real responsibility attached to it. As he put it:

> 'Ce n'est plus le marteau et l'enclume.' ('It's not the hammer and anvil anymore').

A final means of diverting power towards the normal chain of command and away from the unions was through enforcing the participative management legislation. For instance, the discussion groups (groupes d'expression) introduced by the Socialist government which came to power in 1981 (since revoked), had been maintained within the plant. The boss saw in them an excellent means of keeping people informed and of allowing them to vent their grievances in an informal setting – thereby outflanking the unions by depriving them of ammunition.

Company 3 : Large provincial plant (FMCG)

Another manifestation of the move towards participative management has been the introduction of quality circles. The plant manager of the cosmetics plant explained how the company had gone along with the trend on the grounds that quality circles made economic and social sense. Unfortunately, the first attempt had floundered, but they were trying to get the circles off the ground again.

This plant manager had decided to hold a seminar together with the entire management group to discuss what had gone wrong the first time and to try to draw lessons for the second generation of circles. He had already listed a number of the lessons from the first abortive attempt and explained them to the authors.

First of all, the launch of the quality circles took place in very different conditions from its subsequent expansion. The launch had identified a favourable group (a small, stable, autonomous unit), with a good team spirit and an enthusiastic 'facilitator'. All the conditions had been united to ensure success – in the hope that this would provide the necessary publicity to encourage subsequent circles. Subsequent attempts had to contend with individuals who were neither convinced of the need for circles nor capable of organizing them.

The pilot group had also benefited from the psychological boost of being under general scrutiny. They were aware that they had been identified as the most likely candidates for success and derived pride from that fact[1]. The boss had regularly referred to them as pioneers – they felt invested with a mission. Under these circumstances, it was hardly surprising that the pilot group made a promising start, but as the plant manager himself conceded, it was insufficient evidence on which to extend the experiment.

It was only when the number of circles increased that the real resistance manifested itself. There were secret objections, for instance, to the fact that the circles upset the traditional flows of information and required managers to surrender information which they considered to be part of their power. This resistance was not confined to the managers – even one group of highly skilled workers had refused to operate the circles. They were involved in the finishing of costly components and were at the summit of the shopfloor hierarchy. Their opposition to the quality circles was on the grounds that it would force them to divulge tricks of the trade to less skilled workers and formalize their methods. A similar phenomenon was noted by Michel Crozier

---

1 There is a close parallel with the First Relay Assembly Test Room in the famous Hawthorne experiments where the flattering attention received by the pilot group was posited as one of the main reasons for its high performance (see Roethlisberger and Dickson, 1939).

(1963) among maintenance men, who declined to give explanations to workers and hid the repair manuals.

Clearly then, the idea of group discussions in the French context was not universally welcomed, and appeared to clash with the prevailing pattern of work relations which tended to be hierarchic and distant. This was particularly the case in the staff functions where open meetings were not the norm – and the personnel seemed inhibited by the informality expected of them. What was more, there was a certain reluctance to adopt methods associated with production – and quality tended to be perceived in terms of product quality, not in a larger sense.

As for the production-related areas, the meetings had proved difficult to hold during working hours and seemed at odds with production imperatives. The plant manager explained how, on the one hand, the production managers are asked to stick to deadlines and cut costs, and on the other, to hold meetings which cost both time and money. What was more, shutting down the production line for two hours for no reason was anathema to the production manager's thinking – as the plant manager explained to the authors, 'If production kick up a fuss about stopping the line for preventive maintenance, you can bet they don't take kindly to stopping it to hold a discussion.'

There was a general view that the circles ran parallel to the normal management processes. This attitude was no doubt encouraged by the fact that efforts by individuals in relation to quality circles were not officially recognized within the appraisal framework. Indeed, this was perhaps the prime reason for the eventual demise of the pilot group. Those involved in the first circle had put in a great deal of personal effort, and when it was not rewarded their enthusiasm understandably flagged.

Once this circle had lost its impetus the whole infrastructure collapsed very quickly. Yet the idea of quality circles retained a great deal of intellectual appeal – hence the determination to relaunch the experiment.

Tying up the threads

The preceding snapshots give a fairly accurate representation of the salient concerns on the French industrial relations scene – certainly through the eyes of a general manager. The ordering of the accounts is no accident – it is intended to reflect the evolution in top management attitudes towards labour relations.

French management was long regarded as the most authoritarian in Europe. But the trauma of May 1968 (euphemistically referred to as 'les événements') sounded the death-knell of the authoritarian attitude to labour relations. The number of old-style, confrontational bosses is dwindling. In the larger firms, at least, most managers today are intelligent enough to swim with the tide, for a variety of motives. Some may feel a genuine concern for their staff's wellbeing. Others have a main eye for profit, and believe that increased worker participation serves to raise productivity and reduce grievances, thus undercutting union influence. Several birds are expeditiously killed with one stone. As the plant manager of company 3 explained with regard to quality circles:

> *'J'y vois un moyen essentiel pour améliorer non seulement l'ambiance mais aussi les résultats économiques.'* ('I consider them a vital means of improving both the work climate and the financial results.')

With these initiatives coming from the employers themselves there seems little incentive for the government to add to the existing consultation structures – which remain fairly rudimentary.

The foundations for worker participation in France were laid just after the War when de Gaulle set up obligatory *comités d'entreprise* (works' councils) for companies with a staff of over fifty. This in fact encouraged many companies to curb their expansion – the so-called 'forty-niners' – so as not to cross what is seen as a fateful threshold.

The membership of these *comités d'entreprise* is chosen by the staff from candidates generally put forward by the unions, and the *comité* has monthly meetings with management. By law, the members of the *comité* should be the first people to be informed of intended company changes, although they no longer have a right of veto (suppressed by the Socialist government, 1981–86). In theory their advice may be sought, but in practice this rarely happens. In terms of actual activities, the *comité's* main function is to supervise welfare and social matters. At a *comité* meeting attended by one of the authors in company 1, the committee first accounted for the spending of its previous year's budget. Then three main activities emerged; these were the organization of presents for Mothers' Day, and for all the children at Christmas, and a subsidized holiday in Austria. And this would seem fairly typical if we are to believe Ardagh, who comments:

> 'All the *comités* do is arrange the Christmas parties' is a jibe one often hears.
>
> (1982, 95.)

All firms with over ten staff also have what are called *délégués du personnel* (works' stewards). This was a post established in 1936 to channel employee grievances about working conditions (safety, hygiene, wage rates, social security, etc.) to the management. In the 1960s, de Gaulle made it clear that these two minor institutions (comités d'entreprise and délégués du personnel) were merely precursors to larger-scale participation – and in 1967, as a step towards it, a law was introduced obliging all firms with a staff of over fifty to distribute to the workforce a small proportion of their profits in the form of shares.

However, de Gaulle's grander plan of participation does not seem to have materialized – little has in fact been added to his framework. And in the later phase, the only real socialist concession to increased participation have been the Auroux laws voted through in 1982. These introduced groupes d'expression (discussion groups) into many companies and extended shop steward (délégués du personnel) power, making this a full-time job. The idea backfired somewhat though, with the union representatives tending to alienate themselves from the workforce, and the groupes d'expression serving as a useful forum for apolitical discussion. Indeed, although the groupes d'expression are no longer obligatory, many companies have kept them running. Therefore, measures intended to reinforce union power have to an extent ended by undermining it.

As regards the unions then, their support has steadily declined since about 1978. A number of causes lie behind this erosion of union power. First, there is the greater sensitivity of top management to personnel matters, and the multiplication of opportunities for giving vent to those concerns. Secondly, there is a greater awareness of economic imperatives. France's recently acquired business culture has filtered through to the general public – workers are better informed on economic matters and have a better grasp of the interdependent factors affecting businesses.

What is more, worker demands are now tempered by the sobering thought of unemployment. The French traditionally set a high moral value on work and French workers are now thinking twice about the implications of striking.

The unions, however, have not really adapted to the new mood. They are staunchly divided along ideological rather than trade lines as in Britain, and the largest union, the Communist-based CGT, remains doctrinally opposed to 'collaboration with capitalism' on the German model. This tends to make effective joint action between the unions virtually impossible – and the rivalries between the unions are often exploited by management. On the other hand, it does mean that French industry is relatively free of the sort of demarcation disputes and workers' closed shops which have plagued British industry, for instance (Lawrence, 1984) – the result of the power and intransigence of the rival craft unions.

❚Chapter Ten

Audit and prospect

> ❚ Animals studied by Americans rush about frantically,
> with an incredible display of hustle and pep, and at
> last achieve the desired result by chance. Animals
> observed by Germans sit still and think, and at last
> evolve the solution out of their inner consciousness.
> (Bertrand Russell, *Philosophy*, 1927.)

Our aim in this last chapter is to draw some sort of evaluative summary
of the distinctive features of French management. This exercise will of
course reflect on personal as well as cultural biases, and readers may
like to keep this in mind. We will roughly speaking retrace the layout
of the book, and also look for hints as to what Britain can profitably
learn from French management.

Distinctive features

French managers have an obvious advantage over their Anglo-Saxon
counterparts in that they wear a legally recognized badge, that of *cadre*.
Managerial status in France is not something that is handed out indis-
criminately, and the word manager has no unflattering associations
with, say, bar managers or floor managers, as in Britain. In France
cadre status is generally acquired with some difficulty and it bestows
social as well as a professional consideration on its incumbent.

The social standing of *cadres* probably helps to account for the quality
of candidates which firms are able to attract – and a virtuous circle is
established with the calibre of these recruits further enhancing the
prestige of managerial careers. The only way to gain immediate *cadre*
status is to graduate from one of the country's leading *grandes écoles*.
This endorses the strong·belief in the value of education and the use of
qualifications for entry and promotion.

Firms generally deny that qualifications hold any water after initial entry;
the reality is that the senior positions in French management are heavily
dominated by graduates of the *grandes écoles* – even though the *grandes
écoles* account for only about 5 per cent of the population in higher education.

The *grandes écoles* are believed to have contributed a great deal to the growth of the French economy in the post-war period. They have ensured that people of the highest quality enter the civil service, business and government. Equally important, the products of the *grandes écoles* are highly mobile between these three sectors. This creates a powerful élite and old-boy network, which some find objectionable. Yet every society has such groupings; at least this one has the advantage that business, government and civil service share the same values and knowledge of each other's problems – something which facilitates cross-sector mobility and dialogue, at least among the higher echelons.

This qualitatively different relationship between industry and government was highlighted in Chapter 1. We have not since then repeatedly hammered the point home, since this is a book about management rather than industry. Yet the French difference is significant in several ways. It allows an exchange of personnel, particularly from civil service to industry, a phenomenon rare in Britain and the USA. This facilitated planning, when industry needed not only to be included in the dialogue but, especially in the earlier post-war days, to think about France as well as the balance sheet. The relationship has also facilitated some of France's particular achievements, a number of which were outlined in Chapter 1, including achievements in aeronautics, space and telecommunications. Finally, an awareness of this feature of French life has a heuristic value: it helps us to understand what French management is like.

This last point should not be exaggerated. It will be clear from the earlier discussion of, for example, l'Air Liquide and Michelin that privately owned industry may exhibit a distinctive identity and purpose, that France is not in this sense a seamless garment. Yet the threshold between government and industry is generally lower than in, say, Britain, the USA or Germany; there is not the sharp contrast in milieu and *modus operandi* that one is conditioned to expect. Indeed, the simplest answer to the question, what is industrial management in France like, is to say it is actually quite like the civil service. It is not an accident that Henri Fayol called management *'l'administration industrielle'* (1916).

This is in marked contrast to the situation in the UK, where the isolation of the three sectors (civil service, business and government) typically continues in training, experience and career paths. What is more, the type of education imparted in the French *grandes écoles* (with its emphasis on applied science, mathematics and engineering or on commercial subjects) is broadly relevant to the subsequent careers of the French élites, especially those entering management – unlike British educational high-flyers, who have tended to be trained in the classics and other humanities subjects and therefore have a weaker grasp of the underlying needs of an industrial society. It is hardly surprising that once selected for top civil service posts, British civil servants rarely move into industry.

Of course, the reliance on the *grandes écoles* as nurseries for would-be leaders raises questions about the rather premature and irreversible nature of managerial selection and the disillusionment it produces among those cast aside. But the system has concomitant advantages – not least the fact that it pumps a high proportion of the best brains from each generation into the most productive areas of the French economy. There is a close and long-standing relationship between education and business in France. When national deficiencies have been identified it has generally been left to the education system to provide a remedy. The tradition of specialist schools is a perfect example – Polytechnique was set up in the 1790s to train engineers for the armed forces; l'ENA was founded in 1945 to turn out high-level administrators, and most recently l'Ecole Nationale de l'Exportation was created by the Socialist government (1981–86) in response to a balance of trade deficit. There was even talk, at the time of the 'American challenge' (J-J. Servan-Schreiber) and France's alleged managerial lag, of setting up a business version of l'ENA. However, the idea was shelved and a co-ordinating body, the Fondation Nationale pour l'Enseignement de la Gestion des Entreprises (FNEGE), was set up instead.

Another virtue of the system is that it allows youngish men with modern ideas to reach positions of influence without dissipating a lot of useless energy in political gamesmanship. The *grande école* graduate is virtually guaranteed an illustrious career and can therefore concentrate on actually doing a good job without having to devote inordinate time to self-publicity. *Grande école* graduates form a very distinct élite and are very conscious of the fact, self-confident and intellectual in outlook.

If we turn to the nature of French work relations we note that they tend to be fairly structured and formalistic. French employees seem to shy away from the sort of workplace familiarity in which Anglo-Saxons indulge. The French do not appear to share the belief that openness in professional relations makes sound business sense.

From an Anglo-Saxon standpoint, the deliberate restraint and rigmarole of French office life would make it quite unbearable. However, in the French mind this lesser investment of the 'self' is considered a means of preserving personal choice and independence – which are perceived as higher order needs than the desire for enriched social contact.

The French believe that friendship obliges, provides a lever for favours, exposes the 'friend' to manipulation, and makes him or her dependent. In other words, they regard informality in the workplace as something of a Trojan horse – outwardly appealing but inherently dangerous.

It is noticeable in France that those companies which do try to impose a more informal style of work relations are often unpopular. There is a widespread belief that cordial relations merely serve as a means of extracting commitment from employees and of encouraging a certain freedom of expression which facilitates decision-making –

in other words, as a manipulative device which gives an illusion of freedom while actually reducing it.

In order to get round this perceived dependence and manipulation, the French have therefore concocted a system of authority relations, based on ritual, which minimizes the personality input, the need for personal interaction.

Rituals include such things as the form of address, use of first names and so forth. The rituals are a means of situating the participants and defining their respective roles, thereby leaving them in no doubt as to which one has the upper hand. These rituals serve to diffuse potential tension since they clearly identify the authority of each party – thereby reducing the need for political manoeuvring or personal involvement. As a result of the preliminary ritualistic power play (exchange of correspondence, business cards and greeting), the participants know exactly where they stand. In other words, the authority of each party stems from their position (as projected by assorted rituals) rather than from their personalities. Authority in France is vested in the role – it does not emanate from the individual.

Clearly, these rituals are more than the trivial concerns for which they are often mistaken. Beneath their apparent banality they reflect and reinforce essential traits of French management – notably its hierarchic and élitist traditions.

In terms of managerial values, the French seem torn between their respect for traditional values and an infatuation with the more modern American ones. On the one hand, the social and cultural norms of the pre-industrialized order seem to have had a pronounced effect on the development of business attitudes – and colour French views of money, authority, mobility and so on. On the other hand, the American managerial ethos based on openness, pragmatism and results is also having an impact on French attitudes now.

This state of tension between past and future is perhaps best illustrated by the contrasting attitudes of French corporate leaders. At one extreme there is the older style of family management, usually authoritarian, wary of expansion and innovation; and at the other there is the 'new wave' of dynamic young entrepreneurs, symbolized by Bernard Tapie, more or less self-made men who, without any élite training, have built up small firms to achieve spectacular results.

When it comes to big business, though, the majority of heads of companies are products of the *grandes écoles* and are parachuted into firms. French companies rely to a large extent on individuals who are alien to the firm, and sometimes even to the private sector. This goes against traditions in the UK, US and especially Japan which all tend to favour established insiders. There are signs, however, that France may be something of a trend-setter in this area. Richard Vancil, a professor at the Harvard Business School, recently published a book about succession at the top called *Passing the Baton* in which he says that in the late 1960s fewer than 10 per cent of American chief executives were outsiders. By the early 1980s the figure was 25 per cent.

One good reason for preferring an outsider to an insider is that when a company needs to make big changes, outsiders are freer to deliver the necessary shocks. Insiders are too often constrained by favours owed to others who have helped them on the way up.

It is customary in Britain to oppose public and private companies. What is noticeable in the French set-up is that this traditional distinction between public and private sector is less clear-cut. Partly, this is the result of the common backgrounds of the heads. In France, a large number of private companies are run by former senior civil servants, two notable examples being the Peugeot-Citroën Group and Moët-Hennessy. This blurring of categories probably helps to account for the ease with which the likes of Péchiney, Rhône-Poulenc and Saint-Gobain have made the transition from the private to nationalized sector and back again.

It might be said that French companies have confided the task of identifying and training its future leaders to the state. This demonstrates a qualitatively different relationship between state and industry from that found in Britain or the USA. Another manifestation of the positive (though perhaps overbearing) influence of the state on business is the legal obligation to spend one per cent of the payroll on training.

Coherent whole

The distinctive features alluded to so far, taken in isolation, appear contrary to received (and mostly American) wisdom regarding sound management practice. For instance, we might consider that French management is too stratified, that qualifications are accorded too much importance, that interpersonal relations are too remote, that corporate mentalities are archaic .... All these remarks are partly justified. However, we should not forget to look at the whole picture.

To take an obvious example, it would be easy to criticize the education system for its rigidity and rather narrow focus. Yet the education system produces what it is asked to produce. It is geared to suit the exigencies of the companies, which seek help in the preselection of an élite of potential top executives. This allows careers to be mapped out at the recruitment stage, based on qualifications. What is expected of the education system is not that it impart particular skills, but simply that it classify students via entry and finalist examinations. Certificates guarantee a career and the most prestigious guarantee the best careers. If the companies decided to recruit and promote, not on qualifications, but on efficiency in the field, creativity and teamwork, the education system would try to develop these qualities. As it is, those qualities are more or less assumed in the French case to be the natural corollaries of high intellect.

What is true for the French education system also applies to the economic system, to career and salary structures, to organizational relations and to the corporate cultures of French companies. They are all attuned to one another. The jigsaw pieces may have wierd configurations but they still interlock and are generally consistent with the industrial needs of the nation.

So, whatever the perceived merits or shortcomings of French management it cannot be isolated from the society that spawned it – compatibility is probably more important than adherence to an ideal in determining national success. The acid test is, does it work, and the evidence – not least France's economic performance since the war – suggests that it does.

Brilliance and its limitations

In discussing the interconnectedness of French management there is a natural emphasis on the role of the *grandes écoles*, which leads on to considerations of contacts, career and exclusiveness. At the same time one should not shy away from defining French management in terms of its dominant quality – brain-power. French management is quite simply marked by a high level of educated cleverness. While in other countries one calculates in terms of the number and proportion of managers who are university graduates, in France most senior managers are the doubly-tested, super graduates of the *grandes écoles*. It is also worth remembering that the educational 'also-rans' of French management, bluntly designated as *autodidactes* or self-taught, are also somewhat different from their titular colleagues in other countries. In, for example, Britain or Germany, Sweden or Israel, this self-taught label designates managers who left school at the statutory school leaving age, without formal educational qualifications of any kind. But the presumptive majority of the French *autodidactes* have been educated to *baccalauréat* standard, equating with high-school graduation in the USA, or 'A' level GCE/university entrance in Britain. If this is the calibre of the self-taught, what of the formally educated!

This French sense of formal intelligence and educated cleverness is manifest in a variety of ways. It shows in the higher numeracy of French management, and in the numerate dimension of strategy formulation. It shows in the *esprit de planification*, in the readiness to systematize and doggedly to correct. It shows in the quality of executive prose, in the treatment of written communication as an end as well as a means, in a penchant for formulation and a capacity for inference. And it shows, of course, in technical virtuosity and a talent for conceptual design.

All this and more has been documented in earlier chapters, yet we are concerned to raise another question. Granted that French management is clever, and it shows, is there a downside?

Aspects of management

The question cannot be answered directly, only apprehended obliquely. And the starting point is that a lot of different processes, underpinned by different personal qualities, are all a part of that thing we call management. But let us be selective.

Management is invariably defined in terms of getting things done with or through people. Now this does not only refer to a rational and purposive deployment of human resources; it also means getting close to people, listening, talking to them, helping to solve at least their operational problems, maintaining their interest and commitment.

Management is not only about strategy, policy and decisions: it is also about implementation. And there seem to be few rules for successful implementation! It is a matter of judgement, experience, intuition. It is variable, it may be opportunistic, having 'been there before' helps but it is not all of the answer.

Management is not only about the orderly pursuit of objectives, but about fire-fighting, about what to do when things are not going according to plan, about solving operational problems, getting by somehow, about improvization, breaking the law or at least the rules and getting away with it.

If these people – implementation – improvisation ideas suggest a focus on middle management and its preoccupations then consider that overriding demand at the top – for leadership. It has many facets: style, brains and credentials matter – indeed they are trump cards. Yet there is also the legitimation of achievement as distinct from career progress, personal dynamism and its manifestations, and the embodiment of certain values, business and human.

Now our evaluation here can be no more than oblique. It is that none of these qualities or dispositions is particularly related to, or significantly underpinned by, that classic French strength of formal cleverness. And what we know about French work relations, the French conception of authority and a certain individuality suggest that a French response to these exigencies will differ from that of managers in Anglo-Saxon cultures.

Universal versus culture-bound: some thoughts

There are both universalist and particularist (culture-bound) views of management. The (universalist) idea that management tends to submerge cultural differences is one which is particularly dear to the Americans with their enthusiasm to convert people and organizations to an ideal model. There are signs, however, that the French do not cherish conformity in the way the Americans do. Lawrence Wylie makes an acute observation in this connection:

> When I was looking for an average French village
> to study, I had to use the expression *'un village
> témoin'*. Everyone would react with hostility to being
> called 'average'. Whereas, in America, one sees towns
> that advertise themselves as being 'All-American'.
>
> (in Santoni, 1981, 61)

As a variation on this theme it was noted that French *cadres* are relatively immobile. While this is often explained in terms of provincial loyalties and regional patriotism, it is also partly because these French managers do not like to think of themselves as interchangeable in the way American managers are prepared to do, since it evokes facelessness, a lack of individuality.

Such fundamental differences in attitude raise serious doubts about the transferability of American management practices. This is not to say that those concepts are irrelevant, but nor are they automatically applicable to other cultures. The image which emerges is of several parallel tracks, rather than a single track with certain obligatory stops. To take an obvious example, the legitimization of wealth creation and the pro-business cult seems to be a widespread phenomenon in Western cultures in the 1980s, just as consumerism was in the 1960s. But that does not mean that each culture has reacted to it in the same way. In France, for instance, the rehabilitation of profit seems to have taken place at an abstract level, but remains taboo at a personal level. It is doubtful that French culture will ever replicate American candour in the matter.

The universalistic theory derives its strength from the assumption that people will react to the same kinds of challenge in the same way. Yet the foregoing chapters show that this does not seem to be the case in France. For instance, although the French adopted American-style management education in the late 1950s, they did not replicate American business schools. The American model did not generate clones, but grafted itself upon the existing infrastructure of *grandes écoles*, – thus preserving the essential characteristics of French higher education. In other words, the expected democratizing influence of management education was countered by the élitist tradition of the *grandes écoles* – although the curricula (in substance) changed, the character of French management education (in form) did not.

This is inevitably the case. American management practices are not filling a void – they are competing against long-standing practices. Management is certainly a source of change, but it is injected into an existing model whose broad outlines remain unchanged.

Universalists have inherited a view of management as having a kind of pure logic which will eventually erode all the negative (cultural) forces which stand in its way. As Sorge and Warner point out (1986, 10), this idea of international convergence makes sense only as long as one is prepared to accept that industrialism *is* a homogeneous base, and that it is different in this from hunting, gathering, agriculture, herding or trading and transport. These activities also possess the magic ingredient of inherent logic – for instance, speed and safety in the case of transport, or yields and consistency for agriculture. That has not prevented them from evolving in different ways, even in ostensibly similar environments. Maurice *et al.* (1986, 257) make a similar analogy with regard to systems of production, claiming that there is no one best way to organize the construction of an automobile or a typewriter.

The most sensible stance on the debate between universal and culture-bound (particularist) theories is of course an intermediary one. Again Sorge and Warner provide a neat summary of the position:

> The conclusion is that system organization is never
> culture-free. If it were, it would be a natural pheno-
> menon, which it is not. On the other hand, it would be
> wrong to propose a totally constructivist model of
> action, in which man can do more or less anything,
> and any organizational arrangement is possible.
>
> (1986, 19.)

Restatement

Any audit of another nation's management is inevitably loaded with the cultural preconceptions of those passing judgement. But awareness of this bias is half of the battle in overcoming it.

While certain parts of the French managerial model may seem archaic or idiosyncratic, the overall effect is one of coherence – the contradictions are complementary. This is reminiscent of the way we dismiss species in nature as parasitic or even repulsive while they serve to maintain the ecological equilibrium. Again, this view is the result of looking at elements out of context and according to myopic perceptions of what is useful, aesthetic and so forth. The aspects of French management cannot be divorced from the society in which they thrive.

Some criticism of French management has been based on the American presumption of universality. Yet one may respond using the French saying 'ne prends pas ton cas pour une généralité' ('don't project your views onto others').

On the other hand, there is the opposite danger of glibly ascribing unexplainable differences to 'cultural factors'. This would be bad logic, and un-French.

A French malaise?

'On passe notre temps à croire qu'on est malade, à gratter nos plaies.' ('We spend our time thinking

212

we're ill and scratching our sores.')
(Conversation with François Delachaux, PDG
Delachaux SA.)

The French undoubtedly have a long tradition of introspection and self-criticism. As Zeldin put it:

> No nation has tried harder to find and express its
> identity, none has looked in the mirror so hard and
> argued so much about what it sees in it.
>
> (1983,6.)

This theme has fascinated writers from Voltaire and de Tocqueville through Ernest Renan, Michel Crozier, Alain Peyrefitte and François de Closets. Hardly a year passes by without some indictment of the shortcomings of French society – the favourite targets being the constitution of the nation's élites or the psychological blockages within the society. And the French public seems to have a high tolerance for self-criticism since these books are almost guaranteed best-sellers.

French people have a habit of putting themselves above the masses and criticizing the nation. The criticism can be quite incisive and scathing but somehow remains impersonal, with commentators cleverly detaching themselves from the population they are criticizing. The archetypal example is the regular publication of polemic books with titles such as *La mafia polytechnicienne*, *L'Enarchie* or *L'Enaklatura* – usually written by ex–alumni, stricken with conscience at their own presence in this privileged upper-crust world. The critics give the impression they are somehow not part of it – rather in the way de Gaulle used to criticize the French as being ungovernable, when he himself was hardly the most accommodating politician in history. Inside every Frenchman is a miniature General who loves France, but hates the French.

Against this backdrop of criticism, France has recovered from decades of underachievement, defeat, occupation, war in Algeria and student riots – and has emerged as a rich and successful country. Given this essential contradiction, are the French '*malades imaginaires*', ('socio-political hypochondriacs')?

France is reluctant to concede that it is no longer a 'superpower' – it harbours dreams of returning to the forefront of world affairs through prestigious science and technology projects and economic prosperity. The French tend to see their country as a great power *en petit*, on a somewhat smaller scale.

Perhaps because of the lack of self-belief described above and the loss of say in world affairs, the French have looked to Europe for support. This may explain the enthusiasm with which France, and its business community in particular, has embraced the concept of a unified European market. The vision of removing all barriers, visible and invisible, physical and technical, and all obstacles to the internal circulation of people, goods, services and capital has really captured the French imagination.

1992 and all that

It is no accident that the idea of 1992 as an *annus mirabilis* coincides with a rather dour and introspective domestic debate about national decline, as witnessed by articles along the lines: *'La France est-elle encore une grande puissance?'* ('Is France still a superpower?' – *L'Express*, 2 February 1984, 24). To a France worried about its faltering economic performance and lack of clear national direction, the challenge of 1992 offers both a fresh goal (to fire up enthusiasm) and a vital lever for implementing internal structural change.

As explained in *Le Point*:

> *Dans une France encore morose, les thèmes mobili-*
> *sateurs se font rares.* (In a down-hearted France,
> rallying calls are hard to come by.)
> (15 June 1988, 56.)

Confirmation that a united Europe is *une idée porteuse* (an inspirational theme) can be seen in the way the presidential candidates seized upon the concept in the build-up to the May 1988 elections. As early as January 1987, François Mitterrand made a speech to the Royal Institute of International Affairs in London, in which he repeatedly stated, *'La France est ma patrie mais l'Europe est mon avenir'* ('France is my country, but Europe is my future'). Not to be outdone, Jacques Chirac decided to incorporate the idea of Europe into his electoral slogan: *'Gagner en 1988 pour réussir en 1992'* ('Winning in 1988 to succeed in 1992'). Indeed, 1992 cropped up so frequently in speeches by the two front-runners that each seemed to be vying to make the issue his own.

France's vision of a united Europe is a long-standing one. While Britain has wavered and dragged its feet, France has remained staunchly committed to the idea of Europe. It has also led the way in terms of providing a common vision as to the direction and distance in which the European member states should travel together. When he was Prime Minister, Georges Pompidou (1969 – 74) once said that France had to play the role of Europe, given the absence of a common European will. There is more than a grain of truth in this statement. One could not imagine, say, Britain emulating France and staging a conference with the purely academic aim of defining a common European identity (*The Financial Times*, 26 January 1988, 19).

In the late 1980s French faith in the idea of a united Europe has been reinforced by two particular concerns: first, the loss of national impact on world affairs, and second, the need to revitalize certain sectors of French industry.

There is a strong nationalistic element in French life. French people buy French cars, eat French food, go on holiday in France. France shows determination to 'remain herself', to preserve distinctiveness, and to pursue a national ambition. But, there is a clear discrepancy between these goals and the resources at her disposal. The French have realized that, in order to be heard, they must use the European amplifier – unlike Britain which benefits from presumed privileged relations with the USA. Thus, from a French viewpoint, Europe is a means of achieving national goals and conserving a central role on the world stage. France has tried, not without success, to pursue a mix of independent, distinctive and autonomous actions wherever possible and of co-operative policies with its European neighbours – in short, to reap the benefits with a minimum of burdens.

Perhaps more important is the perspective of the single European market as a catalyst to activate French businesses. Some areas of French business are still backward and cloistered, and it is hoped that 1992 will help shock them into modernizing – in much the same way that the prospect of increased competition from the Common Market accelerated French modernization in 1957. The exaltation of 1992 may, therefore, amount to little more than a device to spur some sections of French industry to do faster what it needs to do anyway – become more self-reliant, internationally minded and responsive to market forces.

In France, with its history of protected and highly regulated markets, the deadline is adding psychological impetus to efforts to shake up corporate thinking and the need to reach a 'critical size' to compete on a European scale – hence, the spate of takeovers in the second half of the 1980s.

In fact, there seems to be little danger of the French underestimating the implications for companies of 1992, since everyone from President Mitterrand down has been beating the drum. In his address to industrial leaders (Palais des Congrès, 18 June 1987), Mitterrand evoked the negative scenario of France becoming a mere subcontractor for other nations – instead of seeing French companies flourish on a global scale. Similarly, Edouard Balladur, the Treasury Minister, has tried to instil a sense of urgency among the bosses by telling them:

> Cinq ans est un délai extraordinairement court,
> compte tenu du redressement à accomplir pour un
> pays affaibli depuis de nombreuses années. (Five
> years is a very short lead time to redress a country
> which has grown weaker over several years.)
> (Dirigeant, numéro spécial, July 1987.)

Not all political leaders are using these scare tactics. Some, like Jacques Delors, emphasized the potential gains for French industry, suggesting that the unified market could pave the way for 'a second French economic miracle' *(L'Usine Nouvelle,* 19 March 1987, 10). His optimism was echoed by Philippe Willaume, President of the Centre des Jeunes Dirigeants (CJD), who believed that 1992 represented *'une chance historique'* for French companies.

It would seem that the message has not fallen upon deaf ears. Perhaps stirred by memories of the inspirational years of post-war reconstruction, the whole concept has struck a particularly loud chord in French business circles.

At every level one can see initiatives to raise national consciousness regarding 1992. These efforts have ranged from high-profile extravaganzas like the invitation of 2,800 political and industrial leaders (including François Mitterrand and Jacques Delors) to attend a colloquium entitled 'Europe-entreprise: objectif 1992', to the setting up of hundreds of working groups and taskforces across industry destined to prepare for the challenge of a Europe without frontiers. Since the start of 1987, virtually every trade association, chamber of commerce (see Figure 10.1) or professional body has turned its attention to the theme of a united Europe. Even the small companies have jumped on the bandwagon. In June 1987, they held a national 1992 awareness day. Further support has come from the business journals all of which have focused heavily on 'European' articles knowing that there is a guaranteed readership eager to be informed.

As a result of this frenetic activity, corporate awareness is high. Assuring shareholders that the company is ready for 1992 has become an almost obligatory feature of the PDG's statement. Of course, the way in which companies view the single market is dependent upon their existing commitment to Europe. There are those companies for which international competition is no novelty, and others which have never yet been exposed to it.

Among the former, one finds all the major corporations in industrial and service sectors which have a European perspective at the heart of their strategy. Within these companies there is a faintly pleasurable sense of expectation which is highly revealing. Only a few years ago, the prospect of a freer European market would have been viewed in France as the prelude to an invasion by West German industry. Today it is talked of as an invigorating challenge and an opportunity for expansion. One tell-tale sign regarding French optimism is the way French companies are looking at the Channel Tunnel. They clearly have their eyes set on the British market. One piece of tangible evidence is to be found in a brochure from a small company in northern France. The brochure has a map showing the distance not only from Paris but also from London.

More surprisingly, practical preparations for 1992 have kept in step with the official rhetoric. French companies are preparing rapidly and

RÉPUBLIQUE FRANÇAISE

CHAMBRE DE COMMERCE ET D'INDUSTRIE DE L'AISNE

le Président

. Saint-Quentin, le 24 Juillet 1987

Cher Monsieur,

Lors de l'Assemblée générale des délégués consulaires du 15 juin dernier et des différentes réunions préparatoires, j'avais informé l'ensemble des participants qu'une réunion de travail se tiendrait, le vendredi 18 septembre 1987 à la Chambre de commerce et d'industrie de l'Aisne en présence de M. Georges CHAVANES, Ministre du commerce, de l'artisanat et des services.

Monsieur le Ministre vient de me faire savoir que pour des raisons impératives, il se trouve dans l'impossibilité de se déplacer le 18 septembre.

Compte tenu de l'intérêt qu'il porte à nos travaux, il m'a proposé d'être parmi nous :

le jeudi 17 septembre 1987

Cette importante réunion sera placée sous le thème : **"les entreprises de l'Aisne face au Marché unique de 1992"**. L'ordre du jour vous parviendra ultérieurement par un prochain courrier.

Je souhaiterai très vivement que vous puissiez être présent à cette réunion qui se tiendra :

au siège de la Chambre de commerce et d'industrie de l'Aisne
83 boulevard Jean Bouin à Saint-Quentin
à 14 heures 30.

Je vous prie de bien vouloir agréer, Cher Monsieur, l'expression de mes sentiments distingués.

Serge RENAUD

83 Bd Jean Bouin-BP 630 - 02322 Saint Quentin Cedex-Tel. 23 62 39 16-Telex CCIA 140 584 F-Télécopieur 23 62 09 25

Figure 10.1 Invitation to attend a conference on 1992.

in detail, incorporating the expected changes into their plans. All the companies the present writers visited had a plan already drawn up or in the offing. Even more striking evidence of the preparation was visible in the takeover wave of the late 1980s which saw virtually every merger or acquisition being cloaked in the colours of Europe.

Whilst they are more apprehensive, small firms are not burying their heads in the sand. They too, are giving considerable thought to the changes which the lifting of barriers will foist upon them. The small manufacturing companies visited were particularly preoccupied by the likely shift in engineering norms from the French system towards the more exacting West German standards. Notwithstanding this sense of foreboding, the companies knew the likely direction of the changes because they were clued up on the nature of the voting process whereby each country was alloted a coefficient from 1 to 3. It would seem that the effectiveness of the propaganda has been such that the small firms are as well informed as their large counterparts.

Our informal findings were corroborated by survey results published in *The Times* (2 March 1988, 26). These showed that French companies were well-informed across the board in contrast to the UK (and Germany) where awareness among smaller firms is significantly lower. The survey also revealed that the proportion of British firms with a strategy to take advantage of the internal market is less than half that in France. In France, 60 per cent of the companies had already drawn up a strategic plan either to protect existing markets or to exploit new opportunities, compared to 30 per cent in the UK. The idea that French companies are already in the starting blocks was further supported by a survey of members of the Paris Chamber of Commerce (*Director*, February 1988, 58) which showed that a full quarter of respondents felt they already had enough information and were equipped for the advent of the internal market.

However, the most striking feature of the French reaction to 1992 is the grass-roots interest it has elicited. For instance, in the companies we visited, interviewees would spontaneously refer to the target date. The event has clearly gripped the public imagination, with middle managers enthusing about the prospect of a united Europe and conscious of the urgency of the situation. As one production manager explained:

> '1992, *c'est pas demain, c'est ce soir.*' ('1992 is not tomorrow but tonight.')

What is more, the information does not stop at management level; primed by corporate chiefs and professional bodies, the middle managers are organizing their own seminars and making sure that the rest of the workforce knows what is afoot.

The volubility of the 1992 debate in France is all the more surprising in view of the comparative silence of France's neighbours. Some of the French senior managers who regularly travelled abroad commented on the relative indifference of their European counterparts from business contacts with them. This leads one to wonder if French paranoia in this matter is a reflection of a certain backwardness – perhaps the lack of fuss elsewhere is a sign that preparations for 1992 started a long time ago, by dropping protectionist measures and by internationalizing operations.

That is probably true. In some respects, the challenge of 1992 seems to have appeared at a singularly opportune moment, for France at least. The date has become synonymous with the challenge of restructuring industry and improving its efficiency in the face of international competition. However, something more fundamental seems to lie behind the enthusiasm over 1992. It is difficult to substantiate, but the French appear to respond very positively to grand designs – as seen in post-war rebuilding and, on a smaller scale, in projects like Concorde and the nuclear energy programme. Apparently, the idea of a single European market has locked into a basic French desire to be involved in an epic production.

So France in the late 1980s has become the yardstick against which other EEC member states gauge their efforts. Taking a snapshot may seem pointless since the differences in preparation will no doubt be effaced as the countdown progresses. Yet there are good grounds for doing so. First, because the difference in initial response reflects a qualitatively different attitude to Europe – the French are effectively broadcasting their commitment to Europe. Second, and more importantly, the differences in response which manifest themselves clearly at a relatively timely stage may serve as explanatory factors when it comes to assessing which member states have most benefited from the levelling of the barriers.

Five or ten years ago it did perhaps make sense to talk of a French disease, of local failure to adapt quickly enough to a new world economic climate, and of antipathy towards business. But now, both right and left in politics have roughly similar aims. Socialists call it democracy, the right calls it liberalism. The country is stable and prosperous, and the business community has been revitalized by the idea of a single European market – which is being invoked as a reason to strip away archaic thinking. The French seem to have come to terms with some loss of French grandeur – and are looking to Europe to replenish it.

Bibliography

Ackermann, K.-F. (September 1988) *Europe ahead. The changing role of human resources management in German companies.* Paper at International Comparisons in Human Resource Management Conference, Cranfield Institute of Technology, September 1988. Excerpts adapted by the authors.

Albert, M. (1982) *Le pari français.* Paris: Seuil.

Archier, G. and Serieyx, H. (1984) *L'entreprise du 3e type.* Paris: Seuil.

Ardagh, J. (1982) *France in the 1980s: The Definitive Book.* Harmondsworth: Penguin.

Ardagh, J. (1987) *France Today.* London: Penguin.

Attali, J. (1978) *La nouvelle économie française.* Paris: Flammarion.

Autrement (1984) *Les héros de l'économie,* no. 59. Paris: Autrement.

Barnard, C. I. (1938) *The Functions of the Executive.* Massachusetts: Harvard University Press.

Bauer, M. and Bertin-Mourot, B. (1987) *Les 200. Comment devient-on un grand patron?* Paris: Seuil.

Baumier, J.(1986) *Ces patrons qui gagnent.* Paris: Plon.

Benguigui, G. and Monjardet, D. (1970) *Etre cadre en France.* Paris: Dunod Actualité.

Benguigui, G., Griset, A., Jacob, A. and Monjardet, D. (1975) *Recherche sur la fonction d'encadrement.* Two volume report by the Groupe de sociologie du travail, Paris: CNRS.

Birnbaum, P., Baruco, C., Bellaiche, M. and Marie, A. *La classe dirigeante française.* Paris: Seuil.

Blanchard, K. (1983) *One Minute Manager.* London: Willow Books.

Blazot, J. (1983) *Cadres sur table.* Nancy: Presses de Berger-Levrault.

Bléton, P. (1956) *Les hommes des temps qui viennent.* Paris: Editions Ouvrières.

Bloch, P., Hababou, R. and Xardel, D. (1986) *Service compris: les clients heureux font les entreprises gagnantes.* Paris: Hachette.

Boltanski, L. (1982) *Les cadres: la formation d'un groupe sociale.* Paris: Editions de Minuit. Translation: Goldhammer, A. (1987) *The Making of a Class.* Cambridge: Cambridge University Press.

Bourdieu, P. and Passeron, J.-C. (1964) *Les héritiers.* Paris: Editions de Minuit.

Bourdieu, P. and Passeron, J.-C. (1970) *La reproduction.* Paris: Editions de Minuit.

Burt, S. (1986) The Carrefour group – the first 25 years. *International*

Journal of Retailing, **1** (3), 54–78.

CEREQ (1975) *Les emplois de cadres*. Paris: Documentation Française.

Challenges (January 1987) No.24, 50–54: Ladovar, R., *Faut-il changer de job?*

Challenges (March 1987) No.2, 30–37: Clousy, P., *Le rôle secret des mafias des grandes écoles*.

Challenges (April 1987) No.3, 30–39: *Réussir sans diplôme*.

Cox, C. J. and Cooper, C. L. (Winter 1985) The irrelevance of American organizational sciences to the UK and Europe. *Journal of General Management*, 27–34.

Crozier, M. (1964) *The Bureaucratic Phenomenon*. Chicago: University of Chicago Press.

Crozier, M. (1970) *La société bloquée*. Paris: Seuil.

Crozier, M. (1979) *On ne change pas la société par décret*. Paris: Grasset. Translation: Beer, W. R. (1982) *Strategies for Change: The Future of French Society*. Massachusetts: MIT Press.

Crozier, M. (ed.) (1985) *Les nouveaux modes d'organisation*. Paris: Institut de l'Entreprise.

Daninos, P. (1960) *Un certain M. Blot*. Paris: Librairie Hachette.

de Closets, F. (1982) *Toujours plus!* Paris: Grasset.

de Gramont, S. (1969) *The French – Portrait of a People*. London: Hodder & Stoughton.

Director (February 1988) 56–58: MacGillicuddy, C., Europe heads for the open market.

Director (July 1988) 70–73: Rock, S., Will l'Oréal get the chemistry right?

d'Iribarne, A. and P. (September–October 1987) *Le mariage du noble et du vil*. *La Revue Française de Gestion*, 44–50.

d'Iribarne, P. (January–February 1985) *La gestion à la française*. *La Revue Française de Gestion*, 5–13.

Dirigeant (July 1987) *Numéro spécial: Objectif 92*.

Doublet, J. and Passelecq, O. (1973) *Les cadres*. Paris: Presses Universitaires de France.

Dyas, G. P. and Thanheiser, H. T. (1976) *The emerging European Enterprise: Strategy and Structure in French and German Industry*. London: Macmillan.

The Economist (9 February 1985) *L'Etat c'est eux: a survey of France*, 1–22.

The Economist (5 March 1988) How companies choose their bosses, 69–70.

Ehrmann, H. W. (1957) *Organized Business in France*. New Jersey: Princeton University Press.

L'Etudiant (December 1986) No.70, 120–127: *Entrer dans une grande école: autres tactiques*.

L'Expansion (July/August 1977) 66–71: Fontaine, J., *Les grandes entreprises jugent les grandes écoles*.

L'Expansion (September 1978) 130–141: Jannic, H., Le triomphe des Peugeots.

L'Expansion (7 September 1979) 101–108: Lalanne, B., Les secrets de Michelin.

L'Expansion (3 April 1980) 99–105: Fontaine, J., Douze portraits de chefs.

L'Expansion (4 June 1981) 104–113: Beaufils, V., Les fils à papa.

L'Expansion (11 November 1982) 117–125: Moatti, G., Faut-il couler les grandes écoles?

L'Expansion (6 October 1983) 109–121: Lalanne, B., Destin de majors.

L'Expansion (7 March 1985) 78–85: Izraelewicz, E., Les universités qui réussissent.

L'Expansion (19 May 1985) 70–77: Alexandre, R., A quoi reconnaît-on les chefs?

L'Expansion (18 July 1985) 44–47: Servan-Schreiber, J.-L., Plus on a de pouvoir, mieux on se porte.

L'Expansion (19 September 1985) 90–99: Beaudeux, P., Les dix patrons les plus durs.

L'Expansion (6 February 1986) 45–47: Rodgers, I., Latins et Anglo-Saxon.

L'Expansion (3 July 1986) 45–47: Civegrel, F., Français et Allemands les yeux dans les yeux.

L'Expansion (11 September 1986) 39–45: Mital, C., Quinze Stars.

L'Expansion (25 September 1986) 79–84: Moatti, G., Vive l'argent!

L'Expansion (23 October 1986) 55–63: Beaufils, V., Combien vaut Tapie?

L'Expansion (December 1986) 119–149: La galerie de portraits des grands patrons.

L'Expansion (19 March 1987) 46–59: Gurviez, J.-J., Le hit-parade des écoles de commerce.

L'Expansion (16 April 1987) 62–68: Jannic, H., L'éternelle jeunesse de l'Air Liquide.

L'Expansion (18 June 1987) 121–131: Gurviez, J.-J., Combien gagnent les débutants.

L'Expansion (16 July 1987) 136–137: Domenach, J.-M., La question des élites.

L'Expansion (8 October 1987) 150–158: Gurviez, J.-J., Les réseaux secrets d'influence.

L'Expansion (22 October 1987) 129–130: Bauer, M., Il faut déréguler le marché des dirigeants.

L'Expansion (3 December 1987) 76–83: L'Oréal: superstar de l'image.

L'Expansion (May 1988) 6–11: Alexandre, R., Meilleure image mondiale: Bibendum superstar.

L'Expansion (19 May 1988) 73–79: Gurviez, J.-J., Combien gagnent les jeunes diplômés?

L'Expansion (16 June 1988) 50–56: Mital, C. and Rouge, J.-F., La France:

paradis des patrons?

L'Expansion (16 June 1988) 141–204: Gurviez, J.-J., *Salaires des cadres 1988.*

L'Expansion (14 July 1988) 85–91: Beaufils, V., *Ces patrons qui s'adorent....*

L'Express (2 February 1984) 24–35: Noc, O., *La France est-elle encore une grande puissance?*

L'Express (1 March 1985) 21–33: *Les dix blocages de la société française.*

L'Express (24 January 1986) 25–34: *Ingénieurs: les aventuriers de l'avenir.*

L'Express (3 October 1986) 41–48: Arnoux, P., *Le vrai salaire des cadres.*

L'Express (1 January 1988) 33–37: Lannes, S., *Pour gagner, changez vos patrons.*

Fayol, H. (1916) *L'administration générale et industrielle*, 2nd edn. Paris. Also (1949) *General and Industrial Management*. London: Pitman.

The Financial Times (3 July 1985) 14: Betts, P. and Rodger, I., A rare interview with the Michelin Man.

The Financial Times (21 May 1986) 20: Business with birch twigs – Survey on Finland.

The Financial Times (2 July 1986) 18: Lorenz, C., Europe warms to business punditry.

The Financial Times (5 November 1987) 26: Thursday book review: *L'ambition internationale* by Lionel Stoleru.

The Financial Times (13 January 1988) 19: Betts, P., Bubbling over in a healthy market.

The Financial Times (26 January 1988) 19: Mortimer, E., Searching for an elusive esprit de corps.

Fixari, D. (March 1986) *Patron, vous avez dit patron? Les aventures de Roger Martin président. Gérer et Comprendre*, 10–19.

Fortune (17 March 1986) 20–29: Business dynasties face the raiders.

Fortune (23 May 1988) 36–43: Tully, S., Europe's best business schools.

Freydet, J.-G. and Pingaud, D. (1982) *Les patrons face à la gauche*. Paris: Ramsay.

Gaillard, J.-M. (1987) *Tu seras président, mon fils*. Paris: Ramsay.

Garnier, B., Van Gigch, J.-P. and de Pourvourville, G. (June 1986) *Faut-il copier les business schools? Gérer et Comprendre*, 70–73.

Gelenier, O. (1965) *Le moral de l'entreprise et le destin de la nation*. Paris: Librairie Plon.

Girard, A. (1965) *La réussite sociale en France*. Paris: Presses Universitaires de France.

Glover, I. (December 1976) Executive career patterns: Britain, France, Germany and Sweden. *Energy World*, 3–12.

Goldsmith, W. and Clutterbuck, D. (1984) *The Winning Streak: Britain's Top Companies Reveal Their Formulas for Success*. London: Weidenfeld and Nicolson.

Graham, J. L. and Herberger, R. A. (July–August 1983) Negotiators abroad – don't shoot from the hip. *Harvard Business Review*, 160–168.

Granick, D. (1972) *Managerial Comparisons of Four Developed Countries: France, Britain, United States and Russia*. Massachusetts: MIT Press.

Graves, D. (ed.) (1973) *Management Research: A Cross-cultural Perspective*. Amsterdam: Elsevier Scientific.

Grunberg, G. and Mouriaux, R. (1979) *L'univers politique & syndical des cadres*. Paris: Presses de la Fondation Nationale des Sciences Politiques.

Grunberg, L. (November 1986) Workplace relations in the economic crisis: a comparison of a British and a French automobile plant. *Sociology*, 503–529.

Gunther, J.-B. (September 1986) *Propos sur la formation des ingénieurs. Gérer et Comprendre*, 51–55.

Harris, A. and de Sedouy, A. (1977) *Les patrons*. Paris: Seuil.

Hofstede, G. (1980) *Culture's Consequences*. London: Sage.

Hofstede, G. (September–October 1987) *Relativité culturelle des pratiques et théories de gestion. La Revue Française de Gestion*, 10–21.

Horovitz, J. (1980) *Top Management Control in Europe*. London: Macmillan.

Howorth, J. and Cerny, P. G. (eds) (1981) *Elites in France: Origins, Reproduction and Power*. London: Frances Pinter.

IFOP (1975) *Les français tels qu'ils sont*. Paris: Fayard.

International Herald Tribune (5 May 1977): Story, J. and Parrott, M., An essay on management in France – does it work?

International Management (December 1987) 44–49: Berger, M., The Michelin Man with a Japanese accent.

Julliand, V. and Sidibe, J. (1985) *Bien choisir son école de commerce*. Paris: L'Etudiant.

Kempner, T. (Winter 1983/84) Education for management in five countries: myth and reality. *Journal of General Management*, 5–23.

Kindleberger, C. P. (1964) *Economic Growth in France and Britain: 1851–1950*. Massachusetts: Harvard University Press.

Kosciusko-Morizet, J.-A. (1973) *La mafia polytechnicienne*. Paris: Seuil.

Kotter, J. P. (1982) *The General Managers*. New York: The Free Press.

Landes, D. S. (1951) French business and the businessman: a social and cultural analysis. In Earle, E. E. (ed.), *Modern France*. New York: Russell and Russell.

Lawrence, P. (1980) *Managers and Management in West Germany*. London: Croom Helm.

Lawrence, P. (1984) *Management in Action*. London: Routledge & Kegan Paul.

Lawrence, P. (1986) *Management in the Netherlands*. Report for the

Technische Hogeschool Twente, the Netherlands.

Lawrence, P. (1986) *Invitation to Management*. Oxford: Blackwell.

Lawrence, P. (1988) In Another Country. In Bryman, A. (ed.), *Doing Research in Organisations*. London: Routledge & Kegan Paul.

Lawrence, P. and Elliott, K. (1985) *Introducing Management*. Harmondsworth: Penguin.

Lawrence, P. and Spybey, T. (1986) *Management and Society in Sweden*. London: Routledge & Kegan Paul.

Lockyer, K. G. and Jones, S. (September 1980) The function factor. *Management Today*, 53–64.

LSA (21 April 1978) No. 666, 17–21: *Carrefour plus que jamais valeur de croissance!*

LSA (13 February 1987) No. 1057, 11–15: *L'Oréal prêt pour une nouvelle montée en gamme*.

MacArthur, J. J. and Scott, B. (1969) *Industrial Planning in France*. Boston: Division of Research, Harvard Business School.

Malraux, A. (1946) *La condition humaine*. Paris: Gallimard.

Mandrin, J. (1967) *L'énarchie ou Les mandarins de la société bourgeoise*. Paris: La Table Ronde.

Marceau, J. (1977) *Class and Status in France: Economic Change and Social Immobility, 1945–1975*. Oxford: University Press.

Marceau, J. (1981) Access to élite careers in French business. In Howorth, J. and Cerny, P. (eds), *Elites in France: Origins, Reproduction and Power*. London: Frances Pinter.

Martin, R. (1984) *Patron de droit divin*. Paris: Gallimard.

Maurice, M., Sellier, F. and Silvestre, J.-J. (1977) *Production de la hiérarchie dans l'entreprise: recherche d'un effet social Allemagne –France*. Laboratoire d'Economie et de Sociologie du Travail, Aix en Provence. Translation: Goldhammer, A. (1986) *The Social Foundations of Industrial Power: A Comparison of France and West Germany*. Massachusetts: MIT Press.

Menissez, Y. (1979) *L'enseignement de la gestion en France*. Paris: Documentation Française.

Mermet, G. (1986) *Francoscopie, les français: qui sont-ils? où vont-ils?* Paris: Larousse.

Meuleau, M. (1981) *Histoire d'une grande école: HEC, 1881–1981*. Paris: Dunod.

Miler, P. Mahé, P. and Cannavo, R. (1975) *Les Français tels qu'ils sont*. Paris: Fayard.

Le Monde (11 February 1981) 1 and 9: Mitterrand, F., *Le triangle du pouvoir*.

Le Monde de l'Education (April 1986) 10–13: Reverchon, A., *Grandes écoles: la puissance des anciens*.

Le Monde de l'Education (July–August 1986) 108–137: Cohen, P., *Le palmarès des universités*.

Le Monde de l'Education (25 June 1987) 36: Gaussen, F., *Le piège de* l'Université.

Moreau, M. (1980) *Le management pratique de l'entreprise*. Paris: Economica.

Müller, K. (1983) *François Mitterrand*. Paris: Flammarion.

National Economic Development Office (1987) *The making of managers: a report on management education, training and development in the USA, West Germany, France, Japan and the UK*. London: NEDO.

Newman, W. H. (March/April/May 1986) *Croyances culturelles et management*. La Revue Française de Gestion, 10–15.

Nourissier, F. (1971) *The French* (trans. Foulke, A.). London: Hutchinson.

Le Nouvel Economiste (12 May 1980) 42–47: *Cadres: la course aux pouvoirs*.

Le Nouvel Economiste (19 April 1982) 76–81: Chabeaud, M., *Les nouveaux dadas de la distribution*.

Le Nouvel Economiste (29 November 1982) 48–51: *Peut-on faire fortune en France?*

Le Nouvel Economiste (29 May 1987) 81–90: *Cadres: comment réussir sa carrière*.

Le Nouvel Observateur (21 January 1983) 14–19: Schemla, E., *Universités: le défi aux grandes écoles*.

OECD (July 1987) *OECD Economic Surveys: the Netherlands*.

Peters, T. J. and Austin, N. (1985) *A Passion for Excellence: The Leadership Difference*. London: Collins.

Peters, T. J. and Waterman, R. H. (1982) *In Search of Excellence*. New York: Harper and Row.

Peyrefitte, A. (1976) *Le Mal Français*. Paris: Plon.

Le Point (5 December 1983) 44–49: Gaetner, G., *Grandes écoles: enquête sur l'élite de demain*.

Le Point (27 January 1986) 50–57: Richard, M., *Secret d'Etat: ce que gagnent vraiment les fonctionnaires*.

Le Point (8 September 1986) 51–56: Jeambar, D., *Ce qui fait marcher les cadres*.

Le Point (29 December 1986) 80–84: Bonjean, C. and Basdevant, V., *Jeunesse: une business génération*.

Le Point (6 April 1987) 62–70: Makarian, C. and Pauchet, C., *160 lycées au banc d'essai*.

Le Point (8 June 1987) 63–66: Makarian, C., *Le salaire des jeunes diplômés*.

Le Point (17 August 1987) 50–51: *Comment les patrons prennent congés*.

Le Point (24 August 1987) 24–28: Coignard, S., *Réussites: le palmarès des sans diplômes*.

Le Point (5 October 1987) 54–61: *Spécial cadres*.

Le Point (15 June 1988) 55–57: Dauvergne, A., *Europe 1992: la France mobilise*.

Points de Vente (1 February 1987) No. 316, 55: Fontana, E., *Café et Management*.

Priouret, R. (1968) *La France et le management*. Paris: Denoël.

Revue Internationale du Travail (January/February 1985), **124** (1), 1–16.

Reynaud, J.-D. and Grafmeyer, Y. (eds) (1981) *Français, qui êtes-vous? des essais et des chiffres*. Paris: Documentation Française.

Riveline, C. (December 1986) *L'enseignement du dur et l'enseignement du mou*. Gérer et Comprendre, 41–45.

Roethlisberger, F. J. and Dickson, W. J. (1939) *Management and the Worker*. Massachusetts: Harvard University Press.

Russell, B. (1927) *Philosophy*. New York: Norton.

Sainsaulieu, R. (1977) *L'identité au travail*. Paris: Presses de la Fondation Nationale des Sciences Politiques.

Saint, G. (1984) *Le gaspillage des élites*. Paris: Laffont.

Santoni, G. (ed.) (1981) *Société et culture de la France contemporaine*. New York: State University of New York Press.

Schell, O. (1984) *To Get Rich is Glorious: China in the Eighties*. New York: Clark.

Scherrer, V. *La France paresseuse*. Paris: Seuil.

Schifres, M. (1986) *L'Enaklatura*. Paris: Jean-Claude Lattès.

Science et Vie Economie (May 1987) 70–78: Hoang, A., Corrolère, C. and Riplais, J., *Le choix des employeurs*.

Ségal, J.-P. (June 1987) *Le prix de la légitimité hiérarchique. Une comparaison franco-américaine*. Gérer et Comprendre, 66–77.

Servan-Schreiber, J.-J. (1967) *Le défi américain*. Paris: Denoël.

SOFRES (1987) *L'état de l'opinion: clés pour 1987*. Paris: Seuil.

Sorge, A. and Warner, M. (1986) *Comparative Factory Organization*. Aldershot: Gower.

Stokman, F. N., Zeigler, R. and Scott, J. (1985) *Networks of Corporate Power*. Cambridge: Polity Press.

Sudreau, P. (1975) *La réforme de l'entreprise*. Paris: Documentation Française.

Suleiman, E. N. (1978) *Elites in French Society: The Politics of Survival*. Princeton: Princeton University Press.

Tapie, B. (1986) *Gagner*. Paris: Laffont.

Tertiel (September 1987) 24–29: Roche, F., *Philippe Bouriez: le marginal*.

Thélot, C. (1982) *Tel père, tel fils*. Paris: Dunod.

The Times (2 March 1986) 26: Lord, R., British firms unaware of EEC change.

Tixier, M. (September–October 1987) *Cultures nationales et recrutement*. La Revue Française de Gestion, 59–68.

Tréanton, J.-R. (1984) *Comparaisons France–Allemagne et France–Angleterre: deux études de sociologie de l'entreprise*. Revue Française de Sociologie, **XXV**, 145–150.

L'Usine Nouvelle (19 March 1987) No. 12, 6–11: de Clapiers, R., *Un marché enfin commun*.

L'Usine Nouvelle (19 March 1987) 56–70: *Ingénieurs: la nouvelle* vague.

Valeurs Actuelles (21 July 1986) 29–32: L'Air Liquide, capitalisme exemplaire.

Vancil, R. F. (1987) Passing the Baton: Managing the Process of CEO Succession. Harvard Business School Press.

Vaughan, M. (1981) The grandes écoles: selection, legitimation, perpetuation. In Howorth, J. and Cerny, P.G. (eds), Elites in France: Origins, Reproduction and Power. London: Frances Pinter.

Vaughan, M., Kolinsky, M. and Sheriff, P. (1980) Social Change in France. London: Martin Robertson.

Verron, J. (Winter 1985) Des difficultés d'être cadre et formateur. Enseignement et Gestion, 31–45.

Villette, M. (1986) La gestion des antagonismes entre fractions concurrentes de l'encadrement d'une entreprise. Revue Française de Sociologie, XXVII, 107–131.

Vincent, C. (1981) La fin des illusions. In Santoni, G. (ed.), Société et culture de la France contemporaine. Albany: State University of New York Press.

Warner, M. (January 1987) Industrialization, management education and training systems: a comparative analysis. Journal of Management Studies, 91–112.

Weber, H. (1986) Le parti des patrons – le CNPF (1946–86). Paris: Seuil.

Weinshall, T. D. (1979) Managerial Communication: Concepts, Approaches and Techniques. London: Academic Press.

Weiss, J. H. (1982) The Making of Technological Man: The Social Origins of French Engineering Education. Massachusetts: MIT Press.

Whitley, R., Thomas, A. and Marceau, J. (1984) Masters of Business: The Making of a New Elite? London: Tavistock Publications.

Wickham, A. and Coignard, S. (1986) La nomenklatura française. Paris: Belfont.

Wickham, A. and Patterson, M. (1983) Les carriéristes. Paris: Ramsay.

Xardel, D. (1978) Les managers. Paris: Grasset.

Zeldin, T. (1983) The French. London: Collins.

Zola, E. (1968) Germinal. Paris: Garnier-Flammarion.

Index